STUDIES ON REGULATION IN CANADA

edited by
W.T. Stanbury

Institute for Research on Public Policy/Institut de recherches politiques
Distributed by
Butterworth & Co. Ltd.
Toronto
1978

ISBN 0-920380-04-2

Legal Deposit Third Quarter 1978
Bibliothèque nationale du Québec

Phototypesetting by Ford Publishing Company Limited, Halifax, Nova Scotia, Canada.

Preface

A year ago the Institute for Research on Public Policy selected regulation and government intervention as one of its four major research areas. This choice was made because of the increasing importance of regulation as a method of implementing federal, provincial and municipal government policies, and because very little analysis has been done in Canada on either the effectiveness of regulation as a public policy tool or on its economic impact on regulated firms and consumers.

Since last fall, the importance of regulation as a public policy issue has increased with the decision of the ten provincial premiers and the Prime Minister, at their meeting in February 1978, to ask the Economic Council of Canada to analyse the effect of those government regulations which appear to be having a substantial impact on the Canadian economy. That a wide range of regulatory issues are in need of analysis is clearly illustrated by the papers in the book. They indicate that much remains to be done before Canadians can know the impact which regulation has on the economy of this country.

Hopefully, however, much will be learned in the next three years. IRPP has already launched more than twenty studies as part of its regulation and government intervention program, and more will be started in the coming months. In addition, the Economic Council of Canada will be conducting studies in response to the reference arising from the First Ministers Conference. (Coordination between the two programs is assured because both are being directed by Dr. W.T. Stanbury, the editor of this book, who has been seconded part-time from IRPP to the Economic Council.)

Thus this set of *Studies on Regulation in Canada* represents one of the first of a series of reports which we hope will shed light on some of the questions which need to be answered about regulatory processes and their economic impact on Canada. These studies also illustrate the dilemma which government always faces in deciding whether or not, and to what degree, it should regulate an industry. At what point does further regulation of the activities of an industry, in order to serve the general public interest, produce a cumulative effect which is not in the public interest?

Michael J.L. Kirby,
President
Institute for Research on Public Policy.
September, 1978.

Préface

Il y a un an, l'Institut de recherches politiques choisissait d'inscrire parmi ses quatre champs de recherche principaux la réglementation et l'intervention gouvernementale. Ce choix était motivé par l'importance croissante de la réglementation, en tant que mécanisme d'application des politiques gouvernementales fédérales, provinciales et municipales, et justifié aussi par la pénurie d'analyses d'origine canadienne traitant soit de l'efficacité de la réglementation comme outil politique, soit de son impact économique sur les entreprises et les consommateurs qui y sont soumis.

Depuis l'automne dernier, l'importance des questions de politiques que suscite la réglementation s'est accrue, par suite de la décision des dix Premiers ministres provinciaux et du Premier ministre du Canada, lors de leur rencontre de février 1978, de confier au Conseil économique du Canada l'analyse des conséquences des réglementations gouvernementales qui semblent avoir une répercussion marquée sur l'économie canadienne. Les articles du présent ouvrage démontrent clairement la nécessité d'analyser un large éventail de questions de cet ordre. Le chemin qui reste à parcourir avant que les Canadiens ne discernent l'influence exercée par la réglementation sur l'économie du pays sera long: les textes qui suivent en témoignent.

Nous espérons toutefois que des progrès appréciables seront accomplis dans les trois prochaines années. L'I.R.P. a déjà entrepris plus de vingt études issues de son programme "Réglementation et intervention gouvernementale" et s'apprête à poursuivre ce travail dans les mois à venir. Pour sa part, le Conseil économique du Canada mènera certaines études en réponse à la demande formulée à son endroit, au moment de la Conférence des Premiers ministres. (La coordination des deux programmes est assurée puisqu'ils se trouvent l'un et l'autre sous la direction de M.W.T. Stanbury, éditeur du présent volume, dont les services ont été mis à la disposition du Conseil économique par l'I.R.P., à temps partiel.)

Cet ensemble d'*Etudes de la réglementation au Canada* constitue donc l'un des premiers d'une série de rapports qui, nous l'espérons, feront la lumière sur certaines des questions pressantes que soulèvent les processus de réglementation et leur impact économique sur le Canada. Ces études illustrent aussi le dilemme auquel s'expose constamment le gouvernement en décidant de l'opportunité et des bornes de la réglementation d'une industrie: quelle est la limite au-delà de laquelle la réglementation des activités d'une industrie au profit de l'intérêt général est susceptible d'engendrer un effet cumulatif préjudiciable à cet intérêt.

Le Président,

Michael J. L. Kirby
Septembre 1978

Table of Contents

Chapter One

Executive Summary: Studies on Regulation in Canada

by
*W.T. Stanbury**
Director, Regulation and Government Intervention Program,
Institute for Research on Public Policy

Mark Twain is said to have stated that, "All generalizations, including this one, are false." Regulation is an instrument of government, presumably utilized to advance the public interest. This generalization surely represents an example of what Mark Twain had in mind when he coined his statement about generalizations. However, if there is any generalization that *can* be made about regulation in Canada, it is that its scope has greatly expanded in the last half century. This book is, in part, a response to the expansion of regulation by all levels of government in the Canadian economy. The papers are diverse, ranging from an analysis of the impact of regulation on technological change in the Canadian grain transport industry to the role of the Canadian Air Transportation Administration in the proposed Pickering airport near Toronto. This diversity is a reflection of the range of economic activity which is directly regulated by one or more levels of government in Canada. The evolutionary nature of regulatory processes, that is, their dynamic character, is reflected in Professor Helliwell's paper entitled "Some Emerging Issues in Utility Regulation and Rate Making" and in Heaver and Nelson's analysis of the recently proposed amendments to the *National Transportation Act*.

The whole field of regulation is presently under review. (Some might argue it is under attack!) In November 1977, the Institute for Research on Public Policy announced that regulation and government intervention would be one of its four research programs. Over a dozen research projects were commissioned on such topics as the regulation of occupational health and safety, the State and nuclear energy, charter airfares, provincial Crown corporations, and consumer intervention in the regulatory process. More recently, on July 12, 1978, the Prime Minister requested the Econmic Council of Canada to "undertake a number of studies of specific areas of government regulation which appear to be having a particularly substantial economic impact on the Canadian economy." This Reference to the Council stemmed

* W.T. Stanbury is also Director, Regulation Reference, Economic Council of Canada, and Associate Professor (on leave) Faculty of Commerce and Business Administration, University of B.C.

from the First Ministers' Conference in February 1978. The Communiqué of February 16, 1978 said, in part,

> The burden of government regulation on the private sector should be reduced and the burden of overlapping federal and provincial jurisdictions should be eliminated . . . . First Ministers agreed that the whole matter of economic regulation at all levels of government should be referred to the Economic Council for recommendations for action, in consultation with the provinces and the private sector.

The Council was requested to prepare an Interim Report by the end of 1979 and a Final Report by the end of 1980. This initiative, which follows the actions of the Ford Administration in the U.S. by several years,[1] is a welcome one. However, the process of analysing the impact of regulation (both from the point of view of allocative efficiency and the distribution of income) is likely to be easier than the process of actually implementing changes in the nature, scope and procedures of regulation in the Canadian economy.[2] Any serious program of policy reform must be based upon a sound conceptual footing and extensive empirical knowledge. The papers in this volume should make at least a modest contribution to the debate about regulatory reform.

CHAPTER TWO: RESCHENTHALER

Perhaps one-fifth of the output of the Canadian economy is subject to direct regulation, that is, "economic regulation that bears directly on pricing and resource allocation." This paper represents the first major survey article of the policies and problems of direct regulation in Canada.

Reschenthaler points out that direct regulation is only one of the systems of economic control; the others are private planning, the competitive market and government ownership. In Canada, there has been a (revealed) preference for public ownership and direct regulation, and a distinct aversion to the use of the forces of competitive markets as a means to effect the social control of industry. "The Canadian economy in a special sense can be said to

---

[1] See, for example, *The Challenge of Regulatory Reform*, A Report to the President from the Domestic Council Review Group on Regulatory Reform (Washington, D.C.: Government Printing Office, January 1977). The DCRGRR was formed in June 1975 to co-ordinate the Administration's government-wide regulatory reform program. A description of some of the process of regulatory reform is contained in Paul H. Weaver, "Unlocking the Gilded Cage of Regulation," *Fortune* (May 1977) pp. 179-82, 186-88. See also "Freedom from Regulation," *Business Week* (May 12, 1975) pp. 74—80, and "The Regulators—'They Cost You $130 Billion a Year," *U.S. News & World Report* (June 30, 1975) pp. 24-28. Many of the most interesting and influential studies of the impact of regulation have been done under the auspices of the American Enterprise Institute.

[2] In a nationally-televised speech on August 1, 1978, the Prime Minister pledged "to remove the intrusions of many Government policies and regulations from individuals and business . . ." (*Globe and Mail*, August 2, 1978, p. 1). A little over a week later, a press statement endorsed by all ten provincial premiers said, "The provincial premiers, recognizing the negative impact duplication of government functions and over-regulation have on the economy of the country and the daily lives of Canadians, today called for immediate action to lessen over-lapping services and regulations" (Montreal *Gazette*, August 10, 1978, p. 4).

have been built upon direct regulation and promotion by government." Direct regulation has taken three forms: "independent" regulatory agencies (Canadian Transport Commission, Canadian Radio-television and Telecommunications Commission, National Energy Board); self-regulation by producer groups (e.g., most marketing boards and professions); and tariff, quota, patent and banking policies under parliamentary control. Relatively few studies of the economic effects of the hundreds of regulatory agencies in Canada have been performed.

From the abundant U.S. literature and lesser volume of Canadian literature, Reschenthaler identifies a host of problem areas associated with direct regulation: capture by the regulated industry, inadequate staff and other resources for the regulators, failure of the consumer interest to organize and operate in the regulatory process, emphasis on adjudication and protection of the regulated industry, restriction of the rate of technical change, over capitalization, too little emphasis on operating efficiency, and extensive cross subsidization for political reasons. Agencies tend to outlive their real justification, the costs of "regulatory failure" may be less than the market failure regulation was designed to correct, and the political accountability of regulatory agencies may satisfy no participant—all these criticisms have been levelled at the process of direct regulation.

Many of the strongest critics (economists and lawyers) of regulation have been associated with the University of Chicago. They have called for extensive deregulation on the grounds that much direct regulation has had little impact or its social costs have exceeded its benefits. They have also argued that allocation by market forces, even if some private monopolies are the result, is both more efficient and more conducive to economic freedom. The Chicago criticisms have become increasingly persuasive as few writers defend the regulatory *status quo*[3] or propose the expansion of regulation. Reschenthaler describes Professor Trebing's criticisms of Posner's proposal to deregulate even natural monopolies. Unregulated monopolies may be subject to a variety of undesirable forms of behaviour—even though the absence of regulation may remove others. The efficacy of an excess profits tax is dubious. The effect of deregulation will depend upon the adequacy of broader constraints on monopoly power. The pressures that are supposed to erode private monopoly power are, in fact, slow to operate. In short, Trebing argues, the net benefits of deregulation have been exaggerated. In addition to these criticisms of the Chicago School, Reschenthaler questions whether the general public is willing to treat the distributional effects of private monopoly as inconsequential.

[3.] In the U.S, A.T&T. and the Bell System and in Canada, Bell C?r̄   have defended traditional public utility regulation and have sought to prevent competiti   it has been offered. They have also tried to expand the scope of regulation to cover wha   otherwise result in unregulated competition.

Reschenthaler states that "the traditional economic rationale for direct regulation can be embodied in three very general propositions." First, some industries, because of their importance in the economic infrastructure, are "affected with the public interest" and should be under direct public control. Second, the case of "natural monopolies" will require direct regulation. Third, regulation is required in situations where competition is perceived as unworkable. These arguments/explanations should not be accepted uncritically. Reschenthaler concludes that "a review of the industries which have been subject to some form of direct regulation by democratic governments in North America and Western Europe in this century leaves little doubt that using the 'affected with the public interest' and 'natural monopoly' rationales, almost any industry can and has been subjected to direct regulation or government ownership."

A variety of other rationale have been used to extend the scope of direct regulation: cross-subsidization, regional planning and development, producer protection, and the "maintenance of cultural and political integrity." Revisionist views of the demand for regulation are becoming increasingly popular, that is, regulation is seen less as a device to achieve economic efficiency than as a vehicle to effect changes in the distribution of income and wealth by those who can manipulate this form of government intervention. Reschenthaler describes a number of cases in both the U.S. and Canada which are consistent with this view.

The men and women who are on the front line of regulation (i.e., members of boards or commissions and their senior staff) may be a major source of weakness in the regulatory process. In the U.S. they may have been closely associated with the industry subject to regulation and in Canada with the public service. Given the broad mandates of most regulatory agencies, the problem of defining, in operational terms, the meaning of "the public interest" is overwhelming. In practice, many regulators seem to adopt a balancing-of-competing-interests approach in their decision-making.

Should regulators adopt an inquisitorial approach in their proceedings or should they act as adjudicators and rely on the contesting parties to elicit all the facts and establish the important arguments? The question is complicated by the concerns for overt due process and the fact that as a public good (in the technical sense), consumer interests are seldom represented in the same way as are the interests of the regulated firms.

While regulation is sometime advocated to *prevent* "unfair price discrimination," Richard Posner has recently reminded us that regulation may be used by a government to effect cross-subsidization, that is, to change the distribution of income by price discrimination. Certainly this is the case with regulated air carriers in Canada where long-haul passengers subsidize short-haul passengers and high-density markets subsidize low-density ones. Regulatory agencies have a number of reasons to prefer cross-subsidization to the payment of overt subsidies by government, as Reschenthaler explains.

Regulation is not a costless activity. There are the budgetary outlays of the agency, compliance costs (a bonanza for lawyers) as well as the social losses associated with the restriction of output under regulation. A possibly more important cost may be the "X-inefficiency" permitted by regulation, but absent in competitive markets. A number of studies in Canada and the U.S. indicate that prices under regulation are significantly higher than they would be under competitive market conditions.

"In recent years, the under-representation of the consumer interest in the regulatory process has been of increasing concern." This is particularly true where the regulators have become judges. Consumer advocacy suffers from the "free rider" problem. As a public good (in the technical sense) it will be underprovided unless financed by government. Even if the financing is available, there are important institutional barriers to active consumer participation in the regulatory process.

In the U.S. over the past four years or so there have been extensive federal analyses of regulation (both of the traditional direct regulation and the "new" areas of regulations) and some reforms have been introduced. Little deregulation has taken place (indeed, in the case of energy, more controls have been applied), but the reforms seem to be having a beneficial impact. Reschenthaler describes changes (or proposed changes) in telecommunications, trucking, and airlines.

In Canada, "most of the studies [of regulation], while informative, focus on general policy, administrative procedure, and accountability; but not on the questions of economic impact which have been central in the United States." The few studies of impact, for example those of marketing boards, "have been rejected by politicians and the public alike as irrelevant."

Efficiency concerns have not had a high priority in Canada, while political sensitivity and accountability have been more important. To contrast the Canadian and U.S. approaches Reschenthaler examines the recent behaviour of the Canadian Transport Commission and the Canadian Radio-television and Telecommunications Commissions. Both have been remarkably protective of the interests of the firms they regulate and unwilling to permit changes which would increase the role of competition. On the other hand, railway tariffs appear to be virtually unregulated under the CTC in Canada compared to the Interstate Commerce Commisssion in the U.S. The CRTC has been less concerned with economic regulation than with Canadian content issues and the like. In cable television, Reschenthaler argues, the CRTC "apparently possesses no financial standards as to what is a reasonable profit . . . [and] has failed to engage in meaningful rate regulation."

In the final section of his paper Reschenthaler reviews the proposals to establish a publicly financed consumer advocate and the limited role such entities have played in Canadian regulation.

Reschenthaler concludes his paper by indicating "four general areas where moderate reforms are possible which will result in improvements in the effectiveness and reliability of direct regulation as a system of control of corporate power." These are: (i) deregulation of commercial airlines, intra-provincial trucking, AM and FM broadcasting, peripheral telecommunications equipment and tie-line services, brokerage services, and federal and provincial marketing boards; (ii) a reorientation of the regulatory agencies from the adjudicatory to the inquisitorial model; (iii) provision for the formal representation of consumer interests in the regulatory process; and (iv) improved public access to information together with a series of careful studies which assess the economic impact of regulation.

CHAPTER THREE: HELLIWELL

This paper explains why "regulated utilities, especially those producing and distributing energy products, are living in difficult times." In the first section, Professor Helliwell surveys "the main elements of the existing economic analysis of regulation" and finds it wanting in that "the literature has not been primarily concerned with the more important current issues" facing regulated utilities. The discussion begins with a look at the Stigler-Posner "economic theory of regulation," which posits that regulation results from the interaction of the demand and supply for this form of government intervention, and then reviews Breton's theory of the supply of regulation. Political parties, Breton argues, trade financial and electoral support from the private sector for benefical laws and regulations. This method of financing political parties encourages regulation and costs consumers and taxpayers more than would a direct means of financing the democratic process.

Helliwell then reviews the Averch-Johnson over-capitalization hypothesis and its succeeding extensions and refinements. Drawing upon the papers of Callen *et al.* and Dobell *et al.*, Helliwell points out that "if, by some means, the prototype Canadian telephone industry . . . followed the efficiency rules rather than the rules for profit-maximization subject to regulatory constraint, then the gains from regulation would be more than doubled . . . to an amount equal to 65 per cent of the total revenues of an unregulated monopolist." This result not only suggests the importance of cost minimization in the tasks of the regulators (who have hitherto placed more emphasis on the rate of return than the level of costs), but also that it may be empirically tested in the Canadian context. After discussing some of the sophisticated work introducing uncertainty into the Averch-Johnson model, Helliwell suggests "it ignores too many important features of the regulatory process," for example, the use of "test year" calculations and fixed rate schedules between rate cases.

Regulated utilities are in trouble with their shareholders, customers, lenders and the public, Helliwell argues, because of four factors:
(i) rate structures with declining blocks;
(ii) inflation with historic cost accounting;
(iii) rate base accounting involving straight-line depreciation; and
(iv) marginal costs, in real terms, that are above average real costs in some utilities, especially in energy supply.
Historically, declining block rate structures were designed to reflect economies of scale (marginal costs falling below average costs) and still ensure that total revenue equalled total costs including the allowable rate of

return to shareholders. The problem now, Helliwell asserts, is that the marginal cost of output from new capacity is greatly above historical average costs, not to mention historical marginal costs. The declining block structure is being eroded by fuel adjustment clauses. The result is a flattening of the rate structure. Furthermore, there is an increased recognition that the old rate structure is now inappropriate for peak-load pricing.

Inflation with historic cost accounting creates problems in allocating costs between old and new plant and in the inflation premium associated with old and new long-term debt. A conflict is raised between allocative efficiency (pricing/costing at the margin) and the distribution of the benefits of older, lower embedded costs.

The effect of straight-line depreciation coupled with the rate return on the rate base in the face of inflation is "to increase the apparent cost of using new plant relative to old plant even when the two are of equivalent efficiency . . . *even if* the cost of new plant is appropriately measured as the discounted present value of all costs over its lifetime."

Public utilities, it has usually been argued, are natural monopolies subject to decreasing average and marginal costs over the relevant range. Yet, current evidence suggests that some regulated utilities are facing rising real costs of supply or decreasing returns to scale as sites become scarce, and the cost of fossil fuels rises.

What can be done to cope with these problems? Helliwell states: "The main pricing principle, for a utility that needs to maintain financial integrity and customer satisfaction, should be that increases in demand should be sold at prices . . . that cover the full long-term marginal costs of that supply." Such costs must reflect environmental costs, that is, the social not merely the private costs of production. There is some evidence that this principle will be applied in practice, but there remains the problem of how to handle the distribution of "surplus revenues" collected from customers. These occur because average costs, reflecting, in part, older, cheaper capital, are below current marginal costs. Helliwell suggests several alternative ways to deal with this problem.

The paper concludes with a brief statement on a number of other issues facing regulators of Canadian utilities: the quality of service; the treatment of social costs; government versus private ownership of utilities; consistency across jurisdictions; the links between investment and pricing decisions; and the efficiency of regulation itself.

CHAPTER FOUR: BORINS

Government ownership is an alternative to government regulation of privately owned enterprise. In Canada, it has been a popular alternative. This paper analyses the behaviour of the Canadian Air Transportation Administration (CATA) which owns and operates all major airports in Canada. Its assets amount to $3 billion, it expenditures in 1978-79 will be $600 million and it currently employs 12,000 people. The paper focuses on the decision (later rescinded) to build a second Toronto airport at Pickering.

The Pickering story began with a 1967 report recommending that additional land be purchased adjacent to the existing Toronto airport (Malton). Adverse response to the proposal to expand Malton saw the federal government announce in December 1968 (four months after the decision was taken to build a second airport for Montreal) that a second Toronto airport would be constructed as soon as possible. In March 1972, the Pickering site was chosen "as something of a compromise between federal and provincial preferences. . . . Each side preferred the other's favourite site or sites least." Vigorous opposition to the decision resulted in an Airport Inquiry Commission. Its report was made public in January 1975 and it supported CATA's position. The federal Cabinet approved CATA's plan and construction was to begin in the summer or fall of 1975. Now the pressure groups shifted their efforts to the Province of Ontario. With a minority government and in the light of both opposition parties' desire not to approve the Pickering site, the Province said it would not build the necessary access roads. The Pickering airport was stopped—for several years at least.

Borins analyzes CATA's behaviour by looking at important factors in the agency's environment and asking questions typical of an economist. Four factors characterize CATA's environment period.

(i) Airport planning is inherently fraught with uncertainty—in particular, CATA had "underestimated demand at Toronto, built too late and experienced several years of unexpectedly long queues in Terminal 1 before Terminal 2 was ready."

(ii) CATA is the focus of a variety of explicit or implicit interest groups, for example, the general aviation lobby, the "travelling public" (particularly those who complain), and the scheduled and charter airlines.

(iii) The agency's ability to satisfy the demands of its clients depends largely upon resources provided by the Treasury Board. The revolving fund established in 1970 "provides the appearance of budgetary change, but not the reality."

(iv) CATA's senior staff are "graduates" of the air transport industry or the military—few are economists. They tend to stay with CATA throughout their careers in the civil service.

Borins asks the following questions in an effort to understand CATA's behaviour in the decision to build Pickering airport period.

(i) Why is there no peak-load pricing of airports? CATA uses a "value-of-service" approach in establishing landing fees. Borins interprets the resulting fee schedule "as an attempt by CATA to raise a given amount of revenue while at the same time minimizing the 'griping' from its client groups." Landing fees are kept low in order to reduce (federally owned) Air Canada's deficits and assist privately owned air carriers. With respect to the peaking of certain international flights, Canada "prefers seeking international agreements to acting unilaterally" as the British have done.

(ii) Why do CATA planners do what they do? Perhaps in response to their under-building at Malton, CATA planners biased their estimates to avoid a similar result with respect to Pickering, for example, the agency used "a very high demand forecast for its planning." CATA's noise forecasts applicable to Malton and Pickering amounted to "the 'worst case' that a reasonable man, with the information available in 1973, might have expected to occur."

(iii) Why Pickering? Why not improve Malton? The noise problem apparently pushed CATA toward Pickering, even at the expense of excess capacity if technical advances would reduce aircraft noise at Malton. This tendency was reinforced by the perception that the intensified use of Malton "would antagonize airport users, because it would imply a lowering of the present standards for airport facilities, and because it would make Malton a more difficult airport to manage." CATA's amenity standards, as compared to many U.S. airports, imply substantial excess capacity.

CATA's environment is changing, Borins asserts. The Treasury Board is tightening up its control; Mirabel has left a bad taste in taxpayers' mouths; and the extension of the Vancouver airport has been delayed. CATA's responses to the new environment consist of both the hard-line, "this-too-shall-pass" approach, and a more adaptive one which incorporates more sophisticated economic analyses of large capital projects. Borins is optimistic that CATA "might be changing in the direction of policies which are both more economically efficient and responsive."

CHAPTER FIVE: MAISTER

Can the process of regulation inhibit the rate of technological and organizational change in a regulated industry? This paper examines this question in the case of the Canadian grain transport industry which is regulated by the Canadian Transport Commission, the Canadian Wheat Board, the Canadian Grain Commission and by several federal statutes, for example, the Crow's Nest Pass Agreement. In particular, it asks whether the substitution of large-scale sub-terminals (or inland terminals) for the older, country elevator system was significantly inhibited by regulatory (and other) barriers. But the paper goes beyond providing evidence to indicate that changes in certain regulatory barriers were necessary before the inland terminal system could be introduced to examine the *dynamics* of regulatory change.

Maister emphasizes "channel theory" in explaining change in regulated industries. This theory, in which power comes to rival economic factors as the dominant element, is based upon the relationships between institutions in a channel of distribution. Conflict occurs because of varying goals and because of role deviance, conflicting perceptions of reality, conflicting expectations, zero-sum competition for scarce resources, breakdowns in communications, differences in channel members' values, differences in status aspirations and conflicts in domain. A principal way in which conflict may be overcome is by setting superordinate goals, obtaining domain concensus among channel members and by unifying perceptions. These are often achieved through the actions of a "channel captain"—the member of the system who has the dominant power (based on coercion, expert knowledge, legitimacy or identification).

The process of change (from the country elevator system to inland terminals) can be divided into three stages: the 'disequilibrating stage''; the "initiation stage"; and an "inter-type competition stage." Maister's model focuses on the first two of these and he sets out a number of specific hypotheses which are tested by the case study.

A major section of the paper is devoted to an analysis of the structure of the Canadian grain transportation industry. The following are its most important characteristics.

- The Canadian Wheat Board (CWB) markets about 90 percent of grain production, principally wheat, barley and oats.
- Farmers deliver their grain to the almost 4000 country elevators in 1500 locations themselves—an average haul of ten miles; an average payload of 200 bushels.
- Movement of all grains out of country elevators is under the control of the CWB which used the "block shipping system" between 1958 and 1976. Rail cars are allocated among the forty-eight blocks and then, among specific companies by the "Bracken Formula."
- Rail freight rates on export grain to Vancouver or the Lakehead or on domestic grain to the Lakehead have been held at 1899 levels under the Crow's Nest Pass Agreement.
- Upon delivery to the country elevator, the farmer receives an initial payment less the rail freight charges and less a handling charge established by the Canadian Grain Commission (CGC). The latter also regulates the maximum storage fees paid by the Board to the elevator companies and the terminal elevator charges and the charge for cleaning.
- Eight companies, four of which are farmer co-operatives, operate the primary elevators. The Alberta, Saskatchewan and Manitoba Wheat Pools share of storage capacity increased from 42 to 61 percent between 1964 and 1976.
- There are twenty-four terminal elevators in the four major export ports. The four farmers' co-operatives account for three-quarters of capacity; competition is limited.
- The movement of grain currently accounts for over 20 percent of the railways tonnage and over 30 percent of total ton-mile output—but only 12 percent of their total revenue. The railways were losing $90 million per year on grain in the mid-1970s.
- Three federal ministries and a larger number of boards or agencies are directly involved in grain transportation. Provincial governments are also involved. They provide the roads over which farmers transport their grain to the country elevators.

Maister identifies a number of problems experienced in the grain transport system in the late 1960s. There were too many small country elevators; many were obsolescent. The railways were plagued with many miles of unremunerative branch lines which they could not abandon. The Crow rate led to a shortage of box cars. Vancouver rail operations were congested and there was insufficient cleaning capacity. The predominant alternative to the inefficient country elevator system is the inland terminal system which consists of (i) bulk accumulation of grain by road in large inland terminals, (ii) inland cleaning of grain, and (iii) the use of unit trains to move the grain to export or distant domestic markets. In terms of 1968-69, it was estimated that a shift to a system of eight inland terminals would save $71 million out of a total cost of $415 million, of which the farmers paid $257 million. Maister's revision of these estimates indicates "that total savings with an inland terminal system may be as much as *twice* that [estimated]."

What were the regulatory barriers to the adoption of the new system? Maister identifies several.

- Under the *Canada Grain Act*, elevator owners could not offer discounts to induce farmers to transport their grain farther to larger and more efficient elevators.
- The CGC had held country elevator handling tariffs at extremely low levels, the resulting losses discouraged new investment.
- The cleaning tariff, unchanged from the early 1920s to 1975, inhibited cleaning grain inland.
- The statutory Crow rate, less than the railroad's costs, meant that a potential inland terminal operator could not capture any of the cost savings going to the railways as the result of the use of unit trains.

Other institutional arrangements also inhibited technological and organizational change in grain transport.

Maister details the origins of the regulatory barriers and the bases of their perpetuation—the attitudes of the participants (farmers, elevator operators, the railways, the federal government and its agencies, and the provinces), and the considerations of each participant's power in the system. Most participants opposed the inland terminal system "on the grounds of threats that it poses to role and domain perceptions and differing goals." With respect to the power of various participants, Maister notes that although the federal government has potentially coercive power, it has been reluctant to utilize it. Like other particpants, it has felt constrained to justify its actions as being "in the best interests of the producer." "The basis of producer power is primarily political, and when mobilized, it can be a strong force," Maister notes by referring to the numerous pieces of legislation benefiting prairie farmers. The grain co-operatives have an identification power source—and a large market share at both the country and terminal elevator level.

How did changes come about in the grain transport industry? They resulted from shifts in power, in goals and in perceptions.

- Producer goals shifted as the average size of prairie farms increased and the West became more urbanized.
- Under the *National Transportation Act* of 1967, the federal government's direct subsidies for branch lines gave it an incentive

to be a more active participant.

- The concentration of ownership of both country elevators and export terminals increased—reducing the number of alternatives open to farmers; the co-operatives became big business.
- Large volume exports to the Soviet Union in the 1960s showed the defects in the existing system: "the system was designed to store grain, not to transport it efficiently." The federal government gradually began to assume the role of "channel captain."
- Legislative changes in 1971 permitted the elevator companies to charge different tariffs at different locations.
- Rising wheat prices (e.g., to $5.00/bu. by 1973-74 crop year) permitted an increase in the maximum primary elevator tariff from 3.75¢/bu. (established in 1971) to 10.5¢/bu. in 1974.
- Both the maximum terminal elevation and cleaning tariffs were increased—particularly the latter (from 1¢ to 5¢ per bushel).
- In 1976, a procedural change in allocating rail cars gave an incentive to build inland terminals.

Late in 1974, after the maximum tariffs had been increased, plans were announced for the first inland terminal at Weyburn, Saskatchewan. It opened in November 1976. Announcements of plans for similar terminals have been made.

Sadly, these are not high storage capacity inland terminals as originally conceived (and in operation in the U.S.). They seem to be designed for only one phase in the world grain cycle. As Maister notes, the potential success of the new system is *not* assured as the Saskatchewan government's recent actions and certain recommendations of the Hall Commission presently militate against rapid adoption of the inland terminal system.

CHAPTER SIX: McMANUS

This paper evaluates the *National Transportation Act* which was passed in 1967 following the *Report* of the Royal Commission on Transportation (the MacPherson Commission) in 1961. McManus points out that the Act incorporates conflicting objectives in Section 3 and Section 23 and that a decade later "it seems we don't know if we have a new transportation policy based on minimizing cost or the old one based on an equitable regional distribution of economic activity."[4] McManus states that, from an economic point of view, there are two competing rationales for government regulation of economic activity: (i) to effect a more efficient allocation of resources, and (ii) to use regulation as an instrument of public finance, that is, to charge ("tax") some consumers of the regulated firms' output more than it costs to supply them and to charge others less than it costs to supply them.

[4.] Amendments to the 1967 Act introduced in 1977 (Bill C-33) clearly give more emphasis to the latter objective. They are analyzed in Chapter Seven by Professors Heaver and Nelson.

Such cross-subsidization through the technique of regulation is an alternative to the usual overt tax/transfer system. While the MacPherson Commission emphasized efficiency as the primary regulatory objective, Mackintosh, writing in 1939, indicates that "taxation by regulation" (Posner's phrase) has been the normal approach to transport regulation by Canadian economists with an interest in public policy issues. The Act of 1967, says McManus, indicates Parliament's indecision about the efficiency and public finance objectives.

McManus goes on to point out that the presence of legal barriers to entry imposed by regulators is inconsistent with the natural monopoly theory of regulation. He indicates why the presence of rents, usually due to entry barriers, is consistent with the proposition that the objective of regulation is to serve as an indirect tax and expenditure mechanism. such rents provide the tax base for redistribution among consumers. The evidence, McManus concludes, supports the "taxation by regulation" approach.

External effects provide only a limited basis for the regulation of railroads. In fact, there are two defects in the externalities justification for regulation. First, "not all damages resulting from an action are 'external' damages"—some occur simply because resources are scarce. The case of the withdrawal of railroad services is discussed. It is pointed out that consumers would like to have the service, but are unwilling to pay for it. Second, the proponents of regulation on the grounds of external effects "often seem to ignore the effects on behaviour of changes in external effects . . . Individuals will adjust their behaviour to reduce the external damages caused them by others and to increase external benefits." McManus illustrates his point with the example of a subsidized commuter service instituted to relieve traffic congestion on a public highway. The result could be no reduction of highway congestion; the subsidies produce no offsetting gains.

In the next section of the paper, McManus reviews the context in which Parliament was motivated to write the *National Transportation Act* of 1967. Technical change, in particular the competition from trucking, was making traditional railway regulation difficult. The MacPherson Commission called for flexibility for the railroads to adapt to more vigorous intermodal competition. Insistence on unremunerative services and "value of service" pricing exemplified the use of the railroads as instruments of public finance. Despite increased rates, between 1959 and 1966, the federal government provided $500 million to subsidize railroad freight rates. These subsidies affected locational decisions. In addition, there were substantial direct and indirect subsidies beyond those associated with the *Freight Rates Reduction Act* of 1959. These are detailed by McManus.

In the succeeding section of the paper, McManus questions whether the 1967 Act really constituted a "new transportation policy." He notes two general changes: (i) some direct subsidies were substituted for cross-subsidization resulting from "value of service" pricing, and (ii) "there is a reduction in regulatory control over the railway companies and an increase in potential regulatory control over other modes, particularly trucking." Under the NTA, the railways were free to adjust their general level of rates which had been frozen since 1959. Virtually all earlier subsidies have been retained; in addition, they received subsidies equal to all losses on branch lines and 80 percent of losses on passenger services. In 1976, these subsidies totalled $260 million. The Canadian Transport Commission, created under the 1967 NTA, administers the subsidies. The NTA also created subsidies to truckers, which in 1976 exceeded $23 million.

McManus describes the maintenance of branch lines and continuance of passenger service subsidies as "sacred cows." The mileage of branch lines protected by Order-in-Council has increased greatly over the past decade. The statutory Crow's Nest Pass rates have contributed to the problem. McManus concludes that the CTC "is making decisions regarding passenger services on a political rather than an economic basis." The hard decisions, involving real trade-offs, have yet to be made.

With respect to freight rates, McManus observes that since 1967, the appeal provisions under Section 23 of the NTA have been used eight times, but only one case was completed. As he illustrates with details from some of the appeals, the process has hardly been satisfactory.

Although Sections 36 to 42 of the NTA gave the CTC potential regulatory control over interprovincial trucking, this power has not been exercised by the federal agency.

McManus concludes, from the 1967 Act, that "there has been no apparent change in the objectives of transport policy, except for a most cursory flirtation with efficiency . . . " In fact, Mackintosh's perceptions of 1939 are quite accurate today—transport regulation is largely an instrument of public finance to effect interregional cross-subsidization.

CHAPTER SEVEN: HEAVER AND NELSON

This paper examines Bill C-33 which was introduced into Parliament on January 27, 1977 and would significantly amend the *National Transportation Act* (NTA) of 1967 (and related Acts.). Although the Bill was not enacted, it appears the federal government does plan to alter the stated objectives of the NTA. Heaver and Nelson argue that the government is "misguided" and that "the changes run the risk of leading to decisions contrary to the efficient provision of transport services while exacerbating regional dissatisfactions . . ." They assert that the efficiency objective should be paramount in transport regulation (specifically freight rates and service conditions) and that regulation should not be used to pursue non-economic objectives.

In reviewing the NTA of 1967, Heaver and Nelson state (contrary to McManus in Chapter Six) that "the emphasis in the existing policy is, clearly, on achieving efficiency in the transportation industry." In Bill C-33, transport is to be "efficient," but it is also to be "an instrument of support for the achievement of national and regional social and economic objectives," and it is to provide "accessibility and equity of treatment of users." A set of eleven principles are set out to assist the Canadian Transport Commission in achieving the objectives of regulation, for example, intermodal competition is acknowledged, as is the desirability of commercial viability and where local monopoly exists, rates must be regulated to protect users. Where government policy requires departures from commercial viability, the additional costs are to be borne by the government.

Heaver and Nelson go on to examine the present working of railway markets. They state that "overall, the railways do not enjoy a monopoly power today that enables them to earn monopoly profits." In most markets, intermodal competition exists or the threat of it has similar results. On the basis of their recent book, Heaver and Nelson conclude, "The evidence is clear that market competition in its various forms is a significant controlling factor on the level of railway rates throughout the country and on a wide range of commodities." However, due to the Crow's Nest Pass rates and other factors, the rate structure is complex and involves an extensive amount of price discrimination. Although there have been a few appeals under Section 23 of the NTA, "most shippers are strongly in favour of reliance on the existing transportation policy."

Heaver and Nelson point out that the relationship between minimum and maximum rates under the *Railway Act* and the policy statements in the Bill is unclear. Agreed charges appear to be subject to the new policy statements embodied in the Bill. The policy statements seem unlikely to affect the criteria by which consolidations are judged. However, "the policy statement of Bill C-33 raises insurmountable problems for application to the regulation of rates in the public interest." This is so because the statement of objectives and principles involves conflicts; because political policy judgments are required which the CTC is not qualified to make; and because the application of the objectives and principles is contrary to the carriers, shippers, and the public's interest in efficiency.

With respect to the conflict of objectives and principles, "the CTC is not likely to make choices between efficiency, various national policies, accessibility and equity, consistent with provincial and federal government views in judging the reasonableness of a particular rate." Heaver and Nelson assert that specific concepts in the policy statement are ambiguous and that "it is not an acceptable position for government to suggest that the meaning of words and expressions in Bill C-33 will be defined over time as the CTC renders its decisions." Two obvious examples of ambiguous terms are: "equity" and "effective competition." It is argued that experience under the NTA of 1967 "has shown reliance on commercial market forces has been conducive to the development of efficiency in the Canadian transportation and distribution systems." However, Bill C-33 threatens to supplant the successful operation of market forces in the pursuit of "the public interest" by a few "prudent men" in the CTC. Heaver and Nelson state that the proposed legislation "does not make clear the conditions under which the public interest should take precedence over the private interest and the profitability of traffic to the railways."

The conclusions drawn by Heaver and Nelson are as follows: (i) "the regulation of railway rates and services by the CTC to achieve social and political ends would not be conducive to efficiency in the transportation industry and, therefore, in Canadian production and distribution systems"; (ii) the government appears to have failed to differentiate between its operational and promotional role in the transportation system and the principles to be applied by a regulatory commission; and (iii) "the solution of regional concerns, attributed to transport regulation, does not lie in the application of the transport policy in Bill C-33 to transport regulation."

Chapitre un

Abrégé: Etudes de la réglementation au Canada

par
W. T. Stanbury*
Directeur du programme Régulementation et intervention
gouvernementale, à l'Institut de recherches politiques

Selon Mark Twain, "Toutes les généralisations sont fausses, y compris celle-ci." L'affirmation selon laquelle les gouvernements auraient recours à la réglementation pour mieux servir l'intérêt général constitue certainement un exemple de généralisation illustrant l'aphorisme de Mark Twain. On peut néanmoins émettre l'idée générale suivante, au sujet de la réglementation au Canada: son champ d'application s'est considérablement agrandi au cours des cinquante dernières années. Le développement des contrôles exercés sur l'économie canadienne par tous les niveaux de gouvernement est, pour une large part, à l'origine de ce rapport. Cette question a fait l'objet d'une gamme d'études diversifiées, allant d'une analyse des effets de la réglementation sur les changements technologiques survenus dans l'industrie canadienne du transport des céréales, à l'examen du rôle joué par l'Administration canadienne des transports aériens dans l'élaboration du projet aéroportuaire de Pickering, près de Toronto. Cette pluralité reflète la diversité des activités économiques directement réglementées par un ou plusieurs niveaux de gouvernement au Canada. Le caractère évolutif ou dynamique des dispositions réglementaires se trouve souligné dans l'exposé du professeur Helliwell, intitulé "Some Emerging Issues in Utility Regulation and Rate Making"**, comme dans l'analyse des récentes propositions d'amendements de la *Loi nationale sur les transports,* effectuée par Heaver et Nelson.

On assiste actuellement à un réexamen complet des domaines soumis aux réglementations (certains affirmeront qu'il s'agit d'une remise en cause!). En novembre 1977, l'Institut de recherches politiques annonça que l'un de ses quatre programmes de recherche serait consacré à l'intervention gouvernementale et à la réglementation. Plus d'une douzaine d'études ont été commandées, concernant entre autres les dispositions réglementaires

---

*M. Stanbury est aussi Directeur responsable du mandat sur la réglementation du Conseil économique du Canada, et Professeur agrégé (en congé) de la Faculté de commerce et d'administration des affaires à l'Université de Colombie-Britannique.
**N.D.T.: "Quelques problèmes posés par la tarification et la réglementation des services publics".

relatives à l'hygiène et la sécurité au travail, le rôle de l'Etat vis-à-vis de l'énergie nucléaire, les tarifs de nolisement, les sociétés de la Couronne provinciales et l'intervention des consommateurs dans l'élaboration des règlements. Dernièrement, le 12 juillet 1978, le Premier ministre pria le Conseil économique du Canada "d'étudier les domaines particuliers de la réglementation gouvernementale dont l'influence sur l'économie canadienne semble spécialement importante". Ces instructions découlent de la conférence des Premiers ministres, du 16 février 1978, dont le communiqué concluait notamment:

> "Il conviendrait de soulager le secteur privé du poids excessif des réglementations gouvernementales et d'éliminer le chevauchement des juridictions fédérale et provinciale . . . Les Premiers ministres ont décidé de confier au Conseil économique le soin d'examiner globalement le problème de la réglementation économique, aux divers niveaux de gouvernement, et de recommander certaines mesures élaborées au terme de consultations auprès des provinces et du secteur privé."

On demanda au Conseil économique de préparer un rapport provisoire avant la fin de 1979 et un rapport final avant la fin de 1980. Quelques années après les mesures de l'administration Ford, cette initiative est certes la bienvenue.[1]

Toutefois, il semble moins facile de modifier vraiment le caractère, l'étendue et les modalités des réglementations appliquées[2] à l'économie canadienne que d'en analyser les conséquences, tant sur la répartition des ressources que sur la distribution des revenus. Mais, tout programme sérieux de réformes des politiques d'action doit être fondé sur des conceptions théoriques bien établies associées à des connaissances empiriques étendues. Les diverses études présentées dans ce compte rendu devraient apporter une modeste contribution au débat sur la réforme de la réglementation.

---

[1] Consulter, par exemple, *The Challenge of Regulatory Reform*, rapport soumis au Président par le Domestic Council Review Group on Regulatory Reform (Washington, D.C., Government Printing Office, janvier 1977). Le DCRGRR a été formé en juin 1975, afin de coordonner le programme de réforme de tous les organismes gouvernementaux. Plusieurs articles donnent une description de certains aspects de ce programme:
- Paul H. Weaver, "Unlocking the Gilded Cage of Regulation", *Fortune*, mai 1977, pp. 179 - 182, 186 - 188;
- "Freedom for Regulation", *Business Week*, 12 mai 1975, pp. 74 - 80; et
- "The Regulators—They Cost You $130 Billion a Year", *U.S. News & World Report*, 30 juin 1975, pp. 24 - 28.
Plusieurs des études les plus intéressantes et les plus pertinentes concernant les effets de la réglementation ont été effectuées sous la direction de l'American Enterprise Institute.

[2] Dans son discours du 1er août 1978, télévisé à tout le pays, le Premier ministre s'engagea à "supprimer de nombreuses dispositions et réglementations importanunt les individus et les entreprises . . . " *(Globe and Mail*, 2 août 1978, p. 1). A peine une semaine plus tard, les dix Premiers ministres provinciaux appuyaient le communiqué de presse suivant: "les Premiers ministres des Provinces, reconnaissant les effets néfastes du dédoublement des responsabilités gouvernementales et de l'excès de réglementations sur l'économie du pays et sur la vie quotidienne des Canadiens, ont réclamé aujourd'hui que soient prises des mesures immédiates afin de restreindre le chevauchement des services et le nombre des réglementations" *(Montreal Gazette*, 10 août 1978, p. 4).

CHAPITRE DEUX: RESCHENTHALER

"La réglementation économique exercée directement sur la tarification et sur la répartition des ressources", c'est-à-dire la réglementation directe, s'applique approximativement à un cinquième de la production canadienne. Ce travail représente la première étude complète des politiques de réglementation directe poursuivies au Canada et des problèmes qu'elles ont rencontrés.

Reschenthaler souligne l'existence d'autres moyens de contrôle économique: la planification privée, les mécanismes des marchés concurrentiels et la nationalisation. On constate, au Canada, une préférence (manifeste) pour les nationalisations et la réglementation directe, associée à une résistance marquée à recourir au mécanisme concurrentiel, pour permettre à la collectivité d'exercer un certain contrôle sur l'économie. "En un sens, on peut dire que l'édification de l'économie canadienne repose sur le soutien du gouvernement et sur la réglementation directe." Cette dernière s'applique de trois manières différentes: par l'intermédiaire d'organismes "indépendants"—comme la Commission canadienne des transports, le Conseil de la Radio-diffusion et des Télécommunications canadiennes et l'Office national de l'Energie—par les producteurs privés eux-mêmes (par exemple, la plupart des offices de commercialisation et des associations professionnelles) et enfin, par la fixation de tarifs, de quotas, l'émission de titres, la définition de politiques bancaires, sous le contrôle du Parlement. Le rôle économique de ces centaines d'organismes de contrôle existant au Canada a été relativement peu étudié.

L'examen de l'importante bibliographie, davantage américaine que canadienne, se rapportant à ce sujet a permis à Reschenthaler de dresser une longue liste de problèmes liés à la réglementation directe: accaparement du marché par les entreprises contrôlées, insuffisance du personnel et des ressources matérielles des organismes de réglementation, incapacité des consommateurs à organiser leur participation active à ce processus, priorité accordée à la désignation et à la protection des secteurs industriels réglementés, ralentissement des changements technologiques, surcapitalisation, stimulation insuffisante de la productivité et développement des mécanismes de financement compensatoire, utilisés à des fins politiques. Les organismes responsables cherchent à défendre leur action, en soutenant que le coût des défauts du marché dépasse sans doute celui de l'insuccès des mesures destinées à les corriger: toutefois cette justification risque de ne satisfaire personne et tous les problèmes énumérés ci-dessus alimentent les critiques à l'encontre des mécanismes de réglementation directe.

Les critiques les plus solidement fondées émanent d'économistes et d'avocats, dont les conceptions relèvent de l'école de Chicago. Ils ont mené une campagne pour l'abolition de la réglementation directe en mettant l'accent sur son manque d'efficacité et sur la faiblesse de ses bénéfices par rapport à ses coûts sociaux. Selon eux, la répartition des ressources, sous l'effet des forces du marché, revêt une plus grande efficacité, tout en respectant davantage la liberté économique, même si cela doit aboutir à la formation de quelques monopoles privés. Ces critiques se sont aiguisées, face à certains auteurs défendant le *statu quo*[3] ou préconisant même une extension des règlements. Reschenthaler rend compte de la position du professeur Trebing qui condamne la levée de toutes les réglementations, jusqu'à celles régissant les monopoles naturels, comme Posner l'avait proposé. Une telle libéralisation peut entraîner toutes sortes de réactions malencontreuses, alors même que certaines réactions pourraient être éliminées par l'absence de disposition réglementaire—ainsi, la taxation excessive des profits ne possède-t-elle qu'une efficacité douteuse. Le succès d'une telle politique dépendra du caractère approprié de mesures de contrainte plus globales destinées à éroder le pouvoir des monopoles; or, dans la pratique, celles-ci mettent un certain temps à fonctionner. Bref, Trebing conclut que les avantages d'une levée des réglementations ont été surestimés. Après avoir examiné la critique des théories de l'école de Chicago, Reschenthaler se demande si le public consent vraiment à accepter les conséquences de la formation de monopoles privés sur la distribution des richesses.

D'après Reschenthaler, "la théorie économique classique donne trois raisons, d'ordre très général, à la réglementation directe". Tout d'abord, certaines entreprises, "d'intérêt général", devraient être directement contrôlées par la collectivité, de par leur importance dans l'infrastructure économique; par ailleurs, les "monopoles naturels" doivent être contrôlés de manière directe; enfin, la réglementation s'impose également, lorsque le principe de la libre concurrence ne semble pas applicable. Ces arguments et ces explications devraient toutefois susciter quelques réserves. Ainsi, affirme Reschenthaler, "après avoir examiné toutes les industries soumises, au cours du XXe siècle, à une forme quelconque de réglementation directe, par les gouvernements démocratiques d'Amérique du Nord ou d'Europe occidentale, il apparaît évident que toutes les activités économiques, pratiquement sans exception, peuvent faire ou ont fait l'objet d'une intervention—réglementation ou nationalisation—soit au nom de l'intérêt collectif, soit en invoquant la notion de monopole naturel".

Le domaine d'application de ce type d'intervention gouvernementale s'est également élargi pour plusieurs autres motifs: financement compensatoire, planification et développement régionaux, protection des producteurs et "maintien de l'indépendance politique et culturelle". Les idées de réformes, préconisant une extension de la réglementation, se font de plus en plus populaires; en d'autres termes, cette politique apparaît davantage comme un instrument, aux mains des responsables, permettant de modifier

---

[3] Les compagnies ATT, Bell System, aux Etats-Unis, et Bell Canada ont soutenu le principe de la réglementation classique des services publics et se sont efforcées d'éviter les situations concurrentielles qui pouvaient se présenter. Ces entreprises ont également tenté d'étendre la portée de la réglementation à des domaines susceptibles de donner lieu à une concurrence non réglementée.

la distribution des revenus et des richesses, plutôt qu'un jeu de dispositions visant à obtenir une efficacité économique certaine. Reschenthaler a relevé aux Etats-Unis et au Canada plusieurs exemples reflétant une conception semblable.

Les personnes confrontées aux responsabilités les plus hautes en matière de réglementation (c'est-à-dire, les membres des commissions et des organismes et leurs collaborateurs immédiats) risquent d'être les plus susceptibles de freiner l'application de ces mesures, pour avoir été associées de près aux industries concernées, aux Etats-Unis, ou bien aux services publics, au Canada. Par ailleurs, il semble fort malaisé de définir en termes pratiques la notion "d'intérêt collectif", étant donné l'imprécision de la mission assignée à ces organismes. Dans les faits, les responsables de la définition des règlements semblent souvent enclins à fonder leurs décisions sur un juste compromis entre les différents intérêts en présence.

Devraient-ils au contraire, dans leurs travaux, adopter un rôle investigateur ou bien se comporter en arbitres, comptant sur les parties en cause pour élucider les faits et développer les raisonnements pertinents? Le souci d'assurer une rigueur évidente au processus de réglementation accroît encore les difficultés, d'autant que les intérêts des consommateurs—ainsi que la défense d'autres biens collectifs (au sens économique)—sont représentés dans des conditions différentes de ceux des entreprises contrôlées.

L'intervention des pouvoirs publics est parfois préconisée, afin *d'éviter* "une discrimination injuste par le mécanisme des prix"; cependant, Richard Posner nous a récemment rappelé qu'un gouvernement pouvait recourir à la réglementation afin d'obtenir un financement compensatoire, c'est-à-dire afin de modifier la distribution des revenus par le biais du mécanisme des prix. C'est sans aucun doute le cas des transports aériens canadiens réglementés: les passagers des vols long-courriers subventionnent ceux des vols à courte distance, et les marchés à forte densité subventionnent ceux à densité plus faible. Pour plusieurs raisons, les organismes de réglementation préfèrent le financement compensatoire à l'octroi de subventions gouvernementales officielles, comme l'explique Reschenthaler.

L'élaboration et la mise en oeuvre d'un règlement ne se font pas gratuitement: déboursés budgétaires de l'organisme responsable, frais d'acquiescement des parties en présence (providentiels pour les avocats) s'ajoutent au coût social entraîné par les limitations ainsi imposées à la production concernée. Ce genre de dispositions provoque également "une certaine perte de productivité", sans doute encore plus coûteuse, mais absente dans un contexte concurrentiel. De nombreuses études, canadiennes et américaines, révèlent d'ailleurs que les prix seraient moins élevés dans un marché régi par la libre concurrence.

"Au cours des dernières années, l'insuffisance de la participation des consommateurs au processus de réglementation a fait l'objet d'une préoccupation croissante", en particulier lorsque les responsables de la définition des règlements ont adopté un rôle d'arbitre; dans ces circonstances la protection des consommateurs (tout comme celle d'autres biens publics, au sens économique) souffrira d'un grave handicap, celui des "causes marginales", à moins de recevoir l'appui financier du gouvernement; même dans cette dernière hypothèse, l'importance des barrières institutionnelles s'oppose à la participation effective des consommateurs.

Au cours des quatre dernières années, il a été effectué, à la demande du gouvernement fédéral américain, une série d'analyses détaillées des réglementations directes classiques, comme de celles appliquées à des domaines "nouveaux"; quelques réformes ont été introduites, dont l'impact semble avoir été bénéfique. Toutefois, peu de dispositions réglementaires furent levées: au contraire, dans le cas de l'énergie, la politique de contrôle s'intensifia. Reschenthaler présente une description des changements intervenus (ou proposés), en matière de télécommunications, de transports routiers et aériens.

Au Canada, "la plupart des études [similaires], certes instructives, s'attachent simplement aux problèmes de politique générale, de procédures administratives et de définitions des responsabilités: elles laissent de côté la question de l'incidence économique des réglementations, objet principal des études effectuées aux Etats-Unis". Les quelques travaux qui s'y rapportent, ceux par exemple des offices de commercialisation, "ont été rejetés par les politiciens et par le public comme hors de propos".

La recherche de l'efficacité n'a pas revêtu au Canada un caractère très prioritaire, à l'encontre de la sensibilité aux questions politiques et de l'intérêt porté à la notion de responsabilité. Reschenthaler examine l'attitude récente de la Commission canadienne des transports et du Conseil de la Radio-diffusion et des Télécommunications canadiennes, afin de mettre en contraste les approches différentes prévalant aux Etats-Unis et au Canada. Ces deux organismes se sont efforcés de protéger les entreprises réglementées, se montrant peu soucieux d'introduire des changements propres à susciter une plus grande concurrence. Par ailleurs, le contrôle de la Commission des transports sur les tarifs ferroviaires semble inexistant comparé à celui de l'Interstate Commerce Commission, aux Etats-Unis, tandisque le C.R.T.C. s'est davantage préoccupé du contenu canadien des émissions et autres questions semblables, que d'exercer un contrôle de nature économique. Dans le cas de la télévision par câble, Reschenthaler met en évidence "l'absence de critère financier définissant un profit raisonnable . . . [et] l'échec de cet organisme à mettre en oeuvre une réelle réglementation des prix".

A la fin de son étude, Reschenthaler analyse les propositions visant à la création d'une fonction de défenseur des consommateurs, rémunérée par le gouvernement, puis examine l'importance restreinte que représentent de tels concepts dans l'élaboration des règlements au Canada.

Reschenthaler conclut en citant "quatre domaines où l'introduction de réformes modérées doit accroître l'efficacité et la fiabilité de la réglementation directe, c'est-à-dire du système de contrôle au service des pouvoirs constitués". Il s'agit de: (1) la levée des règlements régissant les compagnies aériennes privées, le transport routier à l'intérieur des provinces, les stations radiophoniques AM et FM, les services de lignes directes et d'équipements périphériques de télécommunications, les services de courtage et les offices de commercialisation fédéraux et provinciaux; (2) la promotion du rôle investigateur des organismes de réglementation, au détriment de leur rôle d'arbitre; (3) la prise de dispositions assurant la représentation officielle des consommateurs; et (4) l'amélioration de l'accès du public à l'information et la mise en oeuvre d'études approfondies des conséquences économiques de la réglementation.

CHAPITRE TROIS: HELLIWELL

Cette étude se propose d'expliquer "les difficultés traversées actuellement par les entreprises de services publics réglementées, et particulièrement par celles de production et de distribution de l'énergie". Dans une première partie, le professeur Helliwell examine "les principales caractéristiques de l'analyse économique actuelle de la réglementation" et en attribue les faiblesses "à une préoccupation insuffisante des écrits dans ce domaine, à l'égard des problèmes majeurs actuels" relatifs aux entreprises de services publics réglementées. Cet examen porte d'abord sur la théorie économique de Stigler-Posner, selon laquelle la réglementation résulterait de l'interaction de l'offre et de la demande dans ce domaine d'intervention publique, puis sur la théorie de Breton, de "l'offre de réglementation"; d'après Breton, les partis politiques proposent au secteur privé, en échange de son appui financier et électoral, de faire passer des lois et des règlements avantageux. Ce mode particulier de financement des partis politiques ne manque certes pas de favoriser l'extension des règlements, mais il coûte davantage aux consommateurs et aux contribuables qu'un système de subventions officielles.

Helliwell étudie ensuite la théorie de la surcapitalisation de Averch-Johnson, puis ses développements et ses perfectionnements ultérieurs. Se reférant aux travaux de Callen et de Dobell, il précise: "si une industrie-type, l'industrie canadienne du téléphone, observait d'une certaine manière les règles de l'efficacité, et non celles de la maximisation des profits—soumises aux règlements en vigueur—les gains induits par la réglementation devraient alors doubler . . . pour atteindre 65 p. cent des revenus globaux d'un monopole incontrôlé". Cette conclusion souligne l'importance que les auteurs des dispositions réglementaires doivent attacher à l'objectif de minimisation des coûts (après avoir davantage mis l'accent sur les taux de rentabilité que sur les coûts) et suggère la possibilité de procéder à une expérimentation de cette théorie dans le contexte canadien. Après avoir passé en revue certains perfectionnements théoriques introduisant la notion d'incertitude dans le modèle de Averch-Johnson, Helliwell y constate "l'absence de trop nombreuses caractéristiques importantes du processus de réglementation" tels les calculs d'évaluation d'une "année-test" et l'usage de barèmes tarifaires choisis entre plusieurs hypothèses.

Les difficultés que rencontrent les entreprises réglementées de services publics, auprès de leurs actionnaires, de leurs clients, de leurs créanciers et de la population, tiennent à quatre raisons identifiées par Helliwell:

(1) utilisation de tarifs dégressifs par paliers;
(2) inflation induite par les dépenses antérieures;
(3) évaluation de la base tarifaire à partir d'un amortissement linéaire;
(4) coûts marginaux, en termes réels supérieurs aux coûts moyens réels, dans certains services publics, notamment d'approvisionnement en énergie.

Historiquement conçue pour tenir compte des économies d'échelle (coût marginal devenant inférieur au coût moyen), la dégressivité par paliers devait garantir l'égalité des recettes totales aux coûts totaux, tout en laissant aux actionnaires un taux de profit raisonable. Or, à présent, la difficulté provient—selon Helliwell—de la hausse du coût marginal de l'actuelle capacité de production, dépassant largement les coûts moyens antérieurs et, *a fortiori*, les coûts marginaux précédemment encourus. De plus, sous l'effet des mesures de rationnement du carburant, la dégressivité tarifaire tend à s'amoindrir, pour quasiment disparaître. Enfin, on reconnaît actuellement davantage l'inadaptation de ce système à la tarification de la charge de pointe.

L'inflation induite par la comptabilisation des dépenses antérieures complique la répartition des coûts entre les installations anciennes et récentes ainsi que le calcul de la dépréciation enregistrée par les dettes à long terme contractées actuellement et par le passé. Le principe de l'efficacité de la répartition des ressources (par la tarification marginale ou l'évaluation marginale des coûts) se heurte à la difficulté de répartir les bénéfices induits par les dépenses antérieures n'apparaissant pas de façon explicite.

L'utilisation d'un amortissement linéaire, associée à l'incidence du taux de profit sur la base tarifaire—compte tenu de l'inflation—entraîne une "augmentation apparente du coût d'utilisation d'une nouvelle installation, par rapport à celui d'une installation ancienne offrant la même productivité . . . *même si* cette évaluation résulte d'une actualisation adéquate des coûts tout au long de sa durée de vie".

On a souvent soutenu que les entreprises de services publics constituaient des monopoles naturels, caractérisés, au cours d'une période de temps déterminée, par une diminution de leurs coûts moyens et marginaux. Cependant, certaines de ces entreprises sont de toute évidence confrontées à une augmentation de leurs coûts réels d'approvisionnement ou à une diminution de leurs rentrées, en raison de la raréfaction des terrains et de la hausse des prix des combustibles fossiles.

Que faire pour venir à bout de ces difficultés? Helliwell déclare: "le principe directeur de la tarification des services d'une entreprise publique— qui doit assurer d'une part son équilibre financier, de l'autre la satisfaction de sa clientèle—devrait consister à vendre la production répondant à un accroissement de la demande, à un prix permettant de couvrir la totalité des coûts marginaux à long terme des biens correspondants". Cette tarification doit refléter les coûts liés à l'environnement, c'est-à-dire non seulement les simples coûts de production, mais aussi les coûts sociaux. Selon toute vraisemblance, ce principe sera adopté, mais sans résoudre pour autant le problème de l'affectation des "surplus de recettes" recueillis auprès des clients: de tels surplus apparaissent à la faveur de coûts moyens inférieurs aux coûts marginaux actuels, en raison notamment de l'utilisation de capitaux plus anciens et moins coûteux. Helliwell suggère plusieurs solutions à ce problème.

Cette étude se termine par une brève présentation de plusieurs autres questions qui se posent aux responsables de la réglementation des entreprises canadiennes de services publics: la qualité des services, l'analyse et la prise en compte des coûts sociaux, l'harmonisation des juridictions, la coordination entre les décisions d'investissement et de tarification et enfin l'efficacité de la réglementation proprement dite.

CHAPITRE QUATRE: BORINS

La nationalisation représente une alternative à la réglementation des entreprises privées, et cette solution s'est révélée populaire au Canada. Cette étude analyse la conduite suivie par l'Administration canadienne des transports aériens (ACTA), qui détient la propriété et assume la direction de tous les principaux aéroports canadiens. Les actifs de l'ACTA s'élèvent à $3 milliards, son personnel actuel à 12000 personnes, ses dépenses seront de $600 millions en 1978 - 1979. La décision (récemment annulée) de construire à Pickering un second aéroport dans la région de Toronto constitue l'objet principal de ce travail.

L'histoire de Pickering remonte en 1967, lorsqu'un rapport recommanda l'acquisition de terrain supplémentaire, adjacent à l'aéroport de Toronto, Malton. Suite à la réponse défavorable au projet d'extension de Malton, le gouvernement fédéral annonça en décembre 1968 son intention de construire aussitôt que possible un deuxième aéroport dans la région de Toronto (déclaration survenant quatre mois après une décision similaire concernant Montréal). En mars 1972, le choix de l'emplacement de Pickering fut décidé à la suite "d'une sorte de compromis entre les préférences fédérales et provinciales . . . chaque partie contestant la (ou les) proposition(s) de l'autre". Une Commission d'enquête sur le choix de l'aéroport naquit d'une vigoureuse opposition à cette décision. Son rapport, appuyant les positions de l'ACTA, fut rendu public en janvier 1975. Le Cabinet fédéral ayant approuvé le projet de l'ACTA, la construction devait commencer en été ou en automne 1975. Les groupes de pression portèrent alors leurs efforts sur le gouvernement provincial de l'Ontario. Ce gouvernement minoritaire ayant dû tenir compte de l'intention des deux partis de l'opposition de ne pas approuver le site choisi à Pickering annonça qu'il refuserait de construire les voies d'accès nécessaires. Le projet d'aéroport de Pickering était arrêté pour plusieurs années au moins.

Borins analyse la conduite adoptée par l'ACTA, en examinant les principaux éléments de son environnement politico-économique et en posant les questions habituellement soulevées par un économiste. Les quatre principales caractéristiques du contexte de l'ACTA sont les suivantes:

(1) L'incertitude représente un aspect inhérent à la planification d'un aéroport—dans le cas présent, l'ACTA ayant "sous-estimé le trafic prévu à Toronto, elle a dû connaître plusieurs années de files d'attente interminables au terminal 1, jusqu'à ce que le terminal 2 soit prêt".

(2) L'ACTA est située au point de rencontre de plusieurs groupes d'intérêt plus ou moins déclarés, comme le lobby de l'aviation, les "voyageurs" (en particulier ceux qui se plaignent), les compagnies de nolisement et les lignes aériennes régulières.

(3) La capacité de cet organisme à satisfaire la demande de sa clientèle dépend, dans une large mesure, des ressources octroyées par le Conseil du trésor. Le fonds de roulement constitué en 1970 "semblait apporter un certain changement budgétaire, lequel s'est avéré illusoire".

(4) Les hauts fonctionnaires de l'ACTA, militaires ou ex-cadres supérieurs de l'industrie des transports aériens, comptent peu d'économistes et tendent à demeurer au sein de l'ACTA durant toute leur carrière dans la fonction publique.

Essayant de comprendre l'approche de l'ACTA dans la décision de construire l'aéroport de Pickering, Borins pose les questions suivantes.

(1) Pourquoi n'existe-t-il pas de tarification de la charge de pointe des aéroports? L'ACTA fixe le montant des droits d'atterrissage à l'aide de la notion de "valeur du service". Le barème qui en résulte apparaît pour Borins comme une "tentative de l'ACTA en vue de recueillir des recettes d'un montant determiné, tout en limitant au minimum le "mécontentement" de sa clientèle". Les droits d'atterrissage sont maintenus à un bas niveau, afin de réduire les déficits d'Air Canada (propriété fédérale) et de soutenir les compagnies aériennes privées. Quant au problème d'affluence de certains vols internationaux, le Canada "préfère la recherche d'accords internationaux aux prises de décisions unilatérales" semblables à celles des Britanniques.

(2) Comment se justifie l'action des planificateurs de l'ACTA? Après avoir sous-dimensionné Malton, sans doute ont-ils infléchi leurs prévisions, afin d'éviter semblable mésaventure dans le cas de Pickering; aussi cet organisme a-t-il "planifié cet aéroport en utilisant des prévisions de trafic très élevées". Le niveau de bruit prévu par l'ACTA pour Malton et pour Pickering "s'identifiait au" pire des cas "raisonnablement envisageable, compte tenu de l'information disponible en 1973".

(3) Pourquoi construire Pickering? Pourquoi ne pas agrandir Malton? Le problème du bruit semble avoir incité l'ACTA à choisir la première solution, quitte à subir le coût d'une capacité excessive,

advenant une réduction du niveau de bruit à Malton, grâce au progrès technique. Par ailleurs, la vision anticipée d'une utilisation intensive de Malton "en accroissait les difficultés d'exploitation et impliquait une diminution de la qualité des services aéroportuaires, se heurtant à une hostilité prévisible de la part des usagers". Enfin, les normes de l'ACTA en matière de commodité offerte aux voyageurs exigent un excès substantiel de capacité, par rapport à de nombreux aéroports des Etats-Unis.

Selon Borins, l'environnement de l'ACTA se transforme: le Conseil du trésor resserre son contrôle; l'aéroport de Mirabel a suscité l'amertume des contribuables et l'extension de celui de Vancouver a été retardée. L'Administration canadienne des transports aériens réagit à cette évolution, à la fois par l'adoption d'une ligne dure—"cela passera!"—et par une approche plus souple, intégrant des analyses plus élaborées des grands investissements. Borins se fie à l'ACTA, "vraisemblablement prête à s'orienter vers le choix de politiques plus souples et d'une plus grande efficacité économique".

CHAPITRE CINQ: MAISTER

Le processus de réglementation risque-t-il de ralentir l'évolution technique et de freiner la réorganisation des industries concernées? Afin de répondre à cette question, cette étude examine le cas de l'industrie canadienne du transport des céréales, activité soumise aux règlements de la Commission canadienne des transports, la Commission du blé, la Commission canadienne des grains et à plusieurs dispositions juridiques fédérales, comme la *Loi de la convention du Nid-de-Corbeau*. Les réglementations (et autres barrières juridiques) ont-elles réellement fait obstacle lors du remplacement des anciens silos-élévateurs ruraux par de grands sous-terminaux (ou terminaux intérieurs)? Déjà auparavant, il s'était avéré nécessaire de modifier certaines barrières réglementaires. Par delà cette mise en évidence, ce travail s'attache à l'étude de la *dynamique* des changements soumis aux dispositions juridiques.

Maister décrit cette dynamique en insistant sur la "théorie de la chaîne de distribution". Selon ce schéma, mettant en jeu les relations entre les diverses institutions impliquées dans une chaîne de distribution, les pouvoirs publics disputent aux forces économiques l'exercice du rôle prédominant. Cette rivalité résulte de la diversité des objectifs poursuivis et des fonctions remplies, de représentations contradictoires de la réalité, et d'attentes différentes; elle provient aussi d'une compétition stérile pour l'obtention de ressources rares, de problèmes de communication et de systèmes de valeurs divergents, comme d'ambitions sociales différentes et des antagonismes qui s'exercent. La fixation de priorités communes, l'obtention d'une consensus des diverses parties en présence et l'harmonisation de leurs conceptions doivent permettre de résoudre les conflits évoqués. Ce résultat sera fréquemment atteint grâce à l'action d'un "leader" de cette chaîne de distribution—il s'agira du protagoniste exerçant une prédominance de par sa position de force ou sa qualité d'expert, prédominance de fait ou reconnue.

On peut distinguer trois phases dans l'évolution ayant conduit du système des silos-élévateurs ruraux aux terminaux intérieurs: une "période de déséquilibre", une "période d'introduction", et une "période de concurrence", entre les deux systèmes. Dans son analyse, Maister s'attache davantage aux deux premières périodes; il énonce plusieurs hypothèses, puis s'efforce d'en vérifier l'exactitude.

Une importante partie de cette étude est consacrée à l'analyse de la structure de l'industrie canadienne du transport des céréales, dont les caractéristiques les plus importantes sont les suivantes:

- La Commission canadienne du blé (CCB) assure la commercialisation d'environ 90 p. cent de la production céréalière, principalement blé, orge, avoine.
- Les cultivateurs remettent leur production à 4000 silos-élévateurs ruraux, situés dans 1500 emplacements différents, après avoir transporté un chargement moyen de 200 boisseaux, sur une distance moyenne de 10 milles.
- A partir des silos ruraux, l'acheminement des céréales est à la charge de la Commission canadienne du blé qui, de 1958 à 1976, eut recours au système "d'expéditions par cantonnements". Les wagons ferroviaires sont répartis dans les 48 cantonnements, puis entre différentes compagnies, suivant la "formule de Bracken".
- Les tarifs ferroviaires de transport des céréales vers Vancouver ou vers les Grands lacs ont été maintenus aux taux de 1899 sous la *Loi de la convention du Nid-de-Corbeau*.
- Lors de la livraison au silo-élévateur local, le versement initial réglé au cultivateur est diminué du montant du fret ferroviaire et du coût de la manutention fixé par la Commission canadienne des grains. Celle-ci détermine également le barème des coûts maximums d'entreposage, payés aux propriétaires des silos par la Commission, ainsi que le prix des services de l'élévateur de tête de ligne et le montant des frais de nettoiement.
- Huit compagnies dirigent les silos-élévateurs ruraux, dont quatre coopératives de cultivateurs. Les groupements de producteurs de blé de l'Alberta, de la Saskatchewan et du Manitoba partagent une fraction de la capacité totale d'entreposage passée de 42 à 61 p. cent entre 1964 et 1976.
- Les plus grands ports d'expédition comportent vingt-quatre silos-élévateurs de tête de ligne, dont les trois quarts de la capacité appartiennent aux quatre coopératives de cultivateurs; aussi la concurrence est-elle restreinte.
- Le transport des céréales représente actuellement plus de 20 p. cent du tonnage du trafic ferroviaire, plus de 30 p. cent du total des tonnes par mille, mais seulement 12 p. cent des revenus des

chemins de fer. Au milieu des années 70, les transports ferroviaires des céréales étaient déficitaires de $90 millions par an.

- Trois ministères fédéraux et un plus grand nombre de commissions ou d'organismes sont directement impliqués dans le transport des céréales. Les gouvernements provinciaux le sont également. Ils fournissent l'infrastructure routière permettant aux cultivateurs d'acheminer leur production céréalière jusqu'aux silos-élévateurs ruraux.

Maister relève plusieurs problèmes auxquels le système de transport des céréales dut faire face vers la fin des années 60: trop grand nombre de petits silos-élévateurs ruraux, souvent vétustes, millage important de lignes secondaires déficitaires constituant un fardeau pour l'administration des chemins de fer contrainte à les maintenir en service, pénurie de fourgons résultant du maintien du tarif défini par la *convention du Nid-de-Corbeau,* congestion du trafic ferroviaire de Vancouver et insuffisance de la capacité de nettoiement. La meilleure alternative au système inefficace des silos-élévateurs ruraux est le système des terminaux intérieurs; celui-ci se caractérise par: (1) le transport routier des céréales en vrac, puis l'entreposage dans des terminaux intérieurs de grande capacité, (2) le nettoiement des céréales dans les terminaux intérieurs, (3) l'utilisation de convois ferroviaires pour acheminer les céréales vers les points éloignés du marché intérieur ou vers les ports d'expédition. Vers 1968 - 1969, la mise en place d'un système de quatre-vingt terminaux intérieurs aurait réduit de $71 millions—selon les estimations alors établies—les coûts totaux de fonctionnement qui s'élevaient à $415 millions, dont $257 millions à la charge des cultivateurs. La mise à jour par Maister de cette évaluation fait apparaître "que les économies totales liées au système des terminaux intérieurs pouvaient s'élever à un montant *deux fois* plus important que les estimations initiales".

Quelles dispositions réglementaires faisaient obstacle à l'adoption du nouveau système? Maister en identifie plusieurs:

- Aux termes de la *Loi sur les céréales,* il était interdit aux propriétaires de silos-élévateurs d'accorder des rabais aux cultivateurs pour les inciter à transporter leurs céréales plus loin et vers des silos plus importants et plus efficaces.
- La Commission canadienne des grains ayant maintenu les tarifs des silos-élévateurs locaux à des niveaux extrêmement bas, les pertes ainsi encourues rebutaient les investisseurs éventuels.
- Le blocage des tarifs de nettoiement survenu de 1920 à 1975 n'incitait pas à procéder au nettoiement des céréales au niveau des terminaux intérieurs.
- Le tarif fixé par la *Loi de la convention du Nid-de-Corbeau,* inférieur aux coûts réels des chemins de fer, entraînait l'impossibilité pour l'éventuel exploitant d'un terminal intérieur de partager une quelconque partie des économies réalisées par les chemins de fer grâce à l'utilisation de convois ferroviaires.

D'autres dispositions administratives freinaient également l'évolution technologique et la réorganisation des transports céréaliers.

Maister explique l'origine des barrières réglementaires, énumère les raisons de leur maintien—attitudes des protagonistes (les cultivateurs, les exploitants des silos-élévateurs, les chemins de fer, le gouvernement fédéral et les organismes qui en relèvent ainsi que les gouvernements provinciaux)—puis examine le pouvoir exercé par les différents acteurs en présence. Pour la plupart d'entre eux, ils s'opposaient au système des terminaux intérieurs, "prétextant que celui-ci mettait en cause leur conception de leur propre fonction et desservait des objectifs différents". Quant au pouvoir des différents protagonistes, Maister remarque l'attitude du gouvernement fédéral, hésitant à faire usage de sa force de coercition potentielle, et contraint à justifier ses interventions en invoquant "la défense des intérêts du producteur", s'alignant en cela sur les autres parties en présence. "Le fondement du pouvoir des producteurs est avant tout de nature politique; leur mobilisation peut s'avérer une menace", ce qui vaut aux cultivateurs des Prairies une législation favorable, rappelle Maister. Les coopératives céréalières jouissent d'un pouvoir de fait et contrôlent une importante fraction du marché des silos-élévateurs ruraux et de tête de ligne.

Comment les changements ont-ils pu survenir dans les transports céréaliers? Ils se produisirent à la faveur d'une modification des rapports de force et des objectifs poursuivis, comme d'une évolution des conceptions:

- La croissance de la taille moyenne des exploitations de la Prairie et l'urbanisation de l'Ouest entraînèrent une modification des objectifs des producteurs agricoles.
- Par la *Loi nationale sur les transports*, de 1967, les subventions directes aux lignes ferroviaires secondaires, accordées par le gouvernement fédéral, encouragèrent une participation plus active des producteurs.
- La concentration de la propriété des silos ruraux et des terminaux d'exportation s'intensifia, réduisant ainsi les choix offerts aux fermiers; les coopératives devinrent de très grosses entreprises.
- Au cours des années 60, l'importance du volume des exportations vers l'URSS révéla les défauts du système en vigueur, "conçu pour stocker les céréales et non comme un système de transport". Progressivement, le gouvernement fédéral entreprit de jouer le rôle de "leader" de la chaîne de distribution.
- La réglementation modifiée en 1971 permit aux entreprises contrôlant les silos-élévateurs d'adopter des tarifs différents selon l'emplacement de leurs installations.
- L'augmentation des prix du blé (portés à $5 le boisseau, au cours de l'exercice 1973 - 74) permit en 1974 d'augmenter le plafond tarifaire des silos locaux de $3.75—fixé en 1971—à $10.50 par boisseau.
- Les tarifs appliqués par les silos-élévateurs de tête de ligne pour l'entreposage et surtout pour le nettoiement des céréales (passé de 1¢ à 5¢ le boisseau) furent relevés.

- En 1976, la construction de terminaux intérieurs fut encouragée par l'adoption d'une méthode différente d'affectation des wagons.

Vers la fin de 1974, suite à l'augmentation des plafonds tarifaires, on annonça le projet de construction, à Wayburn, Saskatchewan, du premier terminal intérieur, qui devait s'ouvrir en novembre 1976. D'autres projets semblables ont été annoncés depuis cette date.

Malheureusement, nous ne disposons pas encore de terminaux intérieurs à grande capacité, répondant aux projets initiaux et semblables à ceux en service aux Etats-Unis. Ce genre d'infrastructure ne semble convenir qu'à un seul stade du réseau mondial de distribution des céréales. Enfin, compte tenu des dernières mesures prises par le gouvernement de la Saskatchewan, et de certaines propositions de la Commission Hall, allant à l'encontre de l'adoption du système de terminaux intérieurs, Maister remarque que le succès de la réorganisation du réseau de distribution des céréales est encore *incertain*.

CHAPITRE SIX: McMANUS

Cette étude examine la *Loi nationale sur les transports,* adoptée en 1967, suite à la publication du *Rapport* de la Commission royale sur les transports (la Commission MacPherson) en 1961. McManus fait observer la contradiction opposant les objectifs de l'article 3 à ceux de l'article 23 de cette loi, affirmant, qu'une dizaine d'années après, "nous ignorons toujours quelle est notre politique des transports: s'agit-il de l'ancienne, visant à répartir équitablement l'activité économique dans toutes les régions, ou d'une nouvelle politique, attachée à réaliser une minimisation des coûts?"[4] Selon lui, la réglementation de l'activité économique par les pouvoirs publics obéit à deux principes concurrents: (1) obtenir une répartition des ressources plus efficace, et (2) recourir à la réglementation pour doter l'Etat d'un instrument de financement, c'est-à-dire fixer, pour certains consommateurs des biens produits par les entreprises contrôlées, un prix supérieur au coût réel (autrement dit les "taxer"), et pour d'autres, un prix inférieur.

Le système classique des transferts sociaux alimentés par la fiscalité trouve ainsi une alternative dans ce genre de financement compensatoire ou de "taxation par la réglementation", selon l'expression de Posner; cette dernière approche de la réglementation des transports, écrivait Mackintosh en 1939, a caractérisé la pensée des économistes canadiens préoccupés des politiques d'intérêt public, alors que la Commission MacPherson mettait l'accent sur l'efficacité en tant qu'objectif principal. D'après McManus, la loi de 1967 révèle l'indétermination du Parlement vis-à-vis de la notion d'efficacité et de la définition des objectifs du financement public.

---

[4] Les amendements de 1977 (projet de loi C-33) à la loi de 1967 accordent explicitement la priorité à ce dernier objectif; ils sont étudiés dans le chapitre sept par les professeurs Heaver et Nelson.

McManus poursuit en soulignant l'incompatibilité entre la réglementation définie suivant la théorie du monopole naturel, et celle visant à dissuader ou à contrôler la consommation de certains biens. De telles mesures, explique-t-il, à l'origine de l'existence de rentes, répondent au principe selon lequel la réglementation doit servir de mécanisme de financement et de taxation indirecte: ces rentes dégagent une masse monétaire susceptible d'être redistribuée aux consommateurs. McManus en conclut à l'évidence du bien-fondé du principe de "taxation par la réglementation".

La réglementation des chemins de fer peut difficilement s'appuyer sur l'utilisation de la notion d'extériorité, et ceci pour deux raisons. En premier lieu, "les effets nuisibles ne sont pas tous des effets externes", certains ne provenant que de la rareté des ressources. Si l'on examine le problème de la fermeture des voies ferrées, les usagers, fait-on remarquer, souhaitent bien disposer du service, mais sans y contribuer financièrement. En second lieu, les tenants d'une réglementation fondée sur ce principe "semblent souvent ignorer comment une modification des extériorités peut influer sur le comportement des individus . . . et se traduire par une adaptation, de manière à réduire les dommages qu'ils subissent des autres et à rechercher des extériorités bénéfiques". McManus illustre son raisonnement par l'exemple de l'ouverture d'un service subventionné de navette afin de décongestionner le trafic routier: il n'en résulte aucune réduction de la circulation et les subventions accordées n'induisent pas de compensations financières.

La suite de l'étude de McManus examine le contexte dans lequel le Parlement fut conduit à élaborer la *Loi nationale sur les transports* de 1967. Les changements technologiques, notamment la concurrence des transports routiers, compliquaient la réglementation classique des transports ferroviaires. La Commission MacPherson exigea un assouplissement de la politique des chemins de fer afin qu'ils puissent s'adapter à une compétition intermodale plus intense. L'importance attachée au maintien de services déficitaires et à une tarification fondée sur "la valeur d'usage" illustrait le rôle assigné aux chemins de fer: celui d'une certaine forme d'assistance financière de la collectivité. En dépit de la hausse des tarifs, le gouvernement fédéral versa, entre 1959 et 1966, $500 millions de subventions au trafic ferroviaire de marchandises. De plus, de substantiels subsides directs et indirects, énumérés par McManus, furent institués, sans parler de ceux associés à la *Loi sur la réduction des taux de transport des marchandises* de 1959.

Ultérieurement, McManus se demande si la loi de 1967 définissait vraiment une "nouvelle politique des transports". Il relève deux changements principaux: (1) certaines subventions directes remplacent le financement compensatoire résultant de la tarification suivant "la valeur d'usage", (2) "on constate une diminution du contrôle exercé sur les compagnies ferroviaires et une extension potentielle de la réglementation affectant les autres modes de transport, notamment le camionnage". La loi sur les transports autorisait les chemins de fer à réviser leurs tarifs, bloqués depuis 1959. Pratiquement toutes les subventions préalablement octroyées ont été maintenues;

une compensation de la totalité du déficit d'exploitation des lignes secondaires et de 80,p. cent des pertes enregistrées par le service aux voyageurs s'y ajouta. Au total, cette assistance financière, dont l'administration est confiée à la Commission canadienne des transports, créée en 1967 par la *Loi nationale sur les transports,* s'est élevée à $260 millions en 1976. Par ailleurs, la loi de 1967 institua des subventions au transport routier, dont le montant dépassa $23 millions en 1976.

McManus qualifie de "vache sacrée" le principe du maintien des lignes secondaires et des subventions accordées au transport des voyageurs. Le nombre des lignes secondaires maintenues en service par décret ministériel a d'ailleurs considérablement augmenté au cours des dix dernières années. Les dispositions tarifaires de la *Loi de la convention du Nid-de-Corbeau* ont partiellement contribué à cette situation. McManus en conclut que "les décisions de la Commission canadienne des transports concernant les services offerts aux voyageurs, répondent à des objectifs plus politiques qu'économiques". Les décisions dures, impliquant de réelles suppressions de service, restent encore à prendre.

En ce qui concerne les tarifs de fret, McManus remarque qu'un seul des huit recours exercés depuis 1967, selon les clauses de l'article 23 de la *Loi nationale sur les transports,* a été mené à terme; du reste, comme l'illustre l'exposé de certains des recours effectués, cette procédure laisse plutôt à désirer.

La Commission canadienne des transports n'a pas exercé le pouvoir que lui confèrent les articles 36 à 42 de la loi de 1967, en matière de réglementation des transports routiers interprovinciaux.

McManus déduit de l'examen de cette loi "l'absence manifeste de changement dans la politique des transports, si ce n'est une brève éruption de coquetterie intellectuelle à l'égard du principe de l'efficacité". Dans la pratique, les conceptions formulées par Mackintosh en 1939 sont toujours parfaitement vérifiées—et la réglementation des transports s'identifie avant tout à une technique d'assistance financière permettant d'assurer une péréquation interrégionale.

CHAPITRE SEPT: HEAVER ET NELSON

Cette étude porte sur le projet de loi C-33, présenté au Parlement le 27 janvier 1977, afin de modifier substantiellement la *Loi nationale sur les transports* de 1967 (et la législation correspondante). Bien que le projet de loi n'ait pas été promulgué, le gouvernement fédéral semble vouloir modifier les objectifs énoncés dans la loi de 1967. Heaver et Nelson affirment que le gouvernement se trompe et que les "changements introduits risquent d'aboutir à des décisions préjudiciables à l'efficacité de l'organisation des services de transports, tout en exacerbant les mécontentements régionaux . . . ." Ils soutiennent que la réglementation des transports (en particulier des tarifs de fret et de la qualité de prestation des services) devrait s'attacher avant tout à la recherche de l'efficacité et servir à la poursuite d'objectifs de nature strictement économique.

Examinant la loi de 1967, Heaver et Nelson affirment (contrairement à McManus, dans le chapitre six), que "la politique actuelle accorde sans aucun doute la priorité à l'obtention de l'efficacité de l'industrie des transports". Dans le projet le loi C-33, les transports sont tenus d'être "efficaces", mais ils doivent aussi servir "d'instruments contribuant à la réalisation des objectifs sociaux et économiques, au niveau régional comme au niveau national", tout en assurant "une absence de discrimination parmi les usagers et l'accessibilité des services". Afin de permettre à la Commission canadienne des transports d'atteindre les objectifs fixés à la réglementation, ce texte définit onze principes d'action, comportant entre autres: l'acceptation de la concurrence intermodale, du bien-fondé de la rentabilité commerciale et la nécessité d'exercer un contrôle des tarifs dans une situation de monopole local, afin de protéger les usagers. Lorsque la politique du gouvernement implique des mesures contraires à la rentabilité commerciale, il devra prendre en charge les coûts supplémentaires correspondants.

Heaver et Nelson étudient ensuite le fonctionnement actuel du marché des transports ferroviaires. Selon eux, les chemins de fer "ne jouissent pas actuellement d'un pouvoir monopolistique leur permettant de réaliser des profits en conséquence". La concurrence intermodale s'exerce sur la plupart des marchés, ou menace de le faire, ce qui revient au même. Se référant à leur dernier ouvrage, Heaver et Nelson concluent que "le caractère concurrentiel du marché, sous ses divers aspects, représente de toute évidence un facteur de contrôle des tarifs ferroviaires appliqués dans tout le pays et relatifs à un large éventail de marchandises transportées". Néanmoins, les dispositions tarifaires de la *Loi de la convention du Nid-de-Corbeau,* entre autres, entraînent une structure complexe des tarifs, à l'origine d'une discrimination tarifaire importante. En dépit des quelques recours aux clauses de l'article 23 de la *Loi nationale sur les transports,* "la plupart des affréteurs soutiennent fermement la politique actuellement pratiquée".

Heaver et Nelson soulignent la difficulté d'établir un rapport précis entre les stipulations de la *Loi sur les chemins de fer* en matière de tarifs minimums et maximums et les politiques énoncées dans le projet de loi C-33: ces dernières semblent en effet devoir concerner les tarifs antérieurement convenus; elles paraissent néanmoins peu susceptibles de modifier les critères d'évaluation de situations bien établies. De toute manière, "les objectifs du projet de loi C-33 soulèvent trop de problèmes insurmontables pour pouvoir être appliqués à une réglementation tarifaire définie dans l'intérêt collectif". Il en est ainsi en raison des contradictions développées dans l'exposé des principes et des buts poursuivis, en raison de l'incompétence de la Commission canadienne des transports à formuler l'indispensable évaluation politique des objectifs à atteindre, comme en raison de l'opposition des transporteurs et des affréteurs et de l'incompatibilité avec le principe d'efficacité, requis par l'intérêt général.

Pour pouvoir résoudre ces contradictions entre les objectifs et les principes, "la Commission des transports n'est pas en mesure de fixer des priorités entre l'efficacité, les diverses politiques nationales, le principe de l'accessibilité et de l'absence de discrimination qui soient compatibles avec les conceptions des gouvernements fédéraux et provinciaux, relatives au choix pertinent d'un tarif déterminé". Evoquant l'ambiguïté de certains concepts figurant dans les objectifs du projet de loi, Heaver et Nelson affirment "qu'il est inacceptable de la part d'un gouvernement de proposer une définition ultérieure des termes du projet de loi C-33, reportée au moment des conclusions de la Commission des transports". La "concurrence effective" et "l'absence de discrimination" constituent deux exemples évidents de formulations ambiguës. L'expérience vécue sous la législation de 1967 avait démontré "que la confiance placée dans le libre jeu des forces du marché favorisait le développement de l'efficacité des transports et des systèmes de distribution au Canada". Or, le projet de loi C-33 menace d'interrompre l'heureux fonctionnement de ce mécanisme, lequel s'exerce dans le sens de "l'intérêt général", pour lui substituer l'action de quelques "sages" de la Commission des transports. De plus, Heaver et Nelson affirment que la législation proposée "n'explicite ni les conditions dans lesquelles l'intérêt collectif prendrait le pas sur les intérêts particuliers, ni celles d'une éventuelle rentabilité des chemins de fer".

Heaver et Nelson tirent les conclusions suivantes: (1) "la réglementation des tarifs et des services ferroviaires, assurée par la Commission des transports dans des buts politiques et sociaux, ne contribuerait pas à l'efficacité de l'industrie des transports ni, *a fortiori,* à celle du système de production et de distribution canadien", (2) le gouvernement semble avoir été dans l'incapacité de distinguer l'ensemble des principes qu'une commission de contrôle est chargée de faire respecter, de son rôle de promotion et de sa fonction pratique dans le système de transport, (3) l'application des politiques du projet de loi C-33 ne permet aucunement de parvenir à une réglementation des transports susceptible de résoudre les problèmes régionaux.

Chapter Two

Direct Regulation in Canada:
Some Policies and Problems

by *G. B. Reschenthaler*
Department of Marketing and Economic Analysis
Faculty of Business Administration & Commerce
University of Alberta

INTRODUCTION: THE REGULATED SECTOR

The Scope of Economic Regulation

In Canada, direct regulation encompasses some of the largest non-financial corporations (Canadian Pacific and Bell Canada are two of the five largest), all financial corporations, all transportation companies, energy industry firms, all private telecommunications companies, most agriculture industries, most firms in the insurance industry, and many professions. Approximately 17 percent of the United States GNP, as estimated by Posner (1975, p. 818), is derived from the regulated sector. The Canadian percentage would certainly not be less.

By direct regulation we refer exclusively to economic regulation that bears directly on pricing and resource allocation. Most sectors of the economy today are affected by what might be termed qualitative or social regulation which involves specification of standards or rules of conduct. The latter types of regulation certainly do affect prices and resource allocation, but in a less direct fashion. We acknowledge that the distinction is somewhat artificial; however, it is traditional and absolutely essential if the study is to be kept within manageable proportions.

Given the large portion of the economy which is subject to direct regulation to some significant degree, the effectiveness of direct regulation as a system of social control of corporate power is of obvious concern.

The Issues

The policy issues raised in the professional literature related to direct regulation include the following:

1. Has direct regulation been effective? Has it achieved its objectives?
2. Is regulation typically introduced as a substitute for the

competitive market which has failed; or, on the contrary, is regulation typically introduced because of effectiveness of the competitive market?

3. Can the members of a regulatory board, over time, avoid becoming captives of the industry being regulated; in effect, must the regulatees ultimately become the regulators?

4. Has regulation tended to protect industries from competition and, as a consequence, simply perpetuated itself and inefficiency in the production processes of the regulated firms?

5. Does regulation have a natural tendency to focus excessively on profits (or rate of return) to the exclusion of far more important questions of economic efficiency?

6. When the administrative costs of regulation are considered in conjunction with tendencies toward inefficiency and over-capitalization alleged to be characteristic of regulated firms, would the public generally be better off with unregulated monopoly?

7. To what extent does the cross-subsidization of different services, which seems to occur invariably in regulated industries, result in special tax subsidy schemes which would be far more appropriately administered directly by the legislature?

8. To what extent should the regulatory process be primarily an adjudicative as opposed to an inquisitorial and legislative process?

9. To what extent should regulatory agencies perform a policy-making role in addition to their traditional administrative roles?

10. If they are to perform a policy-making role, what weights should be attached to equity, income distribution, and economic development goals relative to the traditional goals of regulation?

11. Should regulatory boards be perceived primarily as arbiters of different economic interests or as technocrats?

12. If the regulatory agencies are to be viewed as adjudicatory boards and primarily as arbiters of political and economic interest, then, to what extent, and by what means does the "public interest" demand that all interested parties be fairly represented in the regulatory process?

13. Do regulatory agencies tend to be self-perpetuating? If yes, then why? What instruments are available to ensure that self-perpetuation does not occur?

14. To what extent does direct regulation result in excessive investment in plant and equipment by regulated companies?

We have surveyed the Canadian literature available, as well as selected references in the American literature, and we discuss most of the questions and issues presented above as they relate to questions which may be of interest to those seeking to appraise direct regulation in Canada. Our concluding observations are found in the last section.

THE ISSUES

The Basis for the Study

Canadians are quite properly interested in the efficacy of direct regulation as an instrument of economic control. The Royal Commission on Corporate Concentration (RCCC) (Privy Council Order 1975 - 879), for example, was asked

> To inquire into the nature and role of major concentrations of corporate power in Canada; [and to determine; *inter alia*],
>
> Whether safeguards exist or may be required to protect the public interest in the presence of such concentrations.

The interest in regulation is at least fourfold. First, federal, provincial and municipal agencies directly regulate the levels and structure of prices of many of the largest corporations in Canada. Two of the companies which presented briefs to the Commission—Canadian Pacific and Bell Canada— are companies whose prices are subject to direct regulatory review. Second, interest is directed to this area by the present Anti-Inflation program. This program represents, *de facto,* a comprehensive system of direct control of the pricing and indirect control of resource allocation decisions of major corporations. While the Government has indicated that this comprehensive program will be terminated in late 1978, there is no reason to assume that other economic events will not occur which will require either the present Government or some future government to introduce a new program of direct controls. Third, given the recent government proposal (DCCA, 1977a) that a National Markets or Competition Board be established to review corporate mergers and certain trade practices, it is only reasonable to assume, in the context of discussions of the problems associated with this proposed competitive practices tribunal, that the whole question of the effectiveness of administrative tribunals will become a subject of debate. Fourth, consumers have been particularly sensitive to rising food, textile and energy prices over the last five years. In Canada, prices of most food and textile products and all energy resources are directly or indirectly affected by government regulatory policies.

In addition to these general reasons for concern, Mr. Robert Bertrand, Director of Investigation and Research, Bureau of Competition Policy, in his brief to the RCCC (*Transcripts* 1976 - 77, vol 1, p. 84), drew attention to others by observing:

> It is possible to identify at least three important reasons why concentration of economic power even in the regulated sector may have economic and social implications which provide grounds for serious concern. In the first place, regulation cannot in the best of circumstances duplicate the unceasing pressures of competition. In the second place, serious grounds for concern are compounded where some of the activities of a firm are regulated and some are not regulated. The danger appears

grievous where different sectors of the economy are involved and important possibilities exist for cross-subsidization. In the third place, the regulation gives a new dimension to entrepreneurship. The decisions subject to regulation may be the most important decisions a company can make, those concerning the scale of operations, the types of products or services provided and the prices or rates to be charged. On the one hand, there may be more to be gained by outsmarting regulation than by reducing costs. On the other hand, instead of fighting the regulatory agency, the industry may cooperate with the agency.

The Economic Council in the *Interim Report on Competition Policy* (1969, pp. 160 - 67) also expressed concern about regulated industries:

> . . . The hidden costs to the economy of poor regulatory performance provide, in our view, a strong justification for applying the underlying principles of competition policy, in suitably modified form, to the regulated sector of the economy, the more so since some parts of this sector, such as regulated communications activities are likely to grow rapidly in relative economic importance over the next few years.

For a variety of reasons, it is appropriate that Canadians should examine the scope, and philosophy of Canadian and foreign experience with direct regulation as a system of economic regulation.

Instruments of Public Policy

In general, Canada, the United States and the countries of Western Europe have relied on four systems of economic control in addition to monetary and fiscal policy. These systems are: private planning, the competitive market, government ownership, and direct regulation. Numerous permutations and combinations of these policy approaches exist and are found in these countries. While all four are used in Canada in varying degrees, a careful review of Canadian history reveals that there has been a tendency to emphasize private planning, government ownership, and direct regulation, and, generally, to limit dependence on the competitive market as a planning and control instrument.

The institutionalized predilection of the Canadian public for private planning, government ownership and direct regulation has been examined in a forthcoming book by Canadian sociologists S. D. Clark and Wallace Clement, historian Alexander Brady, and political scientists Lipset, Presthus, Horowitz and Doern. Their analyses have been critiqued in the political science and sociological literature and need not be reviewed here. However, the attitude toward the competitive market does deserve special comment in the context of this study.

The ineffectiveness of Canadian competition policy has been noted in several studies. Three of the more recent studies are the *Interim Report on Competition Policy* prepared by the Economic Council of Canada (1969) and an article and a book by Professor W.T. Stanbury (1976b; 1977). The general ineffectiveness of the Canadian anti-trust legislation and the difficulties encountered by reformers in their efforts to attain revisions of the legislation, provide revealing insights into the public's attitudes about the relative roles of the four systems of economic control.

While the magna carta of American anti-trust, the *Sherman Act* of 1890, explicitly recognizes the role of competitive markets in national policy, no comparable language is found in the first Canadian anti-trust legislation passed in 1889. Canadian anti-trust legislation has not been directed to establishing a competitive market regime; the law has, when effective, simply attempted to insure that private planners possessing market power use that power in a responsible manner, which means without the imposition of "undue" restraints on the public. Mackenzie King, in discussing the 1923 revisions to the combines legislation, expressed the attitude aptly when he noted that, " . . . the legislation does not seek in any way to restrict just combinations or agreements between business or industrial houses and firms, but it does seek to protect the public against possible ill-effects of the combinations" (see Skeoch, 1966, p. 30). In effect, King's philosophy was that market planning power is acceptable provided it is not abused. There is no commitment to competitive market structures as such. In practice, this lack of commitment to the competitive market as an instrument of public policy is reflected in the failure of Parliament to apply Canadian combines laws to other than the most flagrant price fixing and monopoly behaviour (Stanbury, 1977).

The preceding brief discussion of systems of social control and their relative acceptance in the Canadian environment permits us to place the role of direct regulation in its proper perspective relative to the other systems of control in Canada. We find that while we have a multiplicity of control systems, the Canadian model exhibits a tendency to downplay the role of the competitive market instrument. While we have not reached the point where the competitive market system is viewed as outdated, we have certainly moved to a position which tends to emphasize planning and regulation in the private and public sectors. In the next section this generalization is examined more closely.

Direct Regulation in the Canadian Context

Michael Trebilcock (*Submission,* 1976, p. 1) has properly identified as myth the view that our economy is largely unregulated. The very wide scope of regulation in Canada today extends from the transportation, energy, telecommunications, broadcasting, insurance, securities, financial, and pharmaceutical industries to most sectors of agriculture. When the impact of regulation of foreign investment, occupation licensing, and the Canadian tariff structure are considered, we find that there are few industries which are not affected directly or indirectly by regulation.

However, as Professor Posner (1969, p. 620) has noted:

> Until relatively recent times, government regulation of prices and other elements of business behavior had been the rule. But beginning in the 18th century, and with increasing momentum, notions of 'laissez faire' gained ascendancy.

The zenith of the free market was probably attained during the middle of the nineteenth century and by the latter part of that century, a clear reaction against the market was observed by many historians (see Polanyi, 1957).

The Canadian economy in a special sense can be said to have been built upon direct regulation and promotion by government. Economic efficiency has historically taken on secondary importance when an apparent conflict with cultural, political or regional economic development objectives was perceived to exist. The development of the entire transportation infrastructure of the country as well as the adoption of the National Policy in 1879 and its concomitant high tariff structure reflect a very early rejection of economic consequences which a free competitive market system might have been expected to produce. The tariff policy (an extreme form of direct economic regulation), the direct regulation of most agricultural production, direct regulation of all transportation and most conventional utilities, restrictive licensing policies in the past for banks, direct regulation of telecommunications and non-print media, regulation of energy industries, the self-regulation by professional groups, and collective bargaining by organized labour—to mention a few—has resulted in an economic structure and system in which direct regulation in some form is more the norm and less the exception in most sectors of the Canadian economy.

Direct regulation of business-corporate power has always been viewed by economists in North America as a second best alternative to the competitive market place and a distant second best (see Posner, 1969 and Stanbury, 1976a). But generally speaking, in Canada we have opted for one of a select set of systems of economic planning and control in addition to traditional fiscal and monetary policy.

In Canada, direct public regulation has taken basically three forms. First, "independent" regulatory boards have been created with the power to determine resource use and/or prices in a variety of industries including petroleum, potash, pipeline, electric power, natural gas, dairy product, trucking, rail, airline, taxi, telephone, telegraph, radio, television, cable television, securities, and insurance. Second, many producer groups have been given powers of self-regulation which extend to price and/or resource use determination. The industries affected are the professions and agriculture (see Grubel and Schwindt, 1977; Forbes, 1974; Shaffner, 1977; and Cohen, 1977). These boards usually possess the ability to influence supply and/or prices. Third, tariff, quota, patent and banking policies have been adopted and managed by Parliament with the goal of directly regulating economic activity.

The agencies which are of particular interest in this study are those in the first group which are regulatory in the sense that they are statutory bodies:

> charged with the responsibility to administer, to fix, to establish, to control or to regulate an economic activity, or a market by regularized and established means in the public interest (Brown-John, 1976, p. 154 and *Black's Law Dictionary*, 852 and 1451).

Lloyd Brown-John (1976, p. 146) in the preliminary stage of a long-term, multifaceted study of government regulatory boards has compiled an inventory of 436 provincial and 117 federal statutory agencies, boards, commissions, advisory agencies, tribunals and directorates. These all apparently have some regulatory aspect. In total he identified 1,317 statutory agencies; however, many were not regulatory in a broad public policy sense. This list included advisory committees, tribunals, commissions, corporations, institutes and foundations.[1]

Using Black's definition of a regulatory agency, Brown-John classifies regulatory agencies into three principal categories: (1) resource and natural product monopoly control (including public utility and services; (2) food and natural product marketing control; (3) hazardous commodity and product control; (4) others individually categorized (including communications).

jthe agencies included in our analysis all possess statutory powers which permit them to directly affect prices in the economy and resource allocation and they are all agencies which hold some form of public hearing in resolving issues (Brown-John, 1976, p. 155).[2]

Only limited analysis has been undertaken to the *economic effects* of regulatory boards in Canada.[3] The Canadian Transport Commission (CTC) has been the subject of study over time (see Feltham, 1970; 1973; 1974; Purdy, 1972; English, 1973; Baldwin, 1975; and Ruppenthal and Stanbury, 1976; Janisch, 1978a; 1978b). In addition, the Canadian Consumer Council sponsored the study of a select group of regulatory boards.[4] However, as Professor Brown-John (1976, p. 143) observes:

> It has become clear . . . that little is known about the intricacies of that [regulatory] process. Moreover, when it comes to such crucial issues as factors involved in rate determination, the components of price determination for marketing boards, assessments of patterns of agency behavior, the relationship of agencies to their clientele, the modes of appointment of agency members, including fitness and representation, and the direction of agency behavior in terms of policy goals, practically nothing of any substance exists in Canada.

His recent study (1977) of members of Canadian regulatory agencies provides insight into some of these areas.

---

[1] For definitions see Brown-John (1976, p. 148) wherein the approaches of the McRuer Committee, Ontario's Committee on Government Productivity, are considered.
[2] For a general discussion of the problems of taxonomy of regulation see Doern (1974) and Doern (1975).
[3] Several case studies appear in Doern (1978) *The Regulatory Process.*
[4] See Brown-John (1972); Cayne (1972); Dawson (1972); McDougall (1972); McManus (1972); Palmer (1972a, 1972b); Palmer and Erkkila (1972); Reschenthaler (1972); Richardson (1972); Westmacott (1972); Huber (1973); Stanbury (1973).

Issues in Regulatory Economics

As reflected by the Canadian Consumer Council studies prepared in 1971, the last decade has seen a resurgence of interest in direct regulation as a policy instrument. However, interest and criticism has been a continuing phenomenon of the last fifty years.[5] Much of the recent interest is attributable to disillusionment of liberals and populists of the "Nader" variety with some of the American regulatory agencies (Green, 1973), the attribution of energy and transportation industry problems to improvident regulation (MacAvoy, 1965; 1970; 1971; and Fellmeth, 1970), and concerted criticism in the writings of the Chicago School (Stigler and Friedland, 1962; Demsetz, 1968; and Posner, 1969). The consensus of these critics is that regulation has frequently been ineffectual (Stigler and Friedland, 1962), expensive relative to the benefits derived from it (Gerwig, 1962; Friedlaender, 1969; MacAvoy, 1971; Phillips, 1975; and Posner, 1975), and inefficient (MacAvoy, 1965; 1970). Many of the critics have recommended deregulation and the introduction of competition as a preferable alternative to much of existing regulation (Trebing, 1974; Kahn, 1971; and Phillips, 1975).

This resurgence of interest in direct regulation has been accompanied by a growing concern about the effectiveness and efficiency of direct regulation as a policy instrument. The critics of existing regulatory schemes have pointed to the following problem areas (Reschenthaler, 1976).

COMMISSION INDEPENDENCE: LEGISLATION

Commissions may be "captured" at their inception by the private interests they are established to regulate. The interest may request regulation as a cloak to legitimize policies which might otherwise be prohibited (Doern, 1974). Regulation may be introduced not because of market failure, but because the market has functioned *too* effectively.

COMMISSION INDEPENDENCE: STAFF

Commissions may be captured as a result of bureaucratic symbiosis, which is the tendency for individuals on staffs of regulating agencies to move on to employment with firms being regulated. Individuals may accept employment with commissions at below market rates in just such anticipation. This is a serious problem in the United States. In Canada, a higher proportion of regulators are drawn from the ranks of the public bureaucracy. However, many also are drawn from the legal field, though apparently a smaller proportion than in the United States (Brown-John, 1977). In the case

---

[5] See Henderson, Sharfman, Cushman, Fesler, U.S. Commission on Organization of the Executive Branch, Bernstein, Williams, Schwartz, Redford (1959), Saloman, Hector, Landis, Friendly, Caves, Krislov, Kim, Cary, Kohlmeier, Redford (1969), Cox, A.B.A., Jordan, Fellmeth, Turner, The President's Advisory Council on Executive Organization, Breyer, and Douglas and Miller. All are referenced in Stanbury (1976a, p. 145, footnote 1).

of lawyers, a problem arises since lawyers who have been "responsible" while serving on boards might expect to return to private practice with firms which suddenly find themselves the beneficiaries of substantial legal fees from regulated firms.[6]

CAPITALIZATION OF THE CONSUMER'S INTEREST

While private interests can foresee and calculate the impact of regulatory policies, consumers typically do not do so in a collective fashion. Consequently, a change in regulatory policy may generate extra net income over time for an interest group with a present value of several million dollars. Of course, consumers collectively will lose the same several million dollars of purchasing power plus a "consumer surplus." Unfortunately, while producers might be expected to assemble together and incur substantial lobbying, propaganda, and legal expenses to obtain the regulatory change, consumers are not likely to organize. As a consequence, producers may appear at a regulatory hearing represented by a large staff of lawyers and other professionals, while consumers go under-represented or not represented at all. (Trebilcock, 1975; Stigler, 1971; Peltzman, 1976; and Stanbury, 1977; Trebilcock, 1978).

THE ADJUDICATORY FRAMEWORK

Most commissions use an adjudicatory or adversarial system as opposed to an investigative or inquisitorial approach. The adjudicatorial system fails if all important interest groups are not represented.

FINANCING

There is a tendency for boards to be underfinanced because of the lack of a political constituency.

THE PROTECTIVE UMBRELLA

There may be a "natural" human tendency for regulators at some point to abjure their negative regulatory role and adopt a positive role of promoting the health of the industry. In fact, many regulatory agencies are responsible for the promotion of the industry they are supposed to regulate.

THE SIZE OF THE TASK

It is possible that some utilities have become so large that effective cost analysis is impracticable and effective regulation is not possible (Lambert, 1972; and Kahn, 1971, Vol. 2).

---

[6] See Stanbury (1976a) and Gellhorn (1972) for a discussion of the problem.

THE DIMENSIONS OF THE PRODUCT

Direct regulation as traditionally conceived as an instrument to prevent the earning of monopoly profits may be a self-defeating or futile exercise. The regulated company may frustrate the regulators by reducing the quality of service, or profits may be concealed through creative accounting involving valuations and expenses (Posner, 1969, pp. 593 - 98; and Reschenthaler, 1972, p. 39).

OVER-INVESTMENT

If regulated firms are permitted a rate of return exceeding even slightly the true cost of capital, they will have incentive to over-invest in physical plant and equipment. This is referred to as the Averch-Johnson-Wellisz Effect or A-J-W Effect[7] (Averch and Johnson, 1962).

DYNAMIC EFFICIENCY

Extremely restrictive regulation may leave regulated firms with little incentive to innovate. As a consequence, technological change and productivity may be slower in these industries than would otherwise be the case (see Posner, 1969, p. 601; Turner, 1969, p. 1231; Kendrick, 1973; Capron, 1971; Noll, 1971; Trebing, 1976a; 1976b; 1974, particularly pp. 211 - 12).

PROFIT FOCUS

Most regulatory efforts focus on profits or rate of return with little interest in efficiency and costs. Unfortunately, a very small amount of slack can offset the benefits of the most restrictive of profit regulation (Comanor, 1970). While excess profits redistribute income, they have no accompanying direct social costs in terms of under or misutilization of resources (social costs); however, inefficiency in operation by regulated companies will impose a net social cost (Posner, 1975).

The regulated firm's interest in efficiency may be diminished by the 100 percent tax rate which regulation can entail.

Posner (1969, p. 595) reflects the consensus of students of regulatory policy on the general attitude of regulators toward cost control when he observes: "A regulatory agency is naturally reluctant to displace corporate business judgement unless it seems reasonably clear that management is wrong." Thus, the regulatory agency will frequently focus on whether a 9.8 or 10.1 percent rate of return on investment is appropriate when, according to Posner: ". . . most consumers would rather pay $1 for a long distance call, 20 cents of which represented a monopoly profit . . . than $1.10, all of which was cost" (p. 619). "X" inefficiency (management slack) (Leibenstein, 1966) may become a pervasive problem in the regulated industry as management

---

[7] See Helliwell's chapter in this volume for a review of the recent 1971-76 literature.

realizes that improved efficiency may yield a small return to the firm (Posner, 1969, p. 617). Regulation in Canada has seldom involved close examination of costs, other than depreciation. The same is apparently true in the United States according to Massel (1968).

POLITICAL PRICING

Pricing may involve more of a concern with the winning of political support than with the attainment of economic efficiency (Posner, 1969, p. 605).

INNOVATION IN PRICING

The regulatory process may discourage innovative pricing (Posner, 1969, p. 606). Electric utilities have only recently accepted comprehensive pricing formulas which permit extensive price discrimination by time of consumption.

THE DEREGULATION DILEMMA

Direct regulation may create problems at a later date if the government should decide to deregulate an industry. This problem arises when restrictions are imposed by the regulatory agency on entry into the industry and the licence assumes a market value. This has happened, for example, in the case of taxicab licensing where market values for licences in Canada have on occasion exceeded $20,000 (see Reschenthaler, 1972, p. 200). When this capitalization of market values of monopoly occur, many of the current holders of licences who have 'bought-in' will be found to be earning no more than a competitive return (the dead hand of monopoly problem). Special equity problems may arise if deregulation of an industry occurs in an industry in which most of the current licence holders are not the original holders. If a regulated industry involves a very large group of what might be labelled innocent bystanders, then deregulation can become extremely difficult politically. This situation may exist currently in agriculture and in some areas of intraprovincial trucking in Canada.

THE PERPETUAL AGENCY

There is a tendency for a regulatory board, once created, to become immortal. There may have existed conditions at some point in the past which justified the establishment of a regulatory board. However, the passage of time may have witnessed the development of new technologies or the occurrence of economic or institutional changes which obviated the need for continued regulation.

An example is the case of milk price regulation in most of the provinces which was introduced in the early 1930s. Changes in the transportation network, the economics of the industry, and the availability of fluid milk substitutes have collectively removed most of the factors which were used originally to justify price regulation; however, the milk control boards and public utility boards live on (see Reschenthaler, 1972, pp. 49 - 110).

POLITICAL ACCOUNTABILITY

The Ash Council (President's Advisory Council on Executive Organization, 1971) and many political scientists (Doern, 1974) have expressed concern over the lack of political accountability of regulatory commissions which are frequently engaged in making political decisions, in that they are establishing priorities in the uses of resources. This lack of political responsibility is, of course, a proper subject of concern under a parliamentary system which places a high value on political responsibility.

CROSS-SUBSIDIZATION

Economic regulation presents two cross-subsidization problems. The first of these involves the subsidization of some customers by the overcharging of other customers (Posner, 1971). The second involves the regulated company which engages in some non-regulated activities but uses some of the same equipment in the provision of both services and incurs numerous joint costs (McDonald, 1971). The possibility exists for unfair competition for competitors in the non-regulated industry (Posner, 1971, p. 23).

COSTS AND BENEFITS

The costs of administering regulatory programs may exceed their benefits (see Gerwig, 1962; Friedlaender, 1969; MacAvoy, 1971; Phillips, 1975; and Posner, 1975).

The preceding list is not exhaustive; however, it does include most of the themes which have dominated the literature in regulatory economics in recent years. Many of these issues will occupy the interest of later sections of this study.

THE CHICAGO CHALLENGE

In recent years, a group of economists and law professors associated with the University of Chicago has been a dominating influence in the identification of issues in regulatory economics. Most of the literature on the problems of regulated industries and particularly the deficiencies of economic regulation and its costs has appeared in the *Journal of Law and Economics,* the *Bell Journal of Economics and Management Science,* the papers of the Brookings Institution, and the Stanford and Yale law journals. The contributors associated with the Chicago school have been among the most prolific writers.

Many of the recommendations for deregulation of industry in recent years have emanated from writings of the Chicago School. In general, the Chicago group oppose most forms of regulation by government. Given the importance of the Chicago exponents in the debates on various regulatory issues, it is desirable to briefly outline the Chicago position. In a recent article, Professor Harry Trebing (1976b, pp. 97 - 113) noted the following principles of the group:

1. State utility regulation has had little impact on prices.
2. Regulation of transport, broadcasting, natural gas and banking is unnecessary and has been used in a restrictive and protective fashion in the United States.
3. Regulation can provide control over entry, restriction of availability of substitutes, and price stability; but potential costs to the firm in the form of time delays, loss of manoeuverability, and the possibility of extraneous public interest considerations may arise. A firm's attitude toward regulation reflects its maximization of an objective function which includes these potential benefits and costs.
4. Unregulated monopoly is preferable to regulated monopoly. Public monopoly is less susceptible to elimination than private monopoly.
5. The evils of unregulated monopoly are less than commonly assumed. Profits can be limited by elimination of government created barriers to entry and the introduction of a modest excess profits tax under special circumstances.
6. Competitive results are also attainable with private monopoly if the monopoly franchise is auctioned. The competitive pressure of bidders will result in the economic rent being paid to the public auctioneer.
7. Government planning and market control are inferior to a market unconstrained by government influence. This is distinctly the case in the energy industries.
8. Public ownership is an inferior alternative since public management pursues inferior objectives of insuring management tenure and maximization of voter support. Price structures will be set to maximize voter support resulting in disregard of costs, excessively broad consumer classifications, and depressed prices which result in economic distortions.
9. Much regulation involves disguised taxation and subsidization.
10. The concept of private economic power is an empty economic box.
11. Any relationship between market concentration and market power is discounted as are all aspects of oligopolistic interdependence.
12. Corporate power aspects of joint ventures, vertical integration, corporate interlocks, and the issues of cross-subsidization and reciprocal dealings are not significant economic problems.
13. Problems associated with imbalance in power between different classes or groups of consumers are ignored or dismissed.
14. The general distribution of economic power embodied in the existing system of property rights and other institutional arrangements are taken as given.
15. The consumer cannot be extorted or intimidated if he has legal

access; thus, the proper procedure for controlling pollution and similar problems (social regulation) is to assess the value of the abuse, identify the resource owner, and permit individual or local bargaining. The right to impose external costs by regulated companies should be available for local purchase at a reasonable level of taxation.

16. Common law remedies now provide the consumer with most forms of required protection from private monopoly.

17. The costs of regulation are to be controlled explicitly or implicitly with competitive market solutions or with a natural monopoly whose excess earnings are neutralized by competitive bidding or an excess profits tax.

18. Commission regulation cannot be reformed. In Friedman's view, the probability of change is no greater than the probability that "cats can be made to bark."

19. Government regulation and other exercises of government power result in economic distortions which are the sources of most economic problems.

At the present time, there is no formally organized school of writers who have written extensively in favour of the *status quo* or expanded reliance on direct regulation as a policy tool. However, a review of existing literature reveals no general enthusiasm in the United States or Canada for the basic Chicago position which calls for complete deregulation of the economy on the assumption that the social costs of unregulated monopoly are inconsequential while the social costs of regulations are usually quite high.

The following excerpts from an article by Professor Trebing reflect some of the basic reservations about the deregulation proposals of the Chicago School which are held by many non-Chicago economists. Trebing comments (1976b, pp. 118 - 21):

> The deregulation of natural monopoly, as recommended by Posner, is premised on the belief that the evils of private monopoly are greatly exaggerated, that abusive practices would be constrained by common law remedies, and that monopoly would be eroded over time by the actions of broader market forces. Although legal barriers to entry would be removed, Posner envisions no entry in practice because of the natural monopoly's cost advantages. Deregulation would also be accompanied by no changes in industry structure.
>
> This type of deregulation suffers from four major deficiencies that make it a poor option for public policy.
>
> First, the effects of unregulated private monopoly on resource allocation, efficiency, innovation, and income distribution should not be minimized despite efforts to deprecate net losses due to allocative and "x" inefficiencies. In the real world, the private monopolist's strategies to maintain a position of dominance through price discrimination, cross-subsidization, entry foreclosure, and political favoritism will set the stage for all of the distortions associated with monopoly power. In addition, such actions are conducive to a redistribution of income from consumers to the monopolist that may become socially and politically intolerable.
>
> Second, the effectiveness of an excess profits tax as a proxy for regulatory control of earnings is dubious, and its superiority is certainly open to challenge. Expenses

(may) rise to camouflage the monopoly return (and if) the monopolist's return is greater than the cost of capital, then the imposition of the tax will produce a nonregulated variant of the familiar Averch-Johnson effect.

If the government proceeds to apply the excess profits tax assiduously, more similarities with the worst features of regulation will appear. It will become necessary to review and approve all legitimate expenses, the application of the tax will require continuous reassessment and refinement, and its administration will ultimately become the basis for lengthy litigation, adversary proceedings, and delays . . .

Third, deregulation of monopoly will suffer from many of the problems *which plague the bidding process.* These include the control of price discrimination, reconciling the imbalance between public and private scales of development, the motivation for superior performance . . . and the impact of corporate and political power. None of these issues can be resolved within the structural context of the public utility industries without some form of government intervention and control.

Fourth, the adequacy of deregulation must be considered in terms of the adequacy of broader constraints on monopoly power which are assumed to be at work. Reliance on common law remedies would appear to be a poor constraint on price discrimination, extortionist pricing, and the restriction of options for consumers. Historically, the inadequacy of this type of solution led to greater government intervention . . . .

With respect to the broader structural, market and institutional pressures which are supposed to erode monopoly power, it is difficult to discern any changes that might accomplish this task during the coming decade. In fact, deregulation will probably concentrate such power to a greater degree and facilitate control by established firms over those facilities which might be utilized by new entrants or substitute sources of supply.

In the electric power industry, deregulation would facilitate monopoly control of transmission networks and grids.

In the natural gas industry, deregulation of production, transmission, and distribution would take place in a setting where prices for gas (a superior fuel) are lower than the prices of alternative fuels. As a result, the demand for gas is inelastic, and deregulation in the short run would do little more than promote price increases without bringing about a corresponding increase in supply. In the long run, deregulation would perpetuate monopoly control over gathering, transmission, and distribution networks by existing firms, thereby performing a restrictive function similar to that noted with respect to electric power networks. Deregulation would also stimulate joint ventures between the major oil companies, pipelines, and distribution companies, with a consequent diminution of arm's-length bargaining. The impact of interindustry competition from other fuels will also be small in the foreseeable future, in part because of the control exercised by energy companies with major investments in gas, oil, coal, shale, and nuclear fuels, and in part because of the higher marginal cost of substitute fuels.

In communications, deregulation would permit AT&T, as the dominant firm with control over all landline transmissions, effectively to control competition. In addition, it is reasonable to assume that intermodal rivalry of the type that might result from IBM's anticipated entry into satellite communications would terminate in tacit oligopolistic coordination and a recognition of mutual interdependence.

Deregulation will not be matched by Schumpeterian gales of creative destruction. Rather, it would tend to make the market structure more intransigent and resistant to change. It is possible to argue that enforcement of antitrust laws might cure all of these problems, but it is important to remember that antitrust measures involve long delays and a limited range of solutions in industries with these cost and demand characteristics. A far more productive solution would involve incorporating structural flexibility and the minimization of monopoly power as objectives within the context of regulatory reform. Reliance on deregulation becomes de facto reliance on the corporate conscience, and that is a most peculiar culmination of the efforts of the members of the Chicago School.

In addition, the Chicago School analysts assume the impact of monopoly on the distribution of income is inconsequential since it does not involve, strictly speaking, a welfare loss. They also assume whatever value a monopoly position has will be equalled and offset by the expenses necessary to obtain the monopoly position. They assume that where this is not the case, the rent position may be taxed or auctioned away. In any case, the belief is held that, given time, any monopoly position will be undermined by technologically innovative firms.

However, the general public may be unwilling to treat distributional effects of monopoly as inconsequential; indeed, the general public may perceive them as of greater consequence than the allocative (efficiency) effects. The expectation (faith) that in the long run all monopoly positions will be undermined may not be acceptable in a society well-acquainted with Keyne's dictum that in the long run we are all dead! Nevertheless, many of the problems raised in the Chicago analysis are incorporated into the analyses of the following sections. In response to the Chicago analysis, however, we find a heterogeneous—in terms of ideology—group of legal, political science and economic writers who foresee the rejection of the major type of deregulation which the Chicagoans advocate for the economy. Professor Stanbury (1976a), in a recent article argues that changes—if they come—will be incremental. Indeed, he[8] draws on the writings of Ivan Feltham and Charles Reich, among others, to argue that the range of government interference or participation in the economy will increase, not diminish.

The distinct lack of interest which regulated industries demonstrate for elimination of regulation; the embracing by all political parties in Canada of direct regulatory control in agriculture and textiles; the increased sensitivity to corporate power—as demonstrated by the appointment of the RCCC; the demise of Bill C-256 which provided for a vigorous competition policy (see Stanbury, 1977); and the rejection of the Economic Council's (ECC) proposals for freer trade (see ECC, 1975 and the *Financial Post*, July 19, 1975, p. 3 and September 27, 1975, p. 6) almost out of hand by spokesmen for the public and private sectors do not augur well for supporters of deregulation.

THE REGULATORY FRAMEWORK

The traditional economic rationale for direct regulation can be embodied in three very general propositions:

1. Certain industries are perceived as so important as components of the infrastructure of the economy that the competitive market has been rejected in favour of direct public control. These industries are perceived as so

---

[8] See Feltham (1973) and Reich (1966) as quoted in Stanbury (1976a, p. 109).

vital to the public welfare that they have become 'clothed with' or 'affected with' the public interest.

2. Certain industries have economic characteristics which qualify them as "natural monopolies." A single supplier will have lower unit costs than a group of suppliers because of economies of scale.

3. Competition for one reason or another is perceived as simply unworkable (Kahn, 1971, vol. 2, p. 11).

Alfred Kahn (1971, vol 2, pp. 11 - 12) in his authoritative text on economic regulation cautions against uncritical acceptance of this categorization. His comments in this regard are deserving of quotation at length since he ably demonstrates some of the ambiguities and inconsistencies which have seldom been appreciated when governments have moved to directly regulate an industry:

> . . . Every part of the rationalization involves an issue or series of issues instead of a settled conclusion. For instance, the public utilities are important; but do they make a greater contribution to national product or economic growth than the provision of food, medical care, housing or education, none of which is regulated in the same fashion? Their importance, clearly, is not a sufficient explanation or economic justification for their subjection to regulation. Nor is it a necessary condition—one could find economic justification for regulating "unimportant" industries such as ticket brokers, except that since it uses resources to regulate, there would be no economic point in doing so for industries so unimportant that the benefits of regulation could not possibly outweigh the costs of administration.
>
> There is no room for doubt that at least some of the public utility industries are in some respects "natural monopolies." But the interesting economic questions are: What makes them so? Is natural monopoly synonymous with long-run decreasing cost tendencies? If so, what about the public utilities, such as the supply of water, that seem to be characterized by long-run tendencies to increasing costs? Does a tendency for costs to decline over time constitute an evidence of natural monopoly? What parts of these industries are natural monopolies, what parts not? Might they be natural monopolies in some static, efficiency sense but "unnatural" ones in terms of the prerequisites for innovation and growth? And how then do we handle, in theory and in practice, the growing competition between "natural monopolists," such as electric and gas distribution companies for the home heating and cooking market, or between international cable and satellite communications? And how do we cope with the historical fact that the prime historic exemplars of the extension of public utility regulation in the United States in the last quarter of the nineteenth century—railroads and grain elevators—were not really natural monopolists?
>
> As we have already suggested, part of the case for regulation and the inappropriateness of competition inheres in the heavy fixed costs that characterize most of these industries. But do heavy fixed costs make monopoly "natural"? Or competition unreliable? What then of agriculture or even the practice of medicine, most of whose costs are likewise fixed? Or trucking, whose fixed costs are only a small proportion of the total, yet which is regulated like a public utility? And does it make any difference whether the fixed costs that must be recovered from the sale of a number of services are mainly common to those various services, or joint?

A review of the industries which have been subject to some form of direct regulation by democratic governments in North America and Western Europe in this century leaves little doubt that using the 'affected with the public interest' and 'natural monopoly' rationales, almost any industry can and has been subjected to direct regulation or government ownership.

In addition to these traditional economic rationales for regulation, regulation has frequently been introduced with the social goals of subsidizing service to special groups (telephone), regional development (transport), regional planning (electric power), producer protection (marketing boards), and the maintenance of cultural and political integrity (communications), among others (Canadian Radio-Television Commission, 1976, pp. 1 - 16). These other considerations are equally valid in a "public interest" context to the purely economic considerations of price and resource use.

The entire economic rationale of a regulatory agency may be overridden by its mandate to attain cultural objectives. An excellent example of this situation is found in the regulation of cable television where the Canadian Radio-Television Commission (CRTC) until recently has made no pretext of serious *economic* regulation (Babe, 1974), even though such responsibility was clearly within its legislative ambit.

A brief further comment on the 'traditional' economic arguments for direct regulation will complement later discussion of specific industries. While direct regulation may 'protect' the public from unfair price discrimination, the rapacious monopolist and economic inefficiencies, it possesses, equally, the capacity to inflict these on the public with the support of the legal authority and judicial sanctions of the State. Thus regulation is a double-edged sword.

In recent years, economists working in this area have become particularly wary of the economies of scale argument. As James Nelson (1966, p. 3) has observed: "One of the most unfortuante phrases ever introduced into law or economics was the phrase 'natural monopoly'. Every monopoly is a product of public policy."

In some industries, select services may be most efficiently provided by a single firm because of economies of scale. This 'natural monopoly' case involves the provision of a good or service to all customers by one firm at a lower unit cost than would be possible if two or more firms were offering identical services or products. The distribution of electric power to a single community is an example of 'natural monopoly'.

Unfortunately, the concept of natural monopoly has been overused and abused. Indeed, only a very small portion of industries currently regulated fall into this category. Extreme care must be taken to avoid abusing the concept. For example, from an economic standpoint it might be desirable not to build two rail lines paralleling each other between two locations. However, this is no reason to prevent commercial trucks or airlines—industries in which economies of scale are insignificant—from serving the two locations or for requiring a single, large rail system.

In recent years, economists and legal scholars have looked upon all the traditional rationales for direct regulation with increasing skepticism. It is probably not extreme to suggest that conventional wisdom today holds that direct regulation has not typically been introduced to prevent the use of monopoly power and to protect the public interest in industries affected with the public interest. But, on the contrary, regulation has been introduced primarily to protect established firms from competition and to create or entrench market power.

This observation emerges from re-examinations of the histories of many regulatory agencies including: their rationales for existence (Kolko, 1965); interest groups which supported their establishment; the decisions made by the agencies over time; and the interest groups which have opposed the dismantling of the agencies.

Many observers of the regulated sector have noted in most of the extensively regulated industries that the regulated firms have demonstrated a preference for regulation over time. Where that regulation involved restrictions on entry, output and price competition, this has become the conventional wisdom. However, it is always hazardous to generalize from a small sample of cases. It is not necessarily true that a preference for regulation is necessarily a preference for a particular regimen of regulation. However, Mr. Robert Bertrand (*Transcripts*, 1, pp. 83 - 84), in his appearance before the RCCC, probably accurately reflected the attitudes of an overwhelming majority of economists and political scientists which have appeared in the professional and casual literature in the last decade when he stated:

> Other scholars point out that however much business may resist the direct regulation initially, firms frequently learn very quickly to prefer the comfort of a regulated environment to the cold winds and rough blows of competition.

Professor Trebilcock, (*Submission,* p. 2) a leading Canadian student of regulatory law, in his brief to the Commission observed that:

> It has been demonstrated time and again that both theoretically and empirically these regimes are a direct response to industry pressure for reduced competition—in effect, for legalized cartelization.

Likewise, Professor George Stigler (1971, p. 3), a leading American authority in regulatory economics, remarks: ". . . . As a rule, regulation is acquired by the industry and is designed and operated primarily for its benefit."

This conclusion of most of the academics in the area is shared by many practitioners. Lewis Engman (as quoted in Trebilcock, 1975, p. 645), former Chairman of the Federal Trade Commission, has stated:

> Though most government regulation was enacted under the guise of protecting the consumer from abuse, much of today's regulatory machinery does little more than shelter producers from the normal competitive consequences of lassitude and inefficiency. . . . The consumer, for whatever presumed abuse he is being spared, is paying plenty in the form of government sanctioned price fixing.
>
> From time to time, proposals have been made to provide direct cash subsidies in lieu of the patchwork of regulatory subsidies that now pervade our economy. Opponents rise indignantly to object that hardworking individuals and business do not

want handouts. Well, a rose by any other name . . . . Our airlines, our truckers, our railroads, our electronics media and countless others are on the dole. We get irate about welfare fraud. But, our complex systems of hidden regulatory subsidies make welfare fraud look like petty larceny. . . . The fact of the matter is that most regulated industries have become federal protectorates, living in the cozy world of cost-plus, safely protected from the ugly spectres of competition, efficiency and innovation.

The American Case

As we have noted previously, most of the comprehensive analyses of regulatory agencies have been undertaken in the United States. At least for the American case, it is clear that most major regulatory boards either were at their inceptions oriented to the protection of established economic interests, or became so oriented within a very short time thereafter (see Green, 1973; Friedman, 1962). It is worthwhile to briefly review some of the evidence which these lawyers and economists draw upon to support their positions.

COMMERCIAL AIR PASSENGER SERVICE

Studies in the United States of licensing in the commercial scheduled airline industry have revealed a pattern of protection in which new applicants for licences have consistently been refused entry into the industry. No new licences were issued by the Civil Aeronautics Board (CAB) in the United States for major trunklines between 1939 and 1972. The CAB has consistently refused to permit competitive rate reductions (Jordan, 1970; Caves, 1962; and Douglas and Miller, 1974).

The impact of this regulation has been vividly demonstrated in two states—Texas and California—where intrastate airlines are not regulated. In the absence of CAB blanket protection, prices declined by up to 50 percent for some classes of service according to Jordan, and Douglas and Miller. We will have occasion to comment further on this situation in a later section.

COMMERCIAL TRUCKING AND RAIL

The Interstate Commerce Commission (ICC) has consistently blocked entry into these industries by new firms and restricted competition further by setting minimum rates, limiting back-hauls, and narrowly defining the types of commodities which may be carried by some carriers (see Meyer, 1964; Moore, 1972; 1975; Gellman, 1971; Fellmeth, 1970; and *Business Week*, November 2, 1974, pp. 86 - 87, and April 4, 1977, pp. 42 - 95). In addition, the ICC has severely limited the ability of the railroads to compete for business with the commercial truckers. In recent years, the result has been economic inefficiency and excessively high prices. The industry is identified currently by regulatory economists of almost every political persuasion as one in which deregulation is of paramount importance. The industry displays little enthusiasm for such deregulation.

In its early years, the ICC served as an industry secretariat for the railroads which had been victims of 'uncontrolled' competition for years prior to the ICC's creation. With the coming of the ICC deviation from posted prices became illegal. Thus, the effective sanctions of government were substituted for the ineffective efforts of the railroad rate bureaus.

U.S. Attorney-General Richard Olney, as quoted in Josephson (1938, p. 526), tried in 1894 to allay the fears of some railroad executives concerned over the creation of the ICC by commenting:

> The Commission is or can be made of great use to the railroads. It satisfies the public clamor for supervision of the railroads at the same time that the supervision is almost entirely nominal. Furthermore, the older such a commission gets to be, the more inclined it will be to take the business and railroad view of things. It thus becomes a sort of barrier between the railway corporations and the people and a sort of protection against hasty and crude legislation hostile to railroad interests. The part of wisdom is not to destroy the Commission, but to utilize it.

TELECOMMUNICATIONS

Studies (Goulden, 1968; and Consumer Reports, 1977)[9] of the telephone industry have revealed a long history of protection of American Telephone and Telegraph companies from private firms desiring to provide competition for cable, microwave, peripheral terminal equipment and tie-line service by the Federal Communications Commission (FCC). Theodore Vail, founder of the Bell System, was an early supporter of direct regulation—largely out of fear of public ownership, according to Posner (1969, p. 622).

The FCC has also been charged with the protection of established broadcasters by inhibiting the development of pay television and the expansion of cable television systems (Comanor and Mitchell, 1971).

BANKING

Some evidence exists that restrictive licensing of banks has resulted in the restraint of competition in certain markets for financial services (Phillips, 1975, chap. 10).

PETROLEUM

The market pro-rationing policies of the Texas Railroad Commission are legend. In concert with the quota system on foreign oil used in the United States through the early seventies, there is little doubt that regulation served essentially the interests of the producers and major petroleum companies (Shaffer, 1972, and references therein).

This brief review, with one exception, has included only major national regulatory boards in the United States. A review of state agencies has not been undertaken. The evidence available for the major national commissions is supportive of the conclusions drawn by Trebilcock, Stigler and Engman.

---

[9] See Kahn (1971, pp. 127-52) for a review of most of the studies.

The Canadian Case

In the Canadian case, there is ample evidence that companies like the 'right' types of regulation. Approximately one-half of Canadian manufacturing firms benefit from the high tariff structure and many others in manufacturing have approached the government directly or indirectly or through the Anti-Dumping Tribunal for special protection against foreign competition.

The provincial transportation commissions in all provinces but Alberta have used their powers to restrict entry. All provinces, with the exception of Alberta, have adopted regulation of entry or rates for intraprovincial motor carriers. The regulatory frameworks in all regulating provinces are similar. Each of the provinces has a quasi-judicial regulatory agency which has the authority to control:

- the granting of operating authority,
- commercial vehicle licensing,
- bonding and insurance,
- commodities, and
- freight rates and routes.

While the regulatory agencies are provided with the authority to regulate in each of these areas, in some instances there is comprehensive regulation while in others there is only a nominal exercise of power.

In the Alberta case, the enabling legislation permits comprehensive regulation. However, the policy of the Alberta Motor Transport Board and the policy of the Government has been to control neither entry nor rates. Following requests from the industry for comprehensive regulation, the Government of Alberta in November 1975 established a legislative committee to study the industry and make recommendations. In its report in March 1977 (especially pp. 6, 8, 10), the Committee recommended that neither rates nor entry be directly restricted. Thus, intraprovincial truck transportation is likely to remain unregulated in Alberta. Neither the substance nor the analysis in the report is impressive, but its recommendations are likely to be accepted by the government.

The costs of this type of regulation to the consumer have been documented.[10] Economist James Sloss' study for 1958 - 1963 estimated that rates in regulated provinces were 10 to 15 percent higher than in unregulated provinces. University of Calgary economist D.L. McLachlan attributes a premium of 20 percent to regulations (see Weiss, 1975). These estimates of Sloss and McLachlan are paralleled in a recent study of truck regulation in Ontario by Bonsor (1978).

The quiet life and inflated prices have left unregulated truckers envious as is reflected in this excerpt from the *Edmonton Journal* (January 27, 1973)

---

[10] See Sloss (1970); Palmer (1973) and McLachlin (1971). See also Maister (1976) and Alberta (1977a, p. 35) for an opposing view.

of the decision of Alberta truckers to seek regulation:

> Tighter government control over the trucking industry will be sought by the Alberta Motor Transport Association in 1973, says AMTA president Alvin Bietz of Calgary.
>
> "Too many trucking firms are going broke in the province, resulting in the long run in increased costs to taxpayers," said Mr. Bietz, who succeeded Bill Sokil of Edmonton as president last November.
>
> "Alberta is the only province in Canada that has no reasonable or effective control of entry into the trucking industry, and we feel this is a major, contributing factor in companies going broke," he said.
>
> "They go in with a lack of proper financing and are not able to compete in the market. If the government and the public just realized that every time a company goes broke it costs the taxpayer money, then maybe there would be some improvement.
>
> I still believe in the free enterprise system, but we have to have some kind of control in transportation," said Mr. Bietz.

The closing paragraph reflects an inconsistency in philosophy commonly encountered in groups seeking regulatory controls.

In a similar vein, a recent appeal by auto wreckers, as reported in the *Ottawa Journal* (June 26, 1976, p. 10) for the government to control 'bodysnatchers' reads as follows:

> Spokesmen for autowrecking companies in the city say competition from private citizens is ruining their business.
>
> Many private individuals are showing up at salvage auctions, bidding higher than auto wreckers are willing to pay, and snapping up vehicles with the idea of putting them back on the road or at least selling the parts.
>
> "We spent eight years telling the provincial government this and demanding legislation to protect our business, but they won't listen," said Roper Clarke, former president of the now-defunct Alberta Automobile Dismantlers' Association.
>
> A spokesman for Western Auto Wreckers agreed there should be government legislation to protect the industry, saying such legislation worked wonders in the United States, particularly California.

And finally, a recent appeal by the Ontario Dump Truck Drivers Association, as reported in the *Financial Post* (November 8, 1975, p. C-6) for regulation:

> An experiment in freer transport-industry competition is likely to end in Ontario this fall.
>
> After eight years of decontrol—free entry and negotiated rates and routes—the Ontario dump trucking industry is expected to be recontrolled, perhaps before year-end.
>
> Strict control, at least, is the recommendation of the Rapoport Dump Truck Inquiry, which tabled its conclusions in the legislature this past June. The inquiry was undertaken after a campaign of vigorous protest by dump-trucking associations—a protest that included ringing the legislature with dump trucks.
>
> Dump trucks associations contend that the dropping of entry controls encourages the entry of more truckers and trucks than demand warrants. This, in turn, lowers rates operators receive. The effect of the lower rates is to (1) decrease safety

consciousness by truckers—trucks are overloaded and maintenance is skimpy and (2) to increase turnover in the industry—as much as 90% in one five-year period.

Most sectors of Canadian agriculture are regulated with their full consent by milk control boards, public utility boards, or marketing boards (see Forbes, 1974, vol. 2). While the petroleum industry appears displeased with federal price control, it has never demonstrated any particular displeasure with the philosophy of market prorationing embraced by the Alberta Energy Conservation Board (Shaffer, 1972).

Canadian bankers have been able to entrench their market positions as a result of the restrictive chartering policies followed, until recently, by the federal government. They may be immune to significant new competition at this point, due to the protection provided by direct regulation during critical periods in their development. This is an area worthy of study.

The CRTC has consistently followed an extremely restrictive licensing policy for radio and television broadcasting. A review of its files on any given new AM radio application in a large market invariably reveals a pattern of established licensees, as intervenors, opposing the applicant. We will examine the CRTC and CTC in more detail in a later section.

It may safely be concluded that extensive evidence exists that a substantial proportion of the direct economic regulation in Canada exists with the blessing of the interests being regulated and, therefore, may be presumed to be protective of their interests. To the extent that the public interest may be equated with their interest, then the public interest is serviced by the regulation. If the public interest incorporates the welfare of the public at large, instead of being limited to the economic welfare of producers in the industry involved, then, to the extent that the regulation results in supra-competitive prices, restricted economic opportunities, economic inefficiency, and retarded technological development, the effects of such regulation may be perceived as not in the public interest.

Who Regulates?

Irrespective of the motives of governments for introducing regulation, once a regulatory board is established a special problem arises with the membership of the board. In theory, only capable persons with no vested interest in the firms being regulated are to be appointed; in reality, they are frequently less than the best and possess mixed interests. As Francis X. Welch (1942, p. 8), an American public utility lawyer and editor of *Public Utilities Fortnightly,* once observed:

> . . . This selection of our regulatory commissioners seems to be among our most democratic practices of government. There is no discernible barrier based on age, . . . politics, nor—what may be more important—previous training.

The appointments of defeated or retired politicians to regulatory boards, while less common in Canada than in the United States, does occur.

It is frequently asserted that members and staff tend to be mediocre at best (Green, 1973). The American Bar Association (ABA) Report on the U.S. Federal Trade Commission quotes one senior official:

> We preferred to hire older men—who had been out in the world for ten years or so and had come to appreciate that they were not going to make much of a mark— because they tended to be loyal and remain with the FTC.

The ABA concluded as quoted in Stanbury (1976a, p. 115): "If there is a formula better designed to avoid hiring bright and energetic young men, we have not heard of it."

A related problem noted frequently in the United States and cited in almost all studies of specific regulatory agencies is the employment of members of the staffs and the commissioners themselves by the regulated industry. Thus, basic questions can be raised about the likely independence of staff and board members if they expect to be seeking employment or legal work at a later date with the very firms they are now regulating. Is it reasonable to assume that some staff and board members will succumb to the obvious temptations? Professor Brown-John, in the study cited previously, is attempting to assemble information which may provide some answers to these questions. The studies of the Canadian Consumer Council revealed few instances involving federal boards or provincial public utility boards where individuals moved freely back and forth to and from the regulated industries or where they were demonstrably incompetent. In the United States, both the problem of incompetence and the special problem of conflict of interest are chronic.

The fact that two recent studies (Andrew and Pelletier, 1978; and Brown-John, 1977) suggest that a much higher proportion of staff and members of Canadian regulatory commissions are drawn from the public sector bureaucracy than is the case in the United States suggests that if a similar problem exists in Canada it may reveal itself in very different and, as yet, not fully understood ways.

Of course, in industries where regulators are drawn from the industry being regulated because of presumed expertise and in instances where regulators succumb to the temptation to be 'reasonable' in expectation of future rewards, the agencies are effectively captured by the regulatees. However, far more subtle processes of capture have been noted by politicians and scholars alike. It is well reflected in the following comment attributed to the former Minister of Finance John Turner in Sack and Sack (1972, p. 37):

> I've looked at a lot of regulatory agencies, and the longer I'm around here, the more I believe that every one of these tends in a period of time to reflect the interests of the industry it is supposed to be regulating.

Professor Trebilcock (1976 - 77, vol. 21, p. 3731), in his testimony before the RCCC said:

> The pattern that emerged from [U.S. studies and studies of the Canadian Consumer Council] was, of course, not a uniform one, but there was sufficient evidence in relation to a number of regulated sectors, that there was askewedness . . . on the part of regulatory bodies towards producer interests against consumer interests.

This askewedness of interest is attributable in part to a convergence of interest and long-term relationships which develop between the lawyers representing the regulated and the regulators, as reported in the RCCC *Transcripts* (1976 - 77, vol. 21, pp. 3753 - 54). To some extent, a mutual 'bond' is alleged to grow out of protracted and frequent hearings involving the same parties. Beyond this, a protective and promotional attitude may emerge on the part of regulators. Indeed, the regulators may abjure the essentially negative function of regulation and seek to promote a healthy industry which, narrowly defined, is equated with the public interest. The process, if it occurs, may be devoid of any malice or conscious pursuit of self-interest by the regulators.

Landis (1960, p. 71) observes:

> It is the daily machine gun impact on both agency and its staff of industry representation that makes for industry orientation on the part of my honest and capable agency members as well as agency staff.

To the extent that this subtle process of capture occurs, the consequences for all interests but those of the regulated industry can obviously be detrimental. While various individuals have speculated on the tendency (Green, 1973), little concrete evidence is available to prove the hypothesis nor is it possible for us to conceive of a practical methodology that would permit its measurement (see Sabatier, 1975, for one model).

In the final analysis, the idea of 'capture' includes a variety of relationships and is simplistic. Clearly, there are many cases in the literature of regulatory agencies pursuing policies opposed by—and against—the interests of the companies being regulated. Examples involving major American agencies include the deliberate underpricing of natural gas wellhead prices by the Federal Power Commission and the adoption of programming guidelines by the FCC. There is a tendency of critiques to focus on deficiencies in regulation and attribute these to capture. In fact, many of the deficiencies may be attributable to mere obtuseness, limited abilities of regulators, limited resources, or bureaucratic tendencies on the part of regulators to become more interested in the process of regulation than in the substance of regulation (Jaffe as quoted in Wilson, 1973, p. 48).

The Public Interest Problem

A recurrent theme in the regulatory economic literature is the question of the meaning of the term public interest (see Stanbury, 1976a and Trebilcock, 1975). In previous sections, we have avoided the issue by referring to the interests of the industry being regulated as contrasted with the interests of all other groups. The problem is broached in most of the studies on regulatory boards undertaken for the Canadian Consumer Council, but not dealt with definitively in any; indeed, we may be addressing a problem that is beyond the abilities of economists and lawyers. However, working in an area such as regulatory economics, the concept regularly presents itself and demands the formation of some explicit assumptions regarding its meaning. A natural temptation is to define the public interest as the long-term interest of the consumer and simply quote Adam Smith (1937, Book IV, chap. VIII):

> Consumption is the sole end and purpose of all production; and the interest of the producer ought to be attended to, only so far as it may be necessary for promoting that of the consumer. The maxim is so perfectly self-evident, that it would be absurd to attempt to prove it.

This approach, which equates the public interest to the consumer interest, in as much as economic matters are concerned, is acceptable to few legal and economic scholars. A more widely accepted concept of the public interest is the balancing of interests concept which is well stated by Charles Reich (1966, p. 1234), who writes:

> As the agencies have sought a meaning for the public interest, they have come to this: the public interest is served by agency policies which harmonize as many as possible of the competing interests present in a given situation. . . . Thus, the agencies have evolved a meaning for their charters which makes them both philosopher-kings searching for the good, and practical politicians trying to please a multi-voiced rabble.

He also notes some of the drawbacks of this approach by observing that:

> The very concept of balancing is in one sense a contradiction of the concept of planning. Fashioning values and goals out of existing interests prevents any really long-range policy-making or planning from ever being done. It equates policy-making with satisfying the majority or the most powerful interest, although the country might benefit more from policies which favour weaker or minority interests, or interests not yet in existence. It tends to place emphasis on those interests which have a commercial or pecuniary value as against intangible interests such as scenery or recreation. The most fundamental infirmity of the present concept of the public interest as a guide for planning is that it defeats planning by responding only to immediate pressures (p. 1239).

Professor Stanbury (1976a, p. 120) has examined the concept and writes as follows:

> Edelman, a political scientist, argues that 'public policy may usefully be understood as the resultant of the interplay among groups.' Gellhorn, a lawyer very familiar with the administrative process in the U.S., indicates that 'the public interest . . .is not a monolith. It involves a balance of many interests. . . .' Manual F. Cohen, formerly the Chairman of the Securities and Exchange Commission, takes the view that 'It is this delicate balancing of various and seemingly competing public policy considerations that is the principal object of regulation.'

The balancing of interests has often been more narrowly construed to include only those interests which are actively represented before the regulatory tribunal. Leo
M. Pellerzi gives his view:

> 'In the approximately 1000 cases that I presided over in almost ten years as an
> administrative law judge, the "public interest" never meant anything of
> substance to me beyond the materially related interests of the parties that were
> before me. Among the parties, all represented by lawyers, were the principal
> motor carriers, all the class-one rail carriers in the United States, and most of
> the 500 largest corporations.'

The balancing of interests concept of the public interest has a great deal of
academic support. It is derived from the view of the state as a device which brings
about the reconciliation of group differences. The government, in this conceptualiza-
tion, was considered as the adjustment or balance of interests. It is taken for granted
that no interest could be considered in the process unless it manifested itself in group
action.

Hence, the public interest 'must necessarily represent a working compromise and
be subject to continuous definition, as need arises, in the process of achieving an often
delicate balance among conflicting interests.' Behind this is the idea that 'the society
itself is nothing other than the complex of groups that compose it.' Bentley's disciple,
David B. Truman, specifically denied that there is an 'interest of the nation as a
whole, universally and invariably held and standing apart and superior to those of the
various groups within it.' Truman recognized the existence of unorganized groups,
but argued that their interests would be asserted by both appointed and elected officials in all branches of government. Alternatively, if sufficiently disadvantaged, la-
tent groups would become organized as a sort of 'countervailing' force against those
groups who are benefitting at their expense. Glendon A. Schubert has described this
facet of Truman's theory as 'a vague but fervent transcendentalism.' Certainly, most
individual consumers and erstwhile consumer groups (e.g., The Consumers' Association of Canada or Consumers Union) would agree.

When Mr. Roberge of the CTC informed the RCCC, "We feel that we
are custodians of the public interest . . . [and] we are judges" (1976 - 77,
vol. 23, pp. 4250 - 51), what precisely did he mean? He obviously perceived
himself and the other Commissioners as balancers of interests—as policy-
makers.

The problem is not as immense as may appear since many times in
legislation involving regulatory agencies the legislatures do spell out the objectives to be served. Unfortunately, the mandates given to a majority of
regulatory boards are extremely ambiguous and so much ground is left to be
charted that the agencies do assume a legislative function of determining the
public interest. We can reasonably ask whether, in a political system which
emphasizes the principle of political responsibility, the leaving to independent boards the weighing of special interests to determine the public interest
in critical economic questions is appropriate? Is it not what is conventionally
perceived as part of the political policy-making process which more appropriately belongs with Parliament? As we note later, the Government has
recently been considering these questions.

The Adjudicative Versus Legislative Functions

Related to the problems of the public interest and its determination is the format of regulation. Essentially, there are two philosophies of the appropriate format for proceedings of regulatory agencies. These may be distinguished as adjudicative and inquisitorial models. In the adjudicative model, the agency is envisioned as a tribunal or court which adjudicates and sets policy after hearing the presentations of interested parties; regulation becomes primarily a judicial function. The inquisitorial model envisions the regulatory agency as more than a judicial agency. In this model, the agency possesses the ability to assume an investigative function in every sense of the word. In the latter case, an agency will maintain a competent and adequate staff and counsel who will perform research, assemble and present evidence and participate in the hearing.

In a special sense, almost all boards have investigative, judicial and legislative functions to perform; however, they vary with the emphasis given them. The legislative function may be distinguished from the others as a general rule-making function, as contrasted with the judicial function which involves case-by-case decision-making.

Professor Trebilcock (1976 - 77, vol. 21, pp. 3735 - 36) in a lengthy exchange before the RCCC, brought the issues into perspective. He rejected the inquisitorial approach as "totally untenable." He continued:

> Without any doubt, in my view, the [Regulatory Agency] should not get involved in a private inquiry on its own which would lead it to a conclusion different from the conclusion to which it would arrive if it just took into consideration the evidence brought before it.

In effect, this statement and Professor Trebilcock's view of hearings as an instrument for determining the public interest, embody the adversarial, legal or adjudicative philosophy of regulation. It is not surprising that some of Professor Trebilcock's (1972 and 1975) greatest contributions to Canadian public policy in this area have been his efforts to right the balance in interest representation before regulatory tribunals.

The multifaceted inquisitorial approach is, however, the approach which is provided for in almost all the legislation. Most boards have the legal authority to be much more than judicial bodies. If the legislation establishing most of these bodies correctly reflects the thinking of the legislators, then the approach which emerges from a comment and a question by the Chairman of the RCCC, as recorded in the *Transcripts* (1976 - 77, vol. 21, pp. 3741 - 42), reflect more accurately the founding philosophies:

> I would like to return, Professor, to the question that Mr. Bériault [The Commission Counsel] had raised, and you were responding to it, about the nature of these regulatory bodies, not just because of the practical problems that Mr. Dickerson [one of the Commissioners] has raised, but maybe my view is affected a little bit by my own history because I participated in the drafting of government proposals to set up a number of them over the years, but as I have understood the concept, these regulatory bodies such as say the CTC, the Canadian Transport Commission, or the National Energy Board, are not set up to be courts. They are given some of the powers of courts, but they are also, however, expected, as I understood the thing, and perhaps I

am wrong, but they are expected to do two things: first, to undertake technical studies and even research, and how good the research has been I will not endeavour to judge; secondly, to themselves endeavour to determine and defend the public interest, and they are not limited to the evidence that the parties put before them. They can develop their own evidence, their own views, and I am, therefore, not clear as to what is implied by you and Mr. Bériault apparently agreeing that they are quasi-judicial and are arbitrating between the two parties. I would have thought they would have been expected to have a more positive role, or a more defensive role in the process themselves, and that was the reason for their staffs of experts and their research and the kind—whether or not they are deficient, the kind of remit they are given by Parliament, to define and defend the public interest.

And further (vol. 21, p. 3747):

> . . . . Now, do they also have a responsibility that goes beyond that of a judge to dig up evidence on their own, to provide expertise in their staff that contributes to the determination of the desirable course of action, even though that evidence, and those arguments, may not have been advanced by the adversaries before them?

Taxation by Regulation—The Problem of Cross-Subsidization

A problem apparently inadequately appreciated by policy makers and laymen is the extent to which regulation involves, in many instances, the *de facto* exercise of the power of taxation. This problem has recently been examined by Professor Posner (1971) in his article, "Taxation by Regulation." In most industries where regulation occurs, some price discrimination occurs.[11] With many joint costs involved in providing a service, there will always remain opportunity for arbitrary judgements.

However, most discrimination by regulatory boards is intentional. It occurs in essentially three forms. First, different prices may be charged to different customers or classes of customers when the costs of serving the different customers are the same. Second, the same price may be charged to different customers when the costs of servicing them are different. Third, service may be provided to customers at a loss who could not, or would not, afford the service if it was provided at a price sufficient to cover all costs. These customers may be disadvantaged on the basis of location or on the basis of time of use of the service, to mention the most common cases (Waters, 1976).

In many of the preceding cases, one class of customers will be required to pay a price vastly exceeding that necessary to produce a reasonable profit for the regulated company in order that residual revenue will be generated to subsidize the service being provided to other classes of customers at prices below full costs.[12]

---

[11] For a discussion of various types of price discrimination see Scherer (1970, pp. 253-72).

[12] An extreme example of cross-subsidization noted by Stanbury (1973), involved the British Columbia Public Utilities Commission awarding a Certificate of Public Interest to a firm to operate a crematorium adjacent to a cemetery near Nanaimo in 1971. The licence was subject to a requirement that part of the profits obtained (estimated at $36,354 over the first five years) from the crematorium be used to offset the losses involved in operating a cemetery which was licensed by the PUC under the *Cemeteries Act*. This is apparently one case the ecologists lost. See Stanbury (1973, pp. 15-16).

In its early years of operation, potential competitors of Air Canada were curbed on the basis of the somewhat dubious reasoning that Air Canada should earn above normal profits on some high density routes in order to be able to serve the then unprofitable West and East Coast, as well as some isolated Central Canada communities.

Common carrier airlines, truckers and railroads have very frequently persuaded regulatory boards to limit competition. This measure is taken on the basis that they require above normal profits on certain high density routes in order to subsidize service to some communities which would otherwise be serviced only at very high rates or not at all. Frequently, these are rural areas which possess substantial political leverage.

The regulatory agencies often find governments encouraging or at least supportive of restricting entry on otherwise competitive routes in order to permit subsidization of the low density service. The government position is easily understood. The presentation of formal legislation in Parliament requesting direct subsidies out of general revenue would invite critical review by opposition parties and the press, as well as by the general public. A "tax" on consumers in the high density markets to subsidize those in the low density market can be done by a regulatory board with a low political profile and the tax, once in place, is not subject to regular review.

Regulation forces one group of consumers to subsidize another without regular review of the subsidization scheme and without the vast majority of those being taxed even realizing the tax is being imposed. This represents a special cost of regulation to the users on the "highly profitable" routes. These can be and should be calculated. A far more rational approach would involve the payment by government to a regulated company a regular and reviewable subsidy to service certain classes of customers which Parliament has decided are in the public interest to service.

Professor Baldwin (1975), in a recent study of the regulation of Canadian air transportation, has explored some of the reasons why such subsidy schemes have been accepted most reluctantly in that industry as a substitute for cross-subsidization. Indeed, Baldwin, as Peltzman (1976, p. 231), finds cross-subsidization tendencies to be inherent in the politics of the regulatory process in transportation.

Baldwin suggests that there are good reasons to expect that any regulatory agency or government will prefer cross-subsidization schemes to subsidies. He traces this predeliction to the genesis of many of the agencies themselves. In effect, he argues that most regulatory agencies are established by governments to resolve either intergroup or interfirm conflicts which could not likely be resolved by a government itself without unacceptably high political alienation costs. By creating a regulatory agency, the resolution of these conflicts is removed one step from the government and, consequently, the government tries to escape responsibility for the decisions which are made by the "independent" board.

If George Stigler's theory of regulation (1971) is accepted, then we may presume that a regulatory agency, once created, will have a paramount interest in perpetuating itself. If this proposition is valid, then explaining regulatory agency behaviour is a matter largely of understanding how the agency determines a minimum policy mix which will maintain the support of a "winning" coalition of politically active interest groups (Downs, 1957).

In any regulatory setting there will be some issues which will be fully understood by some groups and not understood by others. In the cases of some groups the costs of obtaining information will exceed the expected benefits, or, in the case of large consumer groups, the individual effects will be so small that the consumer interest will not be represented. Under these circumstances, two types of actions will be very visible: price discrimination and service quality. Significant variance from the mean in either case will be visible readily, and inexpensively detected by almost all consuming groups involved. They are likely to organize and politically challenge the regulatory agency.

The regulatory agency, however, may easily perceive that extra revenue may be obtained from the main service market and used to subsidize the groups who would under normal market circumstances receive lower quality and/or more expensive service. The groups in the major service market often will discover only at great expense that they are being overcharged. In fact, they probably will have little basis upon which to evaluate the fairness of the prices they are charged. All groups are satisfied. Service is reasonable and rates per unit of service are comparable; the regulated firm attains adequate system revenue, the government avoids confrontation with consumer groups, and the agency has served its goal of self-preservation.

On the other hand, to annually provide subsidies for certain classes of users invites confrontation. As we noted above, if subsidies are necessary then the government will be unable to conceal costs and will be unable to disclaim responsibility for the result. The prices cease to be the result of technical decisions which are being made by an objective independent tribunal one step removed from the government. Within this model, some regulatory agencies become an integral part of the political process with the role of permitting government to divest itself of conflicts which can be resolved only at unacceptable political costs.

Direct subsidies can be a liability to the agency since they invite continual appraisal of and interference in the operation of the agency. In this sense, they are also not welcomed by the regulated interests which must be concerned that in the process of reviewing subsidies, the effectiveness of the regulatory process itself is likely to be evaluated.

The Costs of Regulation

As noted in the introduction of this study, increasing interest has been directed in recent years to the costs of regulation and to the relative costs of unregulated monopoly. The costs of regulation may be perceived to take several forms. There is a cost associated with maintenance of the agency, hearings, and costs to the regulated firms of participation as well as the costs of other intervenors. In addition, if regulation is protective in nature, then the prices charged may exceed those which would prevail if free entry was permitted. Regulation may also result in what the economist labels static inefficiency, which reflects itself in lower productivity or inefficient use of resources by the firm. Another cost involves inflated expenditures associated with "X" inefficiency.

If management knows that it can pass most costs on to the consumer, it may spend unnecessarily to provide itself and labour with the 'good life'. It may be excessively generous in collective bargaining. Management may also be induced to overinvest in physical plant and equipment if the rate of return exceeds the actual cost of capital. Regulation may also result in 'dynamic' inefficiency, which involves primarily retarded technological development. The economist's measure of cost focuses on "social" cost which involves welfare loss. It is much more narrowly defined than the cost measures mentioned above (see Posner, 1975, pp. 809 - 15).

When all of these costs are considered, it would be surprising indeed if the costs of regulation did not in some instances exceed the benefits. It is surprising that interest in preparation of balance sheets—Regulatory Impact Statements—has only emerged in the last decade. Many of the studies referred to previously of regulatory activity in the United States have included efforts to measure the costs of regulation.

In a recent article on measuring the social costs of monopoly, Richard Posner (1975, p. 819) admits that many of the estimates of the social costs are very crude. They are most assuredly not applicable universally. However, in many of the studies of American regulatory agencies, the estimates of the impact of regulation on prices have been impressive.

A sample of American studies reviewed by Posner reveals estimates that the regulation of motor carriers has caused prices to be up to 62 percent above competitive levels (Moore, 1972; Farmer, 1964; Moore, 1975); and oil prices at times to be up to 62 percent above competitive levels.[13] Airline prices were estimated to be up to 66 percent above competitive levels (Jordan, 1970; Douglas and Miller, 1974). Kessel (1967, p. 73) estimated milk prices to be up to 11 percent above competitive levels. Benham (1973, p. 19) estimated eyeglass prices to be up to 34 percent above competitive levels. Kessel (1972, p. 119) also estimated physician services to be up to 40 percent above competitive levels.

It should be noted that high prices do not necessarily mean high profits, since the higher prices may mask inefficiency or new costs associated with non-price competition which can occur in a regulatory environment. For example, the American airline industry is heavily regulated and prices vastly exceed those which would prevail in a competitive environment. Nevertheless, it has been one of the least profitable American industries over the

---

[13] See the Report of the Cabinet Task Force on Oil Import Controls (1970) as reported in Posner (1975).

past decade according to Gritta (1975) and Douglas and Miller (1974). This may also be said of the Canadian industry.

No regulatory impact statements as such have been prepared in Canada. The studies by Palmer (1973), Sloss (1970), McLachlin (1971), and Bonsor (1978) of the impact of provincial government regulation of intraprovincial trucking on prices indicate supra-competitive price margins of 10 to 20 percent. However, Maister (1976) using a different methodology challenges these findings.

The studies of the impact of agricultural marketing boards prepared in 1973 and 1974 are available but should be updated. These early studies indicate costs in the millions of dollars annually. In a recent study of the B.C. Milk Control Board's pricing policies, Professors Grubel and Schwindt (1977) estimate the annual costs in inflated prices of provincial dairy policies at \$12 million. This estimate ignores some of the administrative costs of the agency (see also Forbes, 1974; Cohen, 1977). Similar effects have been found in studies in Ontario (Broadwith, 1978) and Alberta (Reschenthaler and Wulff, 1977).

Recent studies of fixed commissions in the securities industry and airline industries in Canada suggest substantial and needless consumer costs.

The Problem of Public Representation

In the preceding discussions we have suggested that the regulatory process assumes an adjudicatory-adversarial format in which commission members, in a constrained environment, seek to determine policies which will serve the 'public interest'. The process is not a free good, and may be extremely expensive. Provincial rate hearings costing in excess of \$750 thousand have occurred, and the decisions of the boards may involve the imposition of substantial taxes and subsidies on consumer groups.

The process is extra-parliamentary, reflects a direct delegation of power by parliament, and, in most instances, in Canada, provincial and the federal cabinets retain the right to review and overrule the regulatory boards or to serve, in effect, as regulatory boards themselves. The reality of the process is, however, that the regulatory boards are rarely overruled. The adversarial approach is contingent upon all significant interests being heard. If some important groups are chronically under-represented, then the process, in practice, fails to measure up to the theoretical model. In fact, it does not measure up.

In recent years, the under-representation of the consumer interest has been of increasing concern. Nicholas Johnson[14] a past member of the FCC, has observed:

---

[14] See Nicholas Johnson, "New Fidelity to the Regulatory Ideal" p. 874, as quoted in Stanbury (1976a, pp. 111-12).

> In terms of the legal and economic talent arrayed against it before this Commission, the public is scarcely represented at all. The battle is not just uneven; it is seldom even drawn.

Furthermore Johnson says:

> Policy-making by agencies is dominated by the so-called subgovernment, a coalescence of lobbyists, specialty lawyers, trade associations, trade press, congressional subcommittee staff members, and commission personnel who cluster around each of the regulated industries.

And in a more general view according to Johnson (1971):

> The crises of the regulatory commission is part of the larger crises of failing government, the central problem of which is that it is too often not responsive and not representative.

Colston E. Warne (1972, p. 297), president of Consumers Union, has expressed similar concern in noting that:

> . . . Long established procedures fit snugly into a pattern of resolving conflicts between competing business interests (rather) than of balancing the equities between producers and consumers.

In a Canadian context, J. S. Grafstein (1974, pp. 348 - 53) of the CTC has commented:

> The regulatory policy has not cast its net wide enough to examine the effects of transport policies or carriers activities on the consumer. In massive rate hearings . . . the public interest intervenors rarely have the resources of regulated corporations. This imbalance would change if an independent office—a "consumer advocate"—were built into the regulatory process.

Professor Trebilcock, in a recent article on the representational imbalance problem, draws on writings of Roger Cramton, Chairman of the U.S. Administrative Conference, and Milton Friedman. Roger Cramton (1972, p. 529) summarizes the reasons for the imbalance as follows:

> For an individual consumer to intervene in a regulatory controversy that will affect him, for example, only in his capacity as an occasional purchaser of auto tires, is irrational behavior on his part, since the costs of effective participation will be much greater than any benefits he might hope to obtain. Moreover, the transaction costs of assembling a group of persons, each of whom will suffer only a modest harm by a threatened administrative action, so that they may participate through a common spokesman are extremely large. Even if the transaction costs of group representation were not so large, a number of potential contributors to a common fund are likely to take a free ride at the expense of others.

Milton Friedman, as quoted in Trebilcock (1972, p. 6), offers the following relatively unsophisticated illustration of the problem:

> The declaration by a large number of different state legislatures that barbers must be approved by a committee of other barbers is hardly persuasive evidence that there is in fact a public interest in having such legislation. Surely, the explanation is different: it is that a producer group tends to be more concentrated politically than a consumer group. This is an obvious point often made and yet one whose importance cannot be overstressed. Each of us is a producer and also a consumer. However, we are much more specialized and devote a much larger fraction of our attention to our activity as a producer than as a consumer. We consume literally thousands if not millions of items. The result is that people in the same trade, like barbers or physicians, all have an intense interest in the specific problems of this trade and are willing to devote considerable energy to doing something about them. On the other hand, those of us who use barbers at all, get barbered infrequently and spend only a minor fraction of our income in barber shops. Our interest is casual. Hardly any of us are willing to devote much time going to the legislature in order to testify against the iniquity of restricting the practice of barbering. The same point holds for tariffs. The groups that think they have a special interest in particular tariffs are concentrated groups to whom the issue makes a great deal of difference. The public interest is widely dispersed. In consequence, in the absence of any general arrangements to offset the pressure of special interests, producer groups will invariably have a much stronger influence on legislative action and the powers that be than will the diverse, widely spread consumer interest.

In his discussion of the logic of collective action, Professor Stanbury (1976a, pp. 118 - 19) notes:

> . . . Stigler is not alone when he remarks, 'I know of no historical example of a viable, continuing, broad-based consumer political lobby.' This is despite the fact that the aggregate gains or losses to consumers resulting from the actions of regulatory agencies often greatly exceed the direct benefits or losses to the regulated firms . . . .
>
> It is a well-worn axiom of public finance that in the absence of a government which levies compulsory charges (e.g., taxes), the amount of public goods which a society will provide for itself will be suboptimal. . . .
>
> Consumers as an interest group face an analogous problem, but they lack the means for its solution. Any voluntary scheme will fail if each individual rationally pursues his own self interest. As Leone points out - 'despite public acceptance of the "product" of public interest advocacy, few are willing to pay the costs of "production".' He concludes that 'the resource constraint ultimately will end the current round of public interest advocacy.'
>
> The staffs of the regulatory commission have not lived up to their mandate; the commissioners have become 'judges' in cases where the 'defendant' (consumer) is unrepresented; and consumers themselves cannot voluntarily organize to represent their interests. Is it surprising that one hears a call for an institutionalized consumer advocate financed by government?

The extent to which this problem burdens consumers as an interest group was reflected in the recent controversy surrounding Bill C-256 which was submitted to Parliament in 1971 and involved proposals for major revisions in the *Combines Investigation Act*. Of 308 briefs submitted to the government, 300 came from business and professional groups opposing the legislation and 8 from economists and consumer groups. The expenses of the 300 were tax deductible; those of the 8 were not. The government ultimately decided not to proceed with the legislation (see Stanbury, 1977, especially chap. 9).

The general problem of organization of interests is exacerbated by practical problems encountered in the regulatory process. The report of the Canadian Consumer Council draws attention to the following problems:

1. There are problems of public notice.

2. The failure of many boards to be explicitly required within their legislative mandates to consider the consumer interest frequently results in no consideration.

3. The standing of public interest groups to initiate judicial review of commission decisions varies widely from commission to commission, but is frequently unrecognized.

4. Consumer groups lack information and expertise.

5. The heterogeneity of the consumer interests, rooted in differences in geography, occupation and age, can cause conflicts in objectives.

6. Information on the criteria used by regulatory boards may not be accessible. In some instances, only decisions are published without reasons and transcripts are not made available (see the Canadian Consumer Council, 1973).

The cost of participation can be a deterrent in itself. Professor Trebilcock (1972, p. 7) observes:

> The specific costs, direct and indirect, which inhibit consumer participation in regulatory processes, embrace the problems of providing effective notice of the timing and nature of proceedings to an amorphous interest group like consumers, the costs entailed in securing counsel expert in the area in issue, the costs of providing expert witnesses and evidence, transcript costs, etc. It has been estimated that a major FTC hearing, which may extend over many months, and involve hundreds of witnesses and generate a record running into tens of thousands of pages, will often cost a fully participating party $100,000.

In hearings before some boards, the interests of consumers are represented by businesses with interests of their own. This is the case in many rate hearings involving transportation companies where business groups frequently appear to contest applications for rate increases. However, in these instances, the consumer interest is only represented to the extent that it coincides with the business interest.

An interesting example of a case where the interests coincided involved the Milk Control Board in Manitoba some years ago. In its early years, the board downplayed the consumer interest and in the first hearing at which the CAC appeared in the early 1950s, its right to appear was challenged by the Chairman. The lawyer representing the Safeway food chain argued the consumers' case and persuaded the board of the legitimacy of the CAC's presence (see Reschenthaler, 1972, p. 101).

The right of consumer interest groups to participate is today recognized by most regulatory agencies. The form of that participation is examined later in this study.

SOME PERSPECTIVES ON REGULATORY APPROACHES: THE UNITED STATES AND CANADA

In the previous discussions, most of the fundamental policy issues in regulatory economics were considered. As noted, a preponderance of the research in recent years has originated in the United States, and some common themes have predominated in the literature. In the first portion of this discussion we will explore some of those themes.

The United States Consensus

There is increasing recognition in the United States that while government regulation is pervasive, it is a mixed blessing. It is increasingly appreciated that there are costs associated with direct regulation be it of the traditional economic variety which this study has focused on, or "social" regulation which includes areas such as occupational health and safety, product quality and safety, and environmental protection (see *Business Week,* May 12, 1975, pp. 74 - 80; and April 4, 1977, pp. 42 - 95).

President Ford, in reaction to recommendations of the National Commission on Productivity and the National Commission on Regulatory Reform and studies we reviewed earlier, urged Congress to undertake extensive regulatory reform. The primary aim of the White House policy—supported widely in academic circles in the formal economic area, but not in the social area—is to deregulate many industries and substitute competition as a regulatory instrument. (This information was reported in *Business Week,* May 12, 1975, pp. 74 - 80; and April 4, 1977, pp. 42 - 95; and in the *Wall Street Journal,* October 9, 1975, p. 3; and November 14, 1975, p. 11).

President Ford asked Congress to open commercial trucking and airline service to new competition. In banking he sought to phase out anti-competitive federal regulations governing thrift institutions and commercial banks. Those recommendations included permitting thrift institutions to provide an expanded variety of services and permitting banks and thrift institutions to compete more actively for savers' dollars. Other prime candidates for deregulation included the insurance industry, farm cooperatives and the cable TV industry.

Congress acted on one of the recommendations by enacting legislation which permitted railroads greater freedom in rate setting and in procedures involving mergers and abandonments, as reported in the *Morgan Guarantee Survey,* (1976, pp. 10 - 14).

Some regulatory boards, admittedly under judicial prodding, have adopted more pro-competitive postures. The most striking example has involved the FCC, since 1968, permitting private unregulated companies to supply telephones, switchboards, automatic-answering machines, data-transmission equipment and other terminal equipment that can be interconnected with the Bell Network (Kahn, 1971, vol. 2, pp. 126 - 53). This market has recently been estimated as worth $3 billion a year; private competitors now have $143 million of it, according to Pauly (1976, p. 58).

Another form of competition has involved the $1 billion a year private tie-line service between major cities. Currently private unregulated firms are offering this service in the United States on non-Bell microwave and satellite facilities at prices substantially below Bell's rates. Bell reacted to this competition by obtaining 148 congressional sponsors for a Consumer Communications Reform Act of 1976 on which Congressional hearings were held in the fall of 1976 (Pauly, 1976, pp. 61 - 62). The proposed legislation would have re-established Bell's exclusive jurisdiction in these areas and thereby reinforced Bell's monopoly position.

The move to deregulate has not resulted in the wholesale dismantling of the regulatory machinery; interestingly, the American Congress rejected deregulation of natural gas field prices and extended price controls on petroleum (with enactment of the *Energy Policy and Conservation Act* of 1975) according to the *Morgan Guarantee Survey* (1976, p. 10).

There are only three areas in which the U.S. Congress appears anxious to proceed with deregulation. The first involves the railroads. Many of these are on the verge of bankruptcy because of the tendency of regulators to prevent them from competing with commercial truckers during the last forty years.

The second area is commercial trucking which has been the focal point of criticism of regulatory economists for thirty years. The National Commission on Productivity in the United States has estimated that at any given time 40 percent of the trucks on the road in the United States are running empty because of government regulations which prevent them from carrying cargo on return trips (back-haul prohibition). This is estimated to cost food retailers alone $250 million a year (Bacon, 1974, p. 1).

The third major candidate for regulatory reform is the commercial airline industry where studies cited in "The Regulatory Framework" discussion of this paper revealed rates 30 to 60 percent lower in competitive regions (see Jordan, 1970; and Douglas and Miller, 1974).

These are all sectors in which the National Commission on Regulatory Reform expressed concern, as reported by the President's Advisory Council on Executive Organization (1971). Transportation economists have estimated that price-fixing and waste allowed under regulatory regimens of the CAB, Federal Maritime Commission and ICC cost consumers in the United States between $8 billion and $16 billion a year (1974) in aggregate (see Bacon, 1974; *Wall Street Journal,* October 9, 1974; *Business Week,* November 2, 1974; Moore, 1975; also Green, 1973, p. 24). Some experts have questioned these estimates, but as John R. Meyer of Harvard University and president of the National Bureau of Economic Research has emphasized *(Business Week,* November 2, 1974) the basic issue is not whether or not they are exact; it is rather that there is a substantial amount of money involved.

The estimates of $8 to $16 billion include only the static inefficiency costs of mis-and underutilization of capital and labour. As Meyer notes in the same article, "the dynamic inefficiencies bill may be even larger."

The uncompromising nature of business resistance to the proposal in the United States is not difficult to understand. In the case of the old or economic regulation, to the extent that the agencies have been captured by the regulated interests, those interests, of course, have no desire to right the representational imbalance. However, the core of the resistance is found in the area of social regulation where the agencies possess considerable flexibility in administering their mandates. The presence of a consumer advocate can severely limit the negotiating space open to the agency. More important, perhaps, would be the loss of ability to do this in private.

The opposition is easily understood if the following excerpt from a 1974 article by Arlen J. Large (1974) in the business publication, *The Wall Street Journal* is considered:

> A checklist of examples of wrongs the agency supposedly could correct is long and ambitious: . . . . Food and Drug Administration foot-dragging on safety rules of X-ray machines, Commerce Department sloth in banning fire-prone clothing, Civil Aeronautics Board tolerance of high air fares and lost luggage, FDA laxity toward dangerous toys, Transportation Department snoozing on rickety school buses, Federal Aviation Administration flabbiness on DC-10 cargo doors that pop open in flight, which proved fatal to 344 people in a crash near Paris (Large, p. 19).

The opposition to the agency by economists associated with the Chicago School is largely a reflection of their predilection for deregulation. However, it is completely inconsistent with their acceptance of the proposition that most regulatory agencies are effectively captured by regulated interests.

In summary the main thrust of the regulatory reform movement underway in the United States focuses on industries which suffer from chronic and obvious over-regulation. The supporters of deregulation range from consumer activist Ralph Nader who has said of the regulatory agencies "Never has so little government had so much bad effect" (Bacon, 1974), to former members of the more prestigious agencies, to leading economists and legal scholars in the area.

A second aspect of regulatory reform in the United States involves major efforts in Congress over several recent years to establish a consumer advocate office as an omnibus agency funded by the federal government to represent the consumer interest before all regulatory boards. The concept has been bitterly resisted by business, but proposed legislation does apparently enjoy majority support in Congress and the support of President Carter, as reported in *Business Week* (April 4, 1977, p. 58). The proposed legislation has failed to pass Congress only because of threatened Senate filibuster by opponents. Professor Trebilcock in a presentation to the RCCC (*Transcripts*, 1976, vol. 21, p. 3771), has comprehensively traced the genesis of this legislation.

In summary, a consensus appears to be emerging in the United States which will likely result in legislative or bureaucratic responses which will lead increasingly to the substitution of competition for regulation. There is some doubt that the omnibus consumer advocate's office will be created; however, it is not a perfect solution as revealed in the criticisms raised by Professor Trebilcock in his submission to the RCCC (vol. 21, especially p. 40). There is no discernible move to completely deregulate the economy and while isolated steps toward deregulation have occurred in the social regulation field (the 1974 seat-belt legislation), these remain the exception and not the rule.

The Canadian Policies

Since most of the research and writing on regulatory boards has emanated from the United States there is a natural temptation to borrow from that experience and assume that what has failed there has failed here and what should be done there should be done here. In reality the experiences, while similar in many respects, are significantly different in other critical ways; as a consequence, the appropriate prescriptions for regulatory ailments may not be the same in each instance. Studies undertaken in the last five years in Canada have enabled us to delineate some of these differences and hopefully avoid the pitfalls of universalist solutions.

Most of the Canadian studies of regulatory commissions have focused on the agency administrative structures, the policy-making processes, relation to government generally (accountability), the goals of regulation, and the question of fair representation of interested groups before the agencies.[15] In some instances a sample of decisions has been studied in an effort to determine the consistency of agency practices with legislative mandates.

There are some studies which have explored specifically the question of costs and benefits of regulation. These are the studies of intraprovincial regulation of commercial truck transportation, the studies prepared on agricultural marketing boards, and one study of the Air Transport Committee.

However, the studies of truck transportation regulation have focused only on the question of the measurement of the differences in freight transportation rates between regulated and unregulated provinces which might be attributable to regulation. Thus, many of the costs of regulation, including the welfare loss which is the exclusive interest of the neoclassical economists, are not considered.

The studies of marketing boards endeavour to measure short-term price effects alone. In this they succeed, but with the limitation that the studies were undertaken within a couple of years of the introduction of comprehensive national marketing coordination. The studies do not address themselves

---

[15] See studies prepared for the Canadian Consumer Council listed in footnote 4; see Babe (1974) on the CRTC; see Sloss (1970), McLachlin (1971), Maister (1976), Alberta (1977a), Feltham (1970), Pickersgill (1969), Silverman (1973), English (1973), Purdy (1972), Baldwin (1975), and Ruppenthal and Stanbury (1976) on the CTC; see Grubel and Schwindt (1977) and Cohen (1977) on marketing boards; see Lucas (1978) on the National Energy Board; see Doern (1977a) on the Atomic Energy Board.

to the question of the costs of administration or to questions of dynamic efficiency.

Baldwin's recent study (1975) of air transport regulation focuses on price effects of regulation. Most of the analysis is qualitative, not quantitative; the question of the costs of administration and the question of dynamic efficiency are not explored in depth.

Indeed, most of the studies, while informative, focus on general policy, administrative procedure, and accountability; but not on the questions of economic impact which have been central to the debate in the United States. Perhaps the contrast can be emphasized by noting that questions of efficiency, and costs-versus-benefit of regulation, have generated far less interest than the questions of legitimacy and due process. A high tariff policy as part of the national policy and the various programs of regional development leave little doubt that there are many factors which consistently have been considered to overshadow economic efficiency which is the economists' almost singular preoccupation.

This question of emphasis, which economists frequently underestimate, is one whose importance should not be underrated. The economic studies on the impact of marketing boards have been rejected by politicians and the public alike as irrelevant. In creating marketing boards the government deliberately—and with the support of all major political parties—delegated power to control supply to agencies composed of members almost all of whom were drawn from the ranks of the regulated.[16]

In effect, the government formalized cartels and made available the full force of the judiciary to impose those sanctions on price cutters which are available only to government. There was a desire to raise food prices and transfer income to a particular group of producers. As defined in "The Regulatory Framework" discussion, the public interest is served and the agencies function with the full support of a majority of interest groups. The rotten egg episode with the Canadian Egg Marketing Agency (CEMA) produced extensive debate of questions of poor management of surpluses but little or no debate on the efficacy of direct regulation as such.

It is important to remember that efficiency is not the primary measure of performance when regulatory regimens are established in Canada. For most of the major federal regulatory agencies their overriding concerns, (either due to legislative or Cabinet directive), have been political integrity, regional and national economic development, and advancement and protection of Canadian cultures.

Another factor that must not be forgotten in examining Canadian regulatory policy is a fundamental difference which exists between most American regulatory agencies and Canadian agencies. In Canada the decisions of almost all regulatory agencies are subject to Cabinet review, while in the United States they are rarely reviewable. Thus in the Canadian

---

[16] The British Columbia Government may be having second thoughts. It has appointed a commission to undertake an inquiry into the operation of its marketing agencies.

instance there is a political accountability—at least in theory—that is important. Indeed, the President's Advisory Council on Executive Organization (Ash Council) in the United States had as one of its major recommendations (1971) the establishment of more formal accountability of regulatory agencies in that country.

In practice, Cabinet Ministers and governments have rarely overruled the agencies. However, it is reasonable to assume that members of some of these commissions will be very sensitive to public statements of members of Cabinet on policies which involve their agencies. In this regard the exchange between Mr. Roberge of the CTC, Mr. Bériault, counsel to the RCCC, and Commissioner Dickerson before the RCCC (*Transcripts*, vol. 23, p. 4227) is revealing and easily appreciated:

> **Mr. Bériault** . . . Would the Commission . . . take announced government policy into consideration in making its decision and, if so, might I ask, would the Commission, would the government make this policy known as part of the evidence before it during the procedure?

> **Mr. Roberge:** Actually we do take into account government policy. I am sure you are talking of announced policy.

> **Mr. Bériault:** Absolutely. I should have said that.

> **Mr. Roberge:** Well, the government has announced a policy several years ago and it has been revised several times, with respect to regional air carriers. Therefore, when we deal with a problem between the trunk carriers, that is, Air Canada, CP and the regional carriers, or the regional carriers and the local or third level carriers, the government policy as to what the role is of various levels of air carriers, we do take into account.
> "For instance, if the government embarks on an anti-inflation policy, I suppose that we do take it into account.

Later Commissioner Dickerson commented: (*Transcripts,* vol. 23, p. 4232):

> When does an announcement become formal enough to be recognized? If it is expressed in law that is clear, but I take it that you don't demand that standard. You are prepared to take statements made; I don't know how to decide that these are government policies, and I don't know how you decide that either, and then presumably take them into account.

In practice Canadian regulators must be more sensitive to government policy; though the differences will be ones of degree. Ultimately governments control the agencies through their budgetary powers as well as their ability to legislate the agencies out of existence.

Next we will examine the recent controversy surrounding the propriety of the CTC setting transportation policy as opposed to limiting itself to the purely technical aspects of transportation regulation. In a parliamentary system, unlike the American political system, vesting policy-making power in the hands of an agency independent of Parliament is incompatible with the concept of government accountability.

An appreciation of some of the differences between the regulatory environment in Canada and the United States, from which much of the analysis we normally encounter is drawn, may be gleaned from a brief review of some aspects of the regulatory policies of the CTC and the CRTC. These are particularly appropriate agencies since most of the studies endorsing deregulation in the United States have focused on telecommunications and transportation industries.

The Canadian Transport Commission

Until recently the CTC was responsible for regulating Bell Canada, the largest Canadian telephone company. In the United States, the American Telephone and Telegraph Co. was protected for years from competitors wishing to provide competitive service of peripheral equipment or tie-line service by the FCC. In Canada, unlike the American situation, by Act of Parliament, the *Bell Canada Special Act* (S.5), and other legislation, (S.32 of the *Railway Act*), Bell is protected against any interconnections or the provision of any peripheral equipment without its approval. It is entirely within Bell's discretion under the Acts whether these are approved or not.

The operation of any microwave service requires special legislation; CN-CP and Ontario Hydro operate their own systems. Apparently, no private company has ever been given the legislative authority to operate a microwave voice communication system *in competition* with Bell Canada. Thus, the protection of Bell Canada from competition is due to an Act of Parliament and is not attributable to the 'capture' of the regulatory agency.

To the extent that deregulation is being seriously considered in the United States there is no parallel in Canada since the protection of Bell Canada is not rooted in CTC policy as much as in legislation. Thus any move to deregulate in telecommunications will necessarily involve new legislation, not a change in the policy of the regulatory agency.

The only comprehensive set of studies (English, 1973a) of regulation in telecommunications in Canada reaches conclusions which, in most respects, are little different from the conventional wisdom in the United States. These studies focus on the structure and performance of the industry and the potential for introducing competition.

In general, the authors of the economic studies referred to above (1973a) conclude that:

1. Natural monopoly conditions do exist in each and every phase of Bell Canada's activities (English 1973a, p. 59).

2. Structural determinants in the industry are such that the opportunities for significant increases in competition lie primarily in the fringe areas of terminal equipment, data processing and attachments (Beigie, 1973, p. 194).

3. The volume of business is found inadequate to justify further competition in transcontinental telecommunication transmission service between the Trans-Canada Telecommunications System and the CN-CP Telecommunications.

4. Sufficient volume does exist on a few local routes to permit the presence of more than one carrier. However, only the Toronto-Montreal route is considered, according to Beigie (pp. 198-99).

5. None of these markets is considered large enough to justify the presence of more than two or three competitors.

6. A serious problem of cross-subsidization exists with long-distance and international rates at unnecessarily high levels. Indeed, one study (McManus, 1973, p. 425) finds that these rates probably exceed industry profit maximizing levels.

7. In Canada, the relation between Bell Canada, the principal telephone firm, and its equipment supplier, Northern Electric, differs significantly from the AT & T — Western Electric case. The costs and revenues of Northern Electric are consolidated with Bell's operating revenues and costs. Therefore, there is little opportunity for Bell to transfer its profits to the unregulated sector. The relation of Bell to Northern Electric remains controversial, however, and is the subject of a current investigation of the Restrictive Trades Practices Commission (see English, 1973b, p. 32; Beigie, 1973, p. 203; and the Director of Investigation and Research—Combines Investigation Act, 1976).

While most of the protection of Bell from competition is found in legislation, there are reasons to suspect that the CTC has possessed little enthusiasm for relaxation of the legislative strictures.

Many of these issues were raised with officials of the CTC by a research associate and myself and their reactions were revealing. One member of the CTC, to whom we were referred by the CTC research department, refused to discuss issues involving Bell and its competitors even if the questions involved a simple summary of current policy at the time jurisdiction was shifted to the CRTC. He then referred us to a senior official in the CTC bureaucracy whose reaction to the questions was in general to suggest that we failed to perceive that the public interest involved the maintenance of a good communications system.

The responses revealed that to some of the regulators these types of proposals represent threats to the system which were described by phrases such as: "these represent the efforts of private interests to grab a piece of the action of the telephone company" . . . ". . . the system is threatened by the efforts of competitors to "carve out" or "hive-off" the cream from the system. If indeed these attitudes prevail at the senior level of the bureaucracy then it is clear that no pressure was imposed on Parliament to review these restrictive legislative provisions. If the regulatory agency had been authorized to set policy in these areas, the attitudes of senior staff, as revealed to us, suggests there would have been resistance to deregulation proposals.

The framework of regulation in the telephone industry is closely paralleled in air transport. Hugh Silverman in his study of Canadian Civil Aviation notes that questions of national unity, not economic efficiency or price levels, have always been paramount in Canadian transportation licensing and regulation. The "CTC is directly under government influence, direction and guidance" according to Silverman (1973, p. 122). He concludes (p. 124):

> . . . [In Canada] there is no problem of many competing airlines as in the U.S.; and no problem of appearing to control aeronautics by an independent regulatory agency such as the CAB; the Federal Government runs the show and there is no independence to be considered.

Efforts to enter the industry or to provide extended freight or passenger service may be expected to encounter Air Canada and CTC resistance.[16a]

J.S. Grafstein, (1974, p. 349), has acknowledged these protective tendencies by observing:

> Since 1967 . . . new regulations have been promulgated which strengthen route protection. The onus of proving competitive damage . . . remains on those who seek entry into the field. Other barriers to entry . . . have not been reduced. Thus, the regulators continue about their business without reference to legislative intent.

There, however, have been cases of the CTC's permitting testing of a market even when there have been previous unsatisfactory attempts to service markets. However, neither the CTC nor its predecessor has ever embraced a philosophy that if someone wants to offer airline service they should have the opportunity to go broke trying.

The direct economic benefits to the consuming public of some degree of deregulation could be significant since economies of scale are not significant in the industry. While an optimal size airline requires more than one jet aircraft, it is unlikely that more than five to ten are required, according to the Wardair Marketing Department. Thus, domestic airlines the size of Air Canada or Canadian Pacific are not required for reasons of economic efficiency. However, deregulation would be required at the local, as well as at the federal level.

In a very simplistic sense airlines make or lose money in large measure as a result of flying their planes a large number of hours daily with high load factors. In Canada landings are restricted in Toronto from 11 p.m. to 7 a.m. Given the geographical dispersion of the national market and the critical placement of the Toronto-Montreal axis as the hub of the transport system, it is difficult to schedule the large number of hours per day per plane required if an airline is to make money. While an inhibiting factor, airport curfews should not prevent some benefits being derived from deregulation.

There is evidence available to suggest that freer entry in Canada with

---

[16a] The CTC's attitude towards competition is made clear by its five to one decision, on July 28, 1978, approving Air Canada's application to acquire Nordair. The purchase price was about $25 million (*Ottawa Citizen* July 29, 1978, p. 8). The decision was criticized by a number of commentators, e.g., Geoffrey Stevens (*The Globe and Mail*, August 2 and 4, 1978, p. 6). In August, both the Province of Ontario and the Consumers' Association of Canada appealed the CTC's decision to the Cabinet.

relaxation of airport curfews could result in very significant fare reductions. Indeed, the introduction of special charter service on the Toronto-Miami route for $99 by Wardair caused Air Canada to introduce a special 'Nighthawk' fare of $120; a reduction from the previous low of $230. A detailed empirical study of the impact in Canada of chartered service might provide the information necessary to confidently answer the question: would freer entry to the commercial air passenger service industry result in fare reduction and improvements in economic efficiency of a comparable magnitude to those that have occurred in Texas and California?

Air Transport Committee regulations until recently have effectively precluded the type of charter service by non-scheduled airlines that is developing and forcing competitive responses in the United States. Supplemental or charter lines are prevented from carrying passengers between terminal points within Canada while the CAB in the United States permits domestic advance booking charters (ABCs) with a *30* day advance purchase requirement. This will decline to *15* days in 1978. International ABC s are permitted in Canada; however, rates for private charter firms may not be below those charged by Air Canada or CP Air.

In response to public pressure for the domestic ABC service and severe financial problems, Air Canada recently introduced a Charter Class Fare (see Table 1). The number of seats offered by Air Canada, however, was so limited that as of May 1, 1977, they were fully booked to September.[17]

In an earlier section, we reviewed Baldwin's conclusions on cross-subsidization in Canadian air transport. In another part of that study (1975, p. 206), he concludes that the introduction of transcontinental competition—a duopoly—in Canada has resulted in choice but at the cost of higher prices to the consumer than would have been the case with regulated monopoly. Baldwin did not, however, explore the question of domestic ABC competition.

A recent directive (January 1978) of the federal Cabinet to the CTC and its Air Transport Committee to introduce domestic advance booking charters on an extensive scale should result in much lower air fares. However, it is worth noting, in light of the preceding discussion, that this was not a pro-competitive measure which the Air Transport Committee was prepared to take on its own initiative, even though it possessed the statutory power to do so. Indeed, the federal directive overruled a highly restrictive decision of the Air Transport Committee of early December, 1977 (see Reschenthaler and Roberts, 1978b).

---

[17] The preceding section on charter competition draws on an unpublished working paper prepared by Bruce Roberts of Alberta Travel. See also *Edmonton Journal* (1977).

Table 1

A Comparison of Air Canada's Charter Class Fares
and American Airlines Super Saver Fares

	AIR CANADA's CHARTER CLASS FARES (no domestic ABCs competition)	AMERICAN AIRLINES SUPER SAVER FARES (domestic ABCs competition)
Advance Purchase Requirement	60 days	30 days
Min./Max. Stay	10-30 days	7-45 days
Percent Discount Available From Economy Fare	32% to 44% depending on distance travelled	35% to 45% depending on day of the week
Minimum Distance	700 miles	limited to New York/ L.A., S.F. route
Other Discount Fares	regular 10-30 day excursion fare cancelled	regular 7-30 day freedom fares still applicable
Capacity Available Minimum	undisclosed	none
Maximum	undisclosed	35% allowed for both discount fare plans (freedom and super saver)

The CTC is also responsible under the *National Transportation Act* for regulation of commercial truck service; however, the section of the Act providing for regulation of the trucking industry has never been proclaimed. In addition, the *National Transportation Act* of 1967 clearly specifies that the guiding light in transportation regulation should be competition between modes.

As Pickersgill wrote in 1969 (p. 79), under the *National Transportation Act* of 1967:

> Competition between the modes (becomes) the essential ingredient of national transportation policy.

The Act clearly specifies, as reported in Pickersgill (p. 80), that:

> . . . regulation of all modes of transport will not be of such a nature as to restrict the ability of any one mode of transport to compete freely with any other modes of transport.

In the case of the railroads, the *National Transportation Act* requires that rates be compensatory which means that they must exceed average variable costs. The Act also specifies that where a shipper has "no alternative, effective and competitive service by a common carrier" of the same or competing mode, that a shipper (captive shipper clause) can request that the CTC set a maximum rate. The rate set cannot exceed 250 percent of variable costs, as stated in the Revised Statutes of Canada (1970, N-17, s. 33 and s.40). All tariffs must be published and no rebates are allowed.

The important provision is the liberal treatment in the law of the minimum rates which can be charged. For practical purposes, railroads are free to compete in prices with commercial trucking firms, but prevented from engaging in predatory pricing practices or setting excessively (monopolistically) high prices.

A regulatory and anti-competitive problem can arise when common ownership in several modes of transport is permitted as in the cases of Canadian National and Canadian Pacific. The potential for cross-subsidization in Canada is constrained by the requirement that for piggy-backing (TOFC) operations, the rail companies must not discriminate in pricing in favour of their subsidiaries. However, many questions involving the possibility of hidden subsidies and unfair competition could be raised. Ivan Feltham, who has explored the problems of multi-modal ownership in transportation in Canada in detail, disagrees. Feltham (1970, p. 118) does not see a serious problem existent in the industry given the large number of private carriers and what is presumed to be CN and CP's relatively small market share.[18]

---

[18] See Purdy (1972, p. 318) for a similar position.

An important factor in transportation regulation and intermodal competition in Canada are government investment and subsidy programs and government policies on rail service termination. As Langford (1976b, p. 44) has noted:

> . . . investment or lack of investment in infrastructure can be almost as powerful a regulatory tool as direct economic regulation.

John Langford (1976a, p. 94) in a recent article questions many of the assumptions widely held about transport regulation in Canada. Langford, in effect, argues that regulation of the transportation industry in Canada is largely irrelevant since there is so little of it. Langford notes that:

1. Responsibility for regulation of extra-provincial bus and truck transportation has never been assumed.
2. No barriers to intermodal acquisitions have been imposed and no acquisitions has been disallowed (1976a, p. 96).
3. In the case of domestic commercial air services, the Air Transport Board of the CTC *has* restricted the development of new air services actively, but has been a passive air fare regulator. It has granted every fare increase which the airlines have requested (1976a, p. 95).
4. Rail regulation has been passive.

In the case of rail regulation, Langford receives support from Westmacott who notes that between 1967 and 1975 only nine applications for investigation of individual rates were made to the Railway Transport Committee and only one captive shipper protested a rate. Westmacott (1976, pp. 62-63), on the basis of personal interviews, attributes this small number of appeals to the cost of an appeal, which was estimated at a minimum of $25,000; the time lags involved in appealing; the widely held perception that the Commission is inclined to be overly sensitive to the interests of eastern shippers; and, the fact that no compensation is provided for the time during which excessive rates were charged.

Having leveled the criticism that transportation regulation in Canada is irrelevant, Langford then concludes (1976a, p. 96) by summing up ten years of experience with the *National Transportation Act* as follows:

> When the *National Transportation Act* was passed in 1967 it was widely touted as an instrument which would encourage the development of an economically efficient national transportation system largely through the medium of modal and inter-modal competition without recourse to intense economic regulation. In fact, what the Canadian public has received since 1967 is neither competition nor effective regulation. Across the transportation system, the market place and the inclinations of the large carriers govern for the most part the establishment of transportation rates and levels of service. The Canadian transportation system is characterized most prominently by an absence of competition (both within modes and intermodally), a high degree of intermodal ownership, and a substantial level of federal government promotion through direct investment, subsidies, and the activities of Crown corporations (notably Air Canada and The Canadian National Railways). It seems to be

generally accepted now, even in Ottawa, that competition has not been and will not be a panacea for the most significant ills of the Canadian transportation system.

Many of Langford's own observations on the state of Canadian transportation and telecommunications, as well as our own in the preceding paragraphs, suggest that the regulatory regime has not been irrelevant. Regulation may have been ineffectual in some cases and undesirable in others, but it has not been irrelevant.

The study of airline regulation by Baldwin, and Westmacott's concern about the direction of regulation cast further doubt on Langford's conclusion. Westmacott (1976) has argued that there is apparently a consensus that parliamentary review of the CTC has been minimal and, indeed, Parliament may have lost control of transportation policy. The recent revisions proposed in the *National Transportation Act* reflect, in part, a response of Parliament to the need to maintain control over the formulation and evolution of transportation policy, to ensure that the policies of the CTC are consistent with the social and economic policies of the government and in the words of the Prime Minister, as quoted in the Toronto *Globe and Mail* (July 12, 1974), to insure that "the Canadian Transportation Commission obey clearly stated government policy guidelines."

Policy formulation in these areas is highly politicized and, again, reflects the extent to which the CTC must be sensitive and subservient to cabinet policy.[19]

In a very real sense, as Feltham points out, the CTC is a branch of the executive arm of government, the recommendations of the Glassco Commission notwithstanding,[20] the CTC might for practical purposes be formally integrated into the Ministry of Transportation. With the removal of jurisdiction over Bell Canada and the failure of the government to proclaim Part III of the *National Transportation Act,* the types of questions to be addressed by the CTC cease to be primarily regulatory in nature and fall more in the arena of broad public policy. It is not surprising that many studies of the CTC, which include the Canadian Consumer Council (1973), Trebilcock (1976) and McManus (1976), have focused on public interest determination and consumer representation.

Recent events indicate that the government will move in this direction. John Munro (1976), in reviewing the recent policy statements on transportation policy notes that among other things they reflect a recognition of the critical role of transportation policy, as an instrument of national and regional economic and political policy, doubt about the virtue of an unequivocal commitment to the virtues of competition in transport regulation, and acceptance of the proposition that the CTC should have a smaller policy role. The proposed amendments to the *National Trans-*

---

[19] See Purdy (1972, pp. 175-82) for a discussion of the politics of the Crow's Nest Pass rates.
[20] See Langford (1976b) for a discussion of the Glassco Commission.

portation Act introduced in early 1977 confirm Munro's expectations (see *Financial Post,* April 2, 1977; April 23, 1977, pp. 1 and 4.[21]

The Canadian Radio-Television Commission

The Canadian Radio-Television Commission (CRTC) was established in 1968, in part, to regulate and to promote radio and television broadcasting (*Annual Report,* 1974-75). The Commission has concerned itself primarily with issues of Canadian content, promotion of Canadian artists, and local programming; unfortunately, it has tended to down-play economic considerations. The apparent lack of interest on the part of the CRTC in economic questions is probably a direct reflection of the composition of the Commission. The Commission has tended to be dominated by members with backgrounds in the arts, the media, and the public service with few members possessing business backgrounds or formal training in economics. The result has been inevitable.

Little appreciation has been given to the value of simply setting guidelines, for example, for Canadian content and good taste and then licensing all applicants who agree to live by the rules. Indeed, the CRTC in outlining rules recently for FM licenses in the future, has established guidelines going far beyond Canadian content. There is the clear indication that the CRTC, as a typical regulator, has very early entered into a protectionist and promotional mold—as contrasted with a regulatory mold—for the established companies in the communications industries.

The protective nature of CRTC policy, as it affects AM radio licence applicants, is revealed by the percentage of AM and FM applications denied or deferred in the decade from 1959 to 1969 by the CRTC and its predecessor the Board of Broadcast Governors (BBG). During that decade the BBG and CRTC dealt with 315 applications and denied or deferred 153 or 48.6 percent. It should be noted that many of the applications approved were for routine renewal of licences.

With this track record, it is reasonable to assume that new applicants would become aware of the 'rules of the game'; nevertheless, some new applicants persist. Some of the reasons given (when reasons are given and frequently they are not) in a sampling of AM application denials in the period 1971 to 1975 are instructive:

... The Commission is of the opinion that due to the economic limitation of the advertising revenue in these areas it could not support the operation of two additional stations. (CRTC decision 71-295, 22 July, 1971).

... the introduction of additional competition which is not likely to generate an increase in overall broadcasting income in that area would not increase the quality of programming services. (CRTC decision 72-220, 20 June, 1972)

---

[21] See also Bill C-33 (Canada, 1977c), introduced January 27, 1977, and Bill C-43 (Canada, 1977d).

. . . the proposals . . . did not indicate a significant awareness of the particular needs of the community. (CTRC decision 72-300, 36 October, 1972)

. . . the applicant would not be able to establish and maintain a satisfactory AM broadcasting undertaking. . . . The Commission is also not satisfied that the proposed . . . service would be a real alternative to that already existing . . . (CRTC Decision 72-365, 21 December, 1972)

. . . the introduction of a new private AM radio service at this time would not be compatible with the orderly development of broadcasting services . . . (CRTC Decision 74-173, 20 June, 1974)

. . . the schedule of . . . programming proposed . . . did not . . . offer a sufficient diversity from what is already available . . . (CRTC Decision 74-433, 3 December 1974)

These restrictive and protective attitudes have resulted in situations exemplified by the City of Edmonton, where, in the past decade, no new private English language AM station has been licensed in spite of significant growth in the size of the potential listening audience.

With unused frequencies there appears to be little reason why an applicant should not receive a licence in some markets. The view of the CRTC is that duplication of format is not in the public interest and simply erodes the revenue bases of established stations. The fact of the matter is that given the public underwriting of the Canadian Broadcasting Corporation, there is no public obligation to protect these broadcasters holding existing licences. Indeed, the owners of those stations are frequently the most outspoken exponents of the free enterprise system.

If new entrants to the industry are not economically viable they will shortly be forced out of the market. However, an interesting consequence might be a fragmentation of the audience with beneficial results. For example, in a market such as Edmonton with four private stations there is a tendency for stations to appeal to one of the three or four largest submarkets: popular music, rock, country and western, and talk telephone call-in. Each station is seeking to obtain the 25 to 35 percent of the market which is perceived as possible. With ten stations, a market share of 10 percent suddenly appears attractive and many broadcasters will begin to search for special interest groups in the market.

The problem is one of does the public interest demand protection of a small number of very profitable broadcasters or an industry offering a wide variety of style and substance to the consuming public?

Another area of the CRTC jurisdiction, cable television regulation, has provided an unusual opportunity to see the bankruptcy of policy of a commission in action. The pattern of fees that have been approved in Canada in the last five years makes no economic sense. The CRTC apparently possesses no financial standards as to what is a reasonable profit and has demonstrated little interest in questions of economies of scale as in the case of the Edmonton market where it arbitrarily divided the city into two sections and required duplication of facilities at extra cost in excess of $600 thousand. The CRTC, while given the authority to set rates and while exercising the right to review requests for rate changes, has failed to engage in meaningful rate regulation. The long-term implications of ineffectual economic regulation of cable television should have been apparent as early as 1970 when aggregate statistics for the community antenna television companies revealed net operating profits of $24,658,710 on operating revenues of $54,940,255 (Dawson, 1972, p. 59).[22]

In this examination we have deliberately focused on AM licencing since the rationale used to justify restricted entry—cultural protection—is least valid in this area. We have reviewed licensing policies which involve Canadian companies requesting licences to broadcast in Canadian markets subject to Canadian content regulations. The recent policy decision to prohibit the introduction of pay television is consistent with the industry protectionist posture adopted in the case of radio as is the attitude toward cable television in general (Babe, 1974). Given this protectionist attitude on the part of the CRTC, it comes as no surprise that the average rate of return on invested capital after taxes has consistently averaged above 30 percent in the mid-seventies for owners of private radio, television and cable licenses.

Summary

In reviewing the domestic regulatory policy we have drawn on what are admittedly sparse recourses. The need for case studies of economic costs and benefits of various regulatory boards should be self-evident. Unfortunately, the usefulness of the economic measures is likely to be limited by the multiplicity of objectives of most major boards; at least, we should know the price of attaining the other objectives.

Consumer Representation: The Canadian Case

Earlier in this study we discussed the problems related to the insurance of adequate representation of all groups with substantial interests before regulatory agencies. The discussion of regulatory reform in Canada has focused on the questions of administrative reform while discussions abroad have focused on deregulation, measurement of costs of regulation, and political accountability.

Professor Stanbury (1976a, pp. 140-41) has outlined and commented on some of the recommendations of the Canadian Consumer Council on possible solutions to the problem of consumer representation:

> In their study for the Canadian Consumer Council entitled "On the Question of Consumer Advocacy—A Working Paper," Edward Belobaba *et al.* (1972) identify four principal alternative mechanisms by which the consumer interest could be advanced in regulated industries:

---

[22] For a general analysis of regulation of cable television, see Comanor and Mitchell (1971).

- a consumer ombudsman
- a staff witness, i.e., an officer of the regulatory agency whose job it is to represent the consumer interest in agency proceedings
- a consumer advocate, i.e., "a government financed litigant with a support staff" . . . having "the right to initiate proceedings, call witnesses, and appeal in regulatory hearings on behalf of the consumer"
- a subsidized decentralized system, i.e., government funding of private agencies which would have legal standing to intervene in all phases of the regulatory process on behalf of consumers.

Belobaba *et al.* opted for the final alternative and the Canadian Consumer Council recommended "the establishment by the federal government of a subsidized office of consumer advocacy within the Consumers' Association of Canada, the office to be financed by a separate federal grant specifically earmarked for the sole purpose of consumer advocacy before federal departments, boards, tribunals and commissions."

How would a consumer advocate (CA) along these lines begin to reverse the tide of regulatory failure? By employing a staff of legal, economic and engineering specialists the CA can substitute expertise for the ignorance of individual consumers about the technical issues involved in regulation. Even the current practices regarding notice of regulatory proceedings will no longer act as a major barrier to consumer participation. The CA will make it its business to read the fine print of legal notices and detect in the effluvia of regulatory agencies the time, place and the nature of the issues to be dealt with. Most importantly, the CA will fit extremely well into the adversarial system which has resulted from the judicialization of the commissions. From mainly 'ex parte' proceedings, largely uncontested by a passive professional staff, we would expect to see substantive matters advocated and defended by worthy protagonists. The creation of a CA carries with it the sensible presumption that such an entity would have legal standing to initiate, intervene and appeal to the courts on the full spectrum of regulatory matters.

It is absolutely crucial that the CA be adequately funded if he is to have any real, as opposed to simply cosmetic impact . . . The Department of Consumer and Corporate Affairs could provide initial grants and sustained financial assistance [for a federal office] . . . .

Individual provincial governments are clearly capable of creating an independent consumer advocate to appear before both provincial and federal regulatory agencies. While some legislators might argue that a consumers' counsel would overlap with the regulatory commissions, it should not be too difficult to indicate that the new agency would be filling a vacuum rather than duplicating existing effort. If the legislature (federal or provincial) supplies the funds on an annual basis one can easily become concerned with the "independence" of the consumer advocate. One way to handle this problem would be for a multi-party committee to review the activities of the agency and to make recommendations to the legislature (under a free vote) as to the appropriate funding the agency should receive. The crucial issue here is not so much dollars, but the commitment of the legislature to find ways to 'advance' consumer interests over those of producers.

On the need to have access to information he comments:

It is correctly alleged that "information is power" . . . (but) . . . it can only be defined by careful technical analysis of documents and records of the regulated firms and the regulatory agencies.

If the regulatory commissions are going to adopt a judicial posture then consumer rhetoric must be replaced by careful analytic reasoning supported by mounds of "hard" documentary evidence. While the consumer advocate can undertake (or commission) research on its own, its principal sources of information will be the regulated firms and their regulators. Without access to such information the consumer advocate's effort will fail or at best fall short of what consumers both need and desire. Most of the veils of corporate secrecy must be removed in the case of regulated firms. As one observer put it, regulated firms "must be reconciled to the gold fish bowl life." One can envisage that unless the consumer advocate is given authority equivalent to those under various public enquiries acts, that each request for information will result in appeals to the courts and lengthy litigation. In regulation as well as in the field of taxation, sufficient delay is almost as good as outright avoidance."

And he concludes by observing:

> . . . we should emphasize that the most desirable format for a consumer advocate agency is one which is (of necessity) publicly financed, but privately produced . . . The dangers of "bureaucratic ossification," "capture" by client groups and goal displacement are too well known. One of the best reasons for keeping consumer advocate agencies outside government—and in particular outside the regulatory agencies themselves, is that they will be uncompromised. The agencies "would have no economic largess to dispense in the form of rates, routes, licences, subsidies and no benefits to grant except those which would flow from its representations of the consumer interest before regulatory agencies." Because the consumer interest is not homogeneous, the government should fund a number of consumer advocates— perhaps one or two concerned with federal boards and tribunals and one for each of the provinces. A monopoly in consumer interest advocacy should not be permitted. Finally, unlike the regulatory agencies themselves, the work of the consumer advocates should be carefully appraised against predetermined standards after such agencies have been in operation for perhaps three years. They should be subject to periodic review subsequently.

In response to the recommendation of the Canadian Consumer Council, the Department of Consumer and Corporate Affairs in 1972 commenced a program of annual grants to the Consumers' Association of Canada (CAC) to finance their participation in regulatory proceedings. Professor Trebilcock (1972; 1976) has traced the developments of those programs, many of which he directed for the CAC. It probably is premature to evaluate the CAC's regulated industry program's effectiveness and no objective appraisals have been undertaken (1977).

In general, Professor Trebilcock (1976) has argued against the omnibus consumer advocate concept and in support of the funding of private consumer interest groups.

In recent years some provincial regulatory boards (Alberta Public Utilities Board) have required utilities to pass on to consumers the costs of consumer and municipal intervenors in regulatory proceedings (R.S.A., 1970, c. 302, ss. 60 and 68). Most major regulatory boards in Canada do not permit the awarding of costs of intervenors; some, such as the CRTC, on occasion have financed the travel and accommodation costs of invited citizen participants in hearings. The enabling statutes for many agencies confer discretionary power to award costs (McManus, 1973; see also Trebilcock, 1977).

Unfortunately, as recent experience with the Alberta Public Utilities Commission has demonstrated, a system of awarding costs is useful to consumer intervenors only if assurances are provided prior to the hearing that the costs will be awarded. In one recent case involving Alberta Government Telephones, the Public Utilities Board in Alberta refused to allow $40,000 of expenses of the Consumers' Association of Canada—Alberta Branch, as reported in the *Edmonton Journal* (February 8, 1977, p. 75, and February 22, 1977, p. 38).[23] Needless to say, with a 1977 operating budget of $27.5 thousand, the Alberta Association will think twice before undertaking an active—and consequently expensive—intervention in another major regulatory case. Indeed, in early May 1977, it declined to participate in a major hearing involving the same company.

Conclusion

We have endeavoured to survey some of the current issues involving specific regulatory agencies in Canada and the United States. In the discussion of the United States we have noted a pervasive anti-government attitude, concern with the costs of regulation and the issue of political accountability, support for deregulation, and some concern with the question of consumer representation in regulatory proceedings. In Canada we have noted that in a preponderance of cases, economic efficiency, as such, is frequently of secondary importance to other political, social and economic growth considerations.

In Canada, unlike the United States, political accountability is provided for since direct ministerial review exists for most regulatory tribunals. However, it is seldom exercised.

CONCLUSIONS

In discussion we will first summarize some of the more important observations which follow from this study respecting the functioning of Canadian regulatory agencies. Then, we will present a review of proposals for regulatory reform which have been made in Canada and abroad in recent years with comments on their applicability in Canada.

In summary, the more important observations that we draw from this study on *Canadian regulatory commissions* include the following:

1. One of the distinguishing features of 'independent' regulatory agencies in Canada is that their independence is typically constrained by provision in their enabling legislation for ministerial review and by their role in the policy formulation process. However, the ministerial review, in practice, does not involve a hearing *de novo* except on the most important of public policy issues. The regulatory agency and its staff determine the format of the hearings, the questions to be asked, the evidence to be accepted, the intervenors to be heard, the vigour of the cross-examination of witnesses and the evalua-

---

[23]See also Alberta Public Utilities Board *Position Paper* (1977b).

tions of evidence and testimony. These functions performed by the regulatory bodies serve to effectively limit the role of the minister involved. Nevertheless, there is an element of accountability present which is absent in some other countries.

2. Increasingly, regulation is addressed to broad public policy questions rather than narrow technical questions. An example is the decision to permit construction of a new gas-fired electric generating facility. A decision to construct involves not only questions of the necessary prices to be charged for the resultant power, but consideration of alternative power sources, environmental effects, and alternative pricing and supply policies which might result in reductions in consumption demand, thus postponing the date of necessary construction. If nuclear power is viewed as an economic alternative, the potential societal costs and benefits associated with it—both short-and long-term—must be gauged.

3. In the transport industries most of the regulatory issues involving the railroads have now been fully politicized; only in the areas of airline service and intra-provincial transport regulation can traditional economic questions be viewed as paramount.

4. The questions which must be addressed by the National Energy Board (NEB) have taken on such broad public interest elements that it no longer is primarily concerned with narrow technical questions of regulatory policy. While we have not examined, in detail, the operations of the NEB in this study, references in the literature suggest that it provides an excellent example of the consequences of the failure to maintain an adequate internal research capability. The willingness to accept, at face value, the regulatees'[24] estimates of energy reserves in the early 1970s led to serious errors in policy.

The Alberta Energy Conservation Board has complemented the NEB in the past by restricting supply and elevating prices above competitive levels under market pro-rationing schemes. Market pro-rationing was utilized in the petroleum industry prior to 1972 to maintain artificially high petroleum prices in certain parts of the country; however, since that date, the control of crude oil prices has effectively been in the hands of Cabinet.

5. Of the Canadian regulatory bodies we have reviewed, the CRTC comes closest to fitting the model of the regulatory agency gone askew which is the stereotype of the American literature. The CRTC, until recently, has shown a consistent lack of interest in economic questions and has acted in a traditionally protective manner toward the firms it regulates.

6. In telecommunications, the regulation of Bell Canada by the CTC, in the past, has witnessed the full protection of the Bell System from competitors able to supply competing peripheral equipment and microwave service. However, Bell is protected in all of these areas not by regulatory edict, but by act of Parliament. Recently, telecommunications regulation has been

---

[24] The industry's optimistic forecasts were apparently based on estimates of D.K. McIvor (1973). See also the Presidential Address by R.E. Folinsbee in the *Proceedings of the Geological Society of America,* November 1976.

shifted to the CRTC. A track record is yet to be established; however, its record with radio-television regulation provides little basis for optimism that it will provide effective regulation.

7. Federal and provincial marketing board schemes are the most pervasive in their economic effects of all regulatory agencies. Available evidence suggests extra-competitive price margins in the millions of dollars. However, the economic results are no secret; the agencies are composed of members drawn predominantly from the ranks of the regulated and they enjoy the full support of Parliament and the major political parties.

8. The Tariff Board and the Anti-Dumping Tribunal were subjects of 1972 reports prepared for the Canadian Consumer Council; however, we have not reviewed them in this study. The studies undertaken for the Canadian Consumer Council noted particular problems with consumer under-representation before these boards. Investigations, hearings and administration of the Anti-Dumping Tribunal are usually conducted in private.

9. Banking regulation, for practical purposes, reflects Cabinet policy and the banking industry is not regulated by an independent regulatory agency. Fortunately, a decennial Parliamentary review of the *Bank Act* is required.

10. Provincial public utility and other provincial regulatory boards generally have had little impact on major corporations outside the electric and natural gas distribution industries. The one notable exception is the liquor control boards, whose potential to shield price fixing agreements was made clear in the *Canadian Breweries* case (see R.v. Canadian Breweries Ltd., 1960, O.R. 601; 33 C.R.1; and Jones, 1967). Whether or not that potential is realized is an empirical question which remains unanswered.

Our review of the Canadian and American literature reveals four general areas where moderate reforms are possible which will result in improvements in the effectiveness and reliability of direct regulation as a system of control of corporate power. The reforms include proposals for deregulation and the substitution of the competitive market for regulation; de-emphasis of the judicial aspects of regulation; more effective representation of consumer interests before regulatory bodies; and the provision for greater accountability to the public of regulatory bodies.

The Deregulation Proposals

There are many sectors of the Canadian economy presently regulated, where, in terms of the traditional indices of economic welfare used by economists, deregulation could result in substantial improvements in the general public welfare. However, in each instance, many members of the special interest being regulated would be adversely affected. Some of these areas include: commercial airline service, intraprovincial trucking, intraprovincial bus service; AM and FM radio broadcasting, peripheral telecommunications equipment and tie-line service; brokerage services; and federal and provincial agricultural products marketing.

Our list of candidates for deregulation is relatively short when contrasted with some of those prepared in the United States where intellectual support for deregulation is most ardent.

Even given our modest list, proposals to deregulate these industries will likely encounter organized resistance in most instances. Commercial airline deregulation proposals will be met by national unity and 'creaming' arguments as well as discussion of possible adverse effects on international airline service, and airport congestion. The interest of the federal and Alberta governments in protecting their own airlines should also not be underestimated. Furthermore, Baldwin believes deregulation will result in higher prices in Canada. In the case of telecommunications, Beigie's analysis of the Canadian industry and Waverman's (1975) in the United States, raise doubts about the economic viability of competition in most sectors.

Intraprovincial transport regulation is a provincial problem. Less than half the provinces have restrictive legislation. In the case of agricultural product marketing, questions of inefficiency and reasonableness of prices have never been at issue.

In some industries formal deregulation may be unnecessary. Competition is likely to be forced upon the stock brokerage industry by the threat of loss of substantial business to brokers in the United States. Peripheral telecommunications attachment equipment competition by non-Bell firms is a reality in the United States and has been accepted in large measure by Alberta Government Telephones in Alberta.

The potential for deregulation in the broadcasting industries is promising. In regions in which all frequencies have been allocated, the public auctioning proposals of Harold Demsetz (1968) may have application. Demsetz's proposal calls for periodic competitive auctioning of franchises which should result in the economic rent being captured by the public. Demsetz's first requirement, that inputs for entry must be readily available to bidders at prices determined in open markets, is met in this industry. His second requirement, that collusion be difficult, is also met because of relatively low capital requirements. While intellectually appealing, the Demsetz deregulation proposal—via auctioning of franchises—prossesses some special problems.

Given the frequency with which this proposal is encountered as a cure-all for special monopoly problems, a few comments on its weaknesses are justified.

While we endorsed consideration of the proposal in the broadcasting industry, Professor Harvey Levin (1970) has observed that special problems exist even in that industry. He observes that in border areas where signals cannot be confined domestically, international coordination would be required before the system could be implemented. Society might reject formal acceptance of the idea that a few wealthy users might come to control the AM frequencies in some areas even if owners are required to pay a relatively high price for the privilege. They are able to do so now; but, the public is not cognizant of the effect.

Levin also forsees equity problems associated with 'vested' rights which existing licensees may believe they possess. He offers a range of 'less radical' alternatives.

Professor Trebing (1976a, pp. 209-13) also has noted several deficiencies in the auctioning proposal:

1. If auctioning does eliminate excess profits, there is no guarantee that unacceptable forms of price discrimination will not be imposed.

2. Auctioning will not insure that the firm will operate at a socially optimal output level.

3. Auctioning may increase uncertainty and, consequently, raise the cost of capital.

4. The bargaining agent for the public may be too diffused, fragmented, or decentralized to perceive all of the issues involved.

5. There is a problem of determining whether the bidding process will result in a scale of development that is socially optimal.

6. The auction system possesses motivation problems. A successful bidder is likely to resist experimentation with new services, new pricing concepts, or new technologies, if the experiments might result in deficits. Static efficiency may be attained at the price of dynamic inefficiency.

7. The auction process may result in the failure to develop marginal resources. This effect has been noted in the production of natural gas and petroleum.

Finally, Trebing (1976a, p. 213) has noted that the process may have implications for competition in related industries and may lead to increased concentrations of corporate power. He observes,

> Bidding will permit the dominant firm to strengthen its position in the overall market. For example, it could utilize low bids as a form of limit-entry pricing to capture markets, services, functions, or resources to assure its continued dominance. The only condition is that such a firm earn monopoly profits in some markets sufficient to cross-subsidize. Given the imperfections in bidding as a means of control as well as the coverage of a giant multiple-product enterprise supplying utility services, this is not an unrealistic assumption. Perhaps the best example of the use of bidding to assure dominance would involve the radio frequency spectrum. It is not unreasonable to assume that the Bell System would pay a bounty to acquire control of this resource through the bidding process if the result were to foreclose entry by specialized common carriers into the private line market. Thus the Stigler theory of economic regulation could have its counterpart for the bidding process.
>
> The British government has also argued that the bidding-auctioning process fosters corporate power and market dominance. Specifically, the British claim that reliance on bidding favors the largest oil companies in the exploration for oil and gas, and therefore it has been necessary to follow a discretionary licensing system that is designed to encourage a large number of firms to develop reserves. The U.S. experience with auctioning gas and oil leases provides evidence that the bidding process is an ineffectual constraint on corporate power.

The Judicialization Process

The tendency, demonstrated by most Canadian regulatory boards, to assume an adjudicatory posture and eschew inquisitorial functions has been noted previously. Lawyers tend to dominate the regulatory process and they bring with them a tradition which embodies the adversarial system. To Professor Trebilcock, the idea that the judge should also be the adversary is "untenable" (see RCCC *Transcripts* 1976-77, vol. 21, p. 3735). Stanbury, an economist, recognizes the problem when he notes (1976a, esp. footnote 27):

> an inherent conflict exists when the same men are called upon to prosecute in the name of the public and at the same time sit as judges upon the questions at issue which they themselves have raised.

It is equally clear, that the regulated firms prefer a judicial emphasis as demonstrated in a recent comment by the President of Bell Canada as reported in the RCCC *Transcripts* (1976-77, vol. 21, p. 3736)

The fact that many aspects of decisions of the regulatory boards are appealable to the courts reinforces an inclination to adopt a judicial approach.

Stanbury (1976a, p. 117) argues that the judicialization tendency is also attributable to the high prestige enjoyed in society by members of the judiciary and by the desire of regulators to be more than bureaucrats: to be judges. Stanbury (1976a), Trebilcock (1975), and Willis (1968) have all explored these judicialization tendencies in some depth.

The tendency toward judicialization has been reinforced by staffing problems. These are reflected in the movement of staff from employment with regulatory agencies to employment with firms in regulated industries and to other sections of government. The expected economic return for an active staff member may be small indeed.

One of the consequences of these observed judicialization tendencies is excessive focus on legal and administrative questions. Professor Trebilcock's observation before the RCCC (*Transcripts,* vol. 21, p. 3781) is revealing when he notes:

> . . . [there is a] disproportionate influence by lawyers in the whole regulatory process, . . . thus excessive concern with procedures and process and institutional reorganization and far too little focus on either the economic aspects of regulation . . . or the political aspects.

The judicialization process, irrespective of its genesis, has resulted in the development of a distorted concept by the public and regulators of the function of the agencies. In their conception, the agencies were not viewed as prosecutors, they were not to be interested in persecution or permitted to imprison or impose fines; they were intended as substitutes for a perceived faulty market mechanism and their concerns were to be mainly economic. In most instances, the judicialization of the agencies was a matter of choice by the agencies themselves; it was not a natural consequence of provisions in the enabling legislation.

In terms of reform, it is difficult to envision internal momentum being generated in the regulatory agencies themselves for adoption of an inquisitorial approach. Legislative changes would be necessary over the opposition of the regulated, most regulators, and administrative lawyers.

We have not explored in any depth the elements which would be necessary in a program designed to reorient major regulatory agencies from a judicial to an inquisitorial model.

The Problem of Consumer Interest Group Representation

If the judicialization of regulatory agencies is accepted as desirable and/or unalterable, and if the opportunities for deregulation are very limited, then other avenues of 'reform' of commission regulation must be sought. The alternative to significant structural change is reform of the adversarial system to insure that there is accountability, and to insure that all parties with substantial interests are provided with sufficient resources to be competently represented before the regulatory bodies.

The preceding is particularly the case if it is accepted that most aspects of regulation, as now practised, involve primarily the weighing of various interest groups' interests in a process that involves the determination of the public interest, and only secondarily technical questions.

If this politicization of agencies is considered legitimate, and desirable, then a number of alternatives present themselves for achieving the objectives of proper interest representation and political accountability.

As discussed previously, the regulatory process for various reasons involves—or is likely to lead to—chronic under-representation of consumer groups. How may this under-representation be overcome?

Several models have been proposed in the literature. These include:

1. The creation of an omnibus Consumer Advocate Office at each of the federal and provincial government levels which will be given a legislative mandate to serve as the consumer interest intervenor at public hearings involving regulatory boards. These agencies would be publicly financed and would be authorized to maintain independent expert professional staffs, as well as draw upon external expert and legal services.

2. The present program of direct funding by the federal government of consumer intervenors can be expanded. This program commenced in early 1974 with a grant of $116,000 to the regulated industries program of the Consumers' Association of Canada. The grant in 1975-76 was for $216,000. The government in this model would identify appropriate consumer interest groups and provide long-term grants to facilitate the establishment of programs outside the government bureaucracy.

3. The federal and provincial governments can amend the enabling legislation of all boards to direct the boards to pass the costs of consumer intervenors on to regulated companies. The latter will incorporate the costs in their prices; thus the beneficiaries (customers) will share in the costs of their representation. Currently, the expenses of regulated companies related to the regulatory process are costed through to the consumer.

4. The boards might be provided with special budgets which could be

used to fund intervenors directly. In this and the preceding case the problems of identifying responsible groups with substantial economic interests should not be overstated. A reasonable set of criteria can be devised as exemplified by the set suggested by the Ontario Task Force on Legal Aid and by the guidelines developed in practice by the Alberta Public Utilities Board.

5. Under recent revisions in the *Combines Investigation Act* the Director of Investigation and Research is authorized to intervene in regulatory proceedings where questions involving competition policy are involved. This intervenor function could be expanded; indeed, the Consumer Advocate Office could be established within the Department of Consumer and Corporate Affairs (Trebilcock, 1972, pp. 58-59). The role of competition policy in regulated industries in Canada recently has been considered in three papers (Kaiser, 1978; Reschenthaler, 1977; and Waverman, 1978).

The preceding suggestions are neither new, nor revolutionary, since most have been proposed in the United States and were discussed in Trebilcock's 1972 study for the Canadian Consumer Council. They do not require major structural or political changes; they simply provide a vehicle to right an imbalance in representation.

With consumer interests formally represented in the regulatory process, the regulatory bodies will be forced to consider a wider range of measures of economic performance; it is reasonable to expect that improved regulatory performance should result.

Access to Information and Regulatory Impact Studies

The preceding proposals while major steps forward, will not be enough, in themselves. To be effective, increased consumer representation—by any route—will necessitate a right of access to information. This access will be necessary to permit the identification of important issues and effective participation in proceedings. Furthermore, the proposals will not provide the public with estimates of what regulation is costing directly and indirectly; and, with the exception of the new provisions for the Bureau of Competition Policy intervenors, they do not permit the identification of regulated activities which might best be deregulated. The access to information deficiency can be remedied, in part, by the adoption of an access to information law similar to that proposed by Mr. Baldwin or along lines proposed in the report entitled, *A Report on Access to Information,* prepared by Heather Mitchell (1977) for the Consumer Research Council.

Currently, economists and the general public are hindered in their ability to evaluate regulatory performance by the unavailability of cost-benefit analysis of regulation. Professor Trebilcock, among others, has proposed the preparation annually by each agency of a regulatory impact study which would provide an evaluation of the agencies' activities during the previous year against the statutory policy objectives. The impact study should reflect as clearly as possible the costs and benefits associated with various programs administered by the agency. If a program involves an artificial restriction on supply, then the agency should be required to estimate the short-term price effects of the restriction as well as long-term effects on prices, efficiency and resource allocation. The impact statement would include, against these costs, the estimated benefits to the suppliers of the service and benefits to the general public. If the regulation involves the taxation or subsidization of particular groups (as is frequently the case in utility regulation), then estimates of the value of the subsidies and taxes should be undertaken.

It is not likely that the estimates that appear in these impact statements will be either precisely accurate or readily acceptable to the various interest groups participating in the regulatory process. However, their preparation will force the regulatory agencies to adopt an entirely new frame of reference for their thinking and provide a research base—a methodology—upon which the various interest groups may develop a public policy dialogue.

The directors of the various agencies, federally and provincially, could be required to appear before appropriate parliamentary committees on regulatory affairs and defend their reports. The publicity and open forum provided by these hearings would provide representatives of other societal interest groups the opportunity to inject criticism (Trebilcock, *Submission,* 1976, p. 12).

A related proposal deserving serious consideration is the introduction of sunset laws. Sunset laws have been endorsed widely in the United States as an important part of regulatory reform (Behn, 1977). These laws are statutes of limitation for the legal life of regulatory agencies. At the end of the specified time period, the agency dies unless new enabling legislation is enacted. The virtue of the legislation—much like that of zero base budgeting—is that it requires the legislature periodically to justify a regulatory program.

While possessing considerable theoretical and political appeal, such laws should not be perceived as a panacea for regulatory woes. In a political milieu in which there does not exist a political will for effective consumer representation in the regulatory process or for an effective anti-combines policy, it seems highly improbable that simply requiring periodic renewal of regulatory mandates is likely to result in significant regulatory reform by itself. However, there can be little doubt that such legislation can contribute to regulatory reform since it is reasonable to assume that at least some of the agencies will receive more than cursory review and automatic renewal.

REFERENCES

Alberta (1977a) *Select Committee Reviewing Intraprovincial Trucking Regulation Report* (Edmonton).

Alberta (1977b) Public Utilities Board, *Position Paper: Interventions and Costs* (Edmonton).

Andrew, Caroline and Réjean Pelletier (1978) "The Regulators" in G. Bruce Doern (ed.) *The Regulatory Process in Canada*, pp. 147-64 (Toronto: Macmillan).

Averch, H. and L. Johnson (1962) "Behavior of a Firm under Regulatory Constraint" *American Economic Review* 52: December, 1053-69.

Babe, R.E. (1974) "Public and Private Regulation of Cable Television: A Case Study of Technological Change and Relative Power" *Canadian Public Administration* 17: 187-225.

Bacon, K.H. and A.R. Karr (1974) "The Regulators" *Wall Street Journal* October 9, p. 1.

Baldwin, John R. (1975) *The Regulatory Agency and the Public Corporation: The Canadian Air Transportation Industry* (Cambridge, Mass.: Ballinger).

Beck, Roger (1978) *Micro-economic Analysis of Issues in Business, Government and Society* (New York: McGraw-Hill).

Behn, R.D. (1977) "The False Dawn of Sunset Laws" *Public Interest*, Fall, 103-19.

Beigie, Carl (1973) "An Economic Framework for Policy Action in Canadian Telecommunications" in H.E. English (ed.) *Telecommunications for Canada*, pp. 37-212 (Toronto: Methuen).

Belobaba, Edward *et al.* (1972) "On the Question of Consumer Advocacy — A Working Paper" (Ottawa: Canadian Consumer Council).

Benham, Lee (1973) "Price Structure and Professional Control of Information" (Chicago: University of Chicago, Graduate School of Business).

Berry, G.R. (1974) "The Oil Lobby and the Energy Crises" *Canadian Public Administration* 17: 600-635.

Black's Law Dictionary (1968) 4th ed. (St. Paul, Minn.: West Publishing).

Bonsor, Norman (1978) "The Development of Regulation in the Highway Trucking Industry in Ontario" in Ontario Economic Council, *Government Regulation: Issues and Alternatives*, pp. 103-36 (Toronto).

Brady, A. (1969) "The State and Economic Life in Canada" in K.J. Rea and J.J. McLeod (eds.) *Business and Government in Canada*, pp. 55-67 (Toronto: Methuen).

Broadwith, Hughes and Associates (1978) "The Ontario Milk Marketing Board: An Economic Analysis" in Ontario Economic Council, *Government Regulation: Issues and Alternatives*, pp. 67-102 (Toronto).

Brown-John, C. Lloyd (1972) "The Canadian Transport Commission Experiment" (Ottawa: Canadian Consumer Council).

Brown-John, C. Lloyd (1976) "Research Note: Defining Regulatory Agencies for Analytical Purposes" *Canadian Public Administration* 19: 140-58.

Brown-John, C. Lloyd (1977) "Membership in Canadian Regulatory Agencies" *Canadian Public Administration* 20: 513-33.

Business Week (1974) "The Economic Case for Deregulating Trucking" November 2, pp. 86-87.

Canada (1970) *National Transportation Act* (R.S.C. 1970 N-17)

Canada 1(1975) Office of the Privy Council, Privy Council Order 1975-875.

Canada (1976-1977) Royal Commission on Corporate Concentration, *Transcripts, Volumes 1-23* (Ottawa).

Canada (1977a) Department of Consumer and Corporate Affairs, *Proposals for a New Competition Act for Canada—Second Stage* (Ottawa: Supply and Services).

Canada (1977b) Department of Consumer and Corporate Affairs, Bureau of Competition Policy "Competition in Agriculture: A Working Paper" (Ottawa).

Canada (1977c) *An Act to Amend the National Transportation Act* (Bill C-33).

Canada (1977d) *Telecommunications Act* (Bill C-43).

Canadian Consumer Council (1973) *Report on the Consumer Interest in Regulatory Boards and Agencies* (Ottawa).

Canadian Radio-Television Commission (1975) *Annual Report 1974-75* (Ottawa: Information Canada).

Canadian Radio-Television Commission (1976) *Annual Report 1975-76* (Ottawa: Information Canada).

Capron, William M. (ed.) (1971) *Technological Change in Regulated Industries* (Washington, D.C.: Brookings).

Caves, Richard E. (1962) *Air Transport and Its Regulators: An Industry Study* (Cambridge, Mass: Harvard University Press).

Cayne, David R. (1972) "Consumer Representation before Quebec Regulatory Agencies" (Ottawa: Canadian Consumer Council).

Clark, S.D. (1968) *The Developing Canadian Community* (Toronto: University of Toronto Press).

Clement, W. (1975) *The Canadian Corporate Elite* (Toronto: McClelland and Stewart).

Cohen, Joan (1977) "Confidential Report Details Marketing Board Damage" *Edmonton Journal* April 28, p. 86.

Comanor, W.S. (1970) "Should Natural Monopolies Be Regulated?" *Stanford Law Review* 22: February, 510-18.

Comanor, W.S. and B. Mitchell (1971) "Cable Television and the Impact of Regulation" *Bell Journal of Economics and Management Science* 2: Spring, 154-212.

Connelly, Mark Q. (1977) "Fixed Versus Negotiated Commission Rates on the Toronto Stock Exchange" *Canadian Business Law Journal* 2: August, 244-61.

Consumer Reports (1977) "Ma Bell's Consumer Reform Bill" January, 40-43.

Consumers Association of Canada (1977) *Report on the Regulated Industries Program 1976-77* (Toronto).

Cramton, Roger (1972) "The Why, Where and How of Broadened Public Participation in the Administrative Process" *Georgetown Law Journal* 60: 525-50.

Dawson, Donald A. (1972) "The Canadian Radio-Television Commission and the Consumer Interest" (Ottawa: Canadian Consumer Council).

Demetz, H. (1968) "Why Regulate Utilities?" *Journal of Law and Economics* 11: April, 55-66.

Director of Investigation and Research — Combines Investigation Act (1976) *The Effects of Vertical Integration on the Telecommunications Equipment Market in Canada* (Ottawa: Dept. of Consumer Affairs, Bureau of Competition Policy).

Doern, G. Bruce (1974) "The Concept of Regulation and Regulatory Reform" in G. Bruce Doern and V. Seymour Wilson (eds.) *Issues in Canadian Public Policy* (Toronto: Macmillan).

Doern, G. Bruce *et al.* (1975) "The Structure and Behaviour of Canadian Regulatory Boards and Commissions: Multidisciplinary Perspectives" *Canadian Public Administration* 18: 189-215.

Doern, G. Bruce (1977) "The Political Economy of Regulating Occupational Health: The Ham and Beaudry Reports" *Canadian Public Administration* 20: 1-35.

Doern, G. Bruce (1977a) *The Atomic Energy Control Board,* Study prepared for the Law Reform Commission (Ottawa: Supply and Services).

Doern, G. Bruce (ed.) (1978) *The Regulatory Process in Canada* (Toronto: Macmillan).

Douglas, G.W. and J.C. Miller (1974) *Economic Regulation of Domestic Air Transport: Theory and Policy* (Washington, D.C.: Brookings).

Downs, Anthony (1957) *An Economic Theory of Democracy* (New York: Harper and Row).

Dussault, René (1974) *Traité de droit administratif: canadien et québécois,* 2 vols. (Québec: les presses de l'Université Laval).

Economic Council of Canada (1969) *Interim Report on Competition Policy* (Ottawa: Queen's Printer).

Economic Council of Canada (1975) *Looking Outward: New Trade Strategy for Canada* (Ottawa: Information Canada).

Edmonton Journal (1973) "Trucking Industry Seeking Regulation" January 27.

Edmonton Journal (1977) "Charter Flights Sold Out" May 4, p. 49.

English, H. Edward (ed.) (1973a) *Telecommunications for Canada* (Toronto: Methuen).

English, H. Edward (1973b) "Canadian Telecommunications: Problems and

Policies" in H.E. English (ed.) *Telecommunications for Canada,* pp. 3-36 (Toronto: Methuen).

Farmer, Richard N. (1964) "The Case for Unregulated Truck Transportation" *Journal of Farm Economics* 46: 398-409.

Fellmeth, R.J. *et al.* (1970) *The Interstate Commerce Omission* (New York: Grossman).

Feltham, Ivan R. (1970) "Common Ownership in Canada with Particular Reference to Regulation and Acquisition of Motor Carriers" *Transportation Law Journal* 2: 113-36.

Feltham, Ivan R. (1973) "The New Regulatory State: Economic and Business Regulation Tomorrow" *Canadian Bar Review* 11: 207-14.

Feltham, Ivan R. (1974) "Transport Regulation in Canada" *Transportation Law Journal* 6: 43-70.

Financial Post (1975) "Ontario Plans to Resume Dump Truck Control" November 8, p. C-6.

Folinsbee, R.E. (1976) "Presidential Address" *Proceedings of the Geological Society of America* (Boulder, Co.).

Forbes, J.D. *et al.* (1974) *A Report on Consumer Interest in Marketing Boards* (Ottawa: Consumer Research Council).

Friedlaender, A.F. (1969) *The Dilemma of Freight Transport Regulation* (Washington, D.C.: Brookings).

Friedman, Milton (1962) *Capitalism and Freedom* (Chicago: University of Chicago Press.)

Gellhorn, Ernest (1972) "Public Participation in Administrative Proceedings" *Yale Law Journal* 81: January, 359-404.

Gellman, Aaron J. (1971) "Surface Freight Transportation" in William M. Capron (ed.) *Technological Change in Regulated Industries* (Washington, D.C.: Brookings).

Gerwig, R.G. (1962) "Natural Gas Production: A Study of Costs of Regulation" *Journal of Law and Economics* 5: October, 69-92.

Gosse, R. (1976) *The Provision of Funeral and Cemetary Services in British Columbia* (Vancouver: Dept. of Consumer Services).

Goulden, Joseph C. (1968) *Monopoly* (New York: Putnam).

Grafstein, J.S. (1974) "Some Issues in the Development of Regulatory Policies: Who Is Regulating What?" in K.W. Studnicki-Gizbert (ed.) *Issues in Canadian Transport Policy,* pp. 346-60 (Toronto: Macmillan).

Green, M.J. (1973) *The Monopoly Makers* (New York: Grossman).

Gritta, Richard D. (1975) "Profitability and Risk in Air Transport: A Case for Deregulation" *Transportation Law Journal* 7: 197-208.

Grubel, Herbert and Richard Schwindt (1977) *The Real Cost of the B.C. Milk Board* (Vancouver: Fraser Institute).

Hartle, Douglas G. (1978) "The Regulation of Communications in Canada" in Ontario Economic Council, *Government Regulation: Issues and Alternatives,* pp. 137-206 (Toronto).

Hilton, George W. (1963) "Transportation Regulation and Private Carriage in Private and Unregulated Carriage" (Evanston, Ill.: Northwestern

University, Transportation Center).

Horowitz, G. (1966) "Conservatism, Liberalism and Socialism in Canada: An Interpretation" *Canadian Journal of Economics and Political Science* 32: May, 156-69.

Huber, Paul B. (1973) "Study of the Consumer Interest and Regulatory Commissions in New Brunswick, Nova Scotia, Prince Edward Island and Newfoundland" (Ottawa: Canadian Consumer Council).

Janisch, Hudson N., assisted by A.J. Pirie and W. Charland (1978a) *The Regulatory Process of the Canaidan Transport Commission,* Study prepared for the Law Reform Commission (Ottawa: Supply and Services).

Janisch, Hudson N. (1978b) "The Canadian Transport Commission" in G. Bruce Doern (ed.) *The Regulatory Process in Canada*, pp. 166-211 (Toronto: Macmillan).

Johnson, Nicholas (1971) "Consumer Rights and the Regulatory Crises" *Catholic University Law Review* 20: 424-48.

Jones, J.C.H. (1967) "Mergers and Competition: The Brewing Case" *Canadian Journal of Economics and Political Science* 33: November, 551-68.

Jordan, William A. (1970) *Airline Regulation in America: Effects and Imperfections* (Baltimore: Johns Hopkins Press).

Josephson, Mathew (1938) *The Politicos* (New York: Harcourt, Brace).

Kahn, A.E. (1971) *The Economics of Regulation: Principles and Institutions,* 2 vols. (New York: Wiley).

Kaiser, Gordon E. (forthcoming) "Competition Law and the Regulated Sector" in J.R.S. Prichard, W.T. Stanbury and T.A. Wilson (eds.) *Canadian Competition Policy: Essays in Law and Economics* (Toronto: Butterworth).

Kendrick, John (1973) *Postwar Productivity Trends in the United States* (New York: National Bureau of Economic Research).

Kessel, Reuben A. (1967) "Economic Effects of Federal Regulation of Milk Markets" *Journal of Law and Economics* 10: October, 51-78.

Kessel, Reuben A. (1972) "Higher Education and the Nation's Health: A Review of the Carnegie Commission Report on Medical Education" *Journal of Law and Economics* 15: April, 115-27.

Kolko, Gabriel (1965) *Railroads and Regulation, 1877-1916* (Westport, Conn.: Greenwood).

Lambert, R.D. (ed.) (1972) "The Government as Regulator" *The Annals of the American Academy of Political and Social Science* 400: March, 1-139.

Landis, J.M. (1960) *Report on Regulatory Agencies to the President-Elect* (Senate Committtee on Judiciary 86th Cong., 2d sess.) (Washington, D.C.: Government Printing Office).

Langford, John W. (1976a) "The National Transportation System: Restructuring for Effective Regulation" in Karl M. Ruppenthal and W.T. Stanbury (eds.) *Transportation Policy: Regulation, Competition, and the Public Interest,* pp. 93-107 (Vancouver: University of British Columbia, Centre for Transportation Studies).

Langford, John W. (1976b) *Transport in Transition* (Montreal: McGill-

Queen's University Press).

Large, Arlen J. (1968) "Do We Need a Consumer's Bureau?" in Roger Beck (ed.) *Micro-economic Analysis of Issues in Business. Government and Society,* pp. 19-21 (New York: McGraw-Hill).

Leibenstein, Harvey (1966) "Allocative Efficiency and X-Efficiency" *American Economic Review* 56: June, 392-415.

Levin, Harvey J. (1970) "Spectrum Allocation without Market" *American Economic Review* 60: May, 209-18.

Levine, M.E. (1965) "Is Regulation Necessary? California Air Transportation and National Regulatory Policy" *Yale Law Journal* 74: 1416-47.

Lipset, S.M. (1968) *Revolution and Counter Revolution: Change and Persistence in Social Structures* (New York: Basic Books).

Lucas, A. (1978) "The National Energy Board" in G. Bruce Doern (ed.) *The Regulatory Process in Canada,* pp. 259-313 (Toronto: Macmillan).

Lucas, A.R. and T. Bell (1977) *The National Energy Board: Policy, Procedure and Practice,* Study prepared for the Law Reform Commission (Ottawa: Supply and Services).

MacAvoy, P.W. (1965) *The Economic Effects of Regulation* (Cambridge, Mass.: MIT Press).

MacAvoy, P.W. (1970) "The Effectiveness of the Federal Power Commission" *Bell Journal of Economics and Management Science* 1: Autumn, 271-303.

MacAvoy, P.W. (1971) "The Regulation Induced Shortage of Natural Gas" *Journal of Law and Economics* 14: April, 167-99.

Maister, David (1976) "An Analysis of Trucking Rates in Canada" (Occasional Paper no. 11) (Vancouver: University of British Columbia, Centre for Transportation Studies).

Massel, Mark (1968) "The Regulatory Process and Public Utility Performance" in Harry M. Trebing (ed.) *Performance under Regulation* (East Lansing, Mich.: Institute of Public Utilities).

McCallum, S.K. and G. Watkins (1975) "Citizens Costs before Administrative Tribunals" *Chitty's Law Journal* 23: 181-90.

McDonald, J. (1971) "A Test of the Averch and Johnson Theory That Regulated Firms Cross-Subsidize Unregulated Competitive Services with Other Services" M.B.A. thesis, University of Alberta.

McDougall, John (1972) "The National Energy Board and the Canadian Consumer" (Ottawa: Canadian Consumer Council).

McIvor, D.K. (1973) "The Hydrocarbon Potential of the Canadian Arctic" paper presented to the Second Annual Meeting of the American Petroleum Institute, *Daily Oil Bulletin* (Calgary) October 22.

McLachlin, D.L. (1971) "Canadian Trucking Regulation" paper presented to the Canadian Economics Association, June.

McManus, John C. (1972) "Federal Regulation of Transport in Canada" (Ottawa: Canadian Consumer Council).

McManus, John C. (1973) "Federal Regulation of Telecommunications in Canada" in H.E. English (ed.) *Telecommunications for Canada,* pp.

389-428 (Toronto: Methuen).

Meyer, John R. *et al.* (1964) *Economics of Competition in the Transportation Industries* (Cambridge, Mass.: Harvard University Press).

Mitchell, Heather (1977) *A Report on Access to Information* (Ottawa: Consumer Research Council).

Moore, Thomas G. (1972) *Freight Transportation Regulation* (Washington: D.C.: American Enterprise Institute).

Moore, Thomas G. (1975) "Deregulating Surface Freight Transportation" in A. Phillips (ed.) *The Promotion of Competition in Regulated Markets,* pp. 55-98 (Washington, D.C.: Brookings).

Morgan Guarantee Survey (1976) "Washington's New Focus on Regulatory Rigidities" March, 10-14.

Munro, John M. (1976) "The 'New' Transportation Policy and the Public Interest" in Karl M. Ruppenthal and W.T. Stanbury (eds.) *Transportation Policy: Regulation, Competition, and the Public Interest,* pp. 215-32 (Vancouver: University of British Columbia, Centre for Transportation Studies).

National Farm Products Marketing Council (1976) *Proceedings of the Public Hearings into the Canadian Egg Marketing Agency's Pricing Formula,* vols. 1-4 and Summary of Findings and Recommendations (Ottawa).

Nelson, James R. (1966) "The Role of Competition in the Regulated Industries" *Antitrust Bulletin* 11: January, 1-36.

Noll, Roger G. (1971) *Reforming Regulation* (Washington, D.C.: Brookings).

Ontario Economic Council (1978) *Government Regulation: Issues and Alternatives* (Toronto).

Ottawa Journal (1976) "Auto Wreckers Want Bodysnatcher Ban" June 26, p. 10.

Palmer, J. (1972a) "Empirically Testing the Effects of Provincial Trucking Regulation: A Further Analysis" (Ottawa: Canadian Consumer Council).

Palmer, J. (1972b) "Taxation by Regulation? The Experience of Ontario Trucking Regulation" (Ottawa: Canadian Consumer Council).

Palmer, J. (1973) "A Further Analysis of Provincial Trucking Regulation" *Bell Journal of Economics and Management Science* 4: Autumn, 655-64.

Palmer, J. and John Erkkila (1972) "The Role of the Consumer in Affecting the Decisions of the Hydro-Electric Power Commission of Ontario" (Ottawa: Canadian Consumer Council).

Pauly, David (1976) "Ma Bell's Big Fight" *Newsweek* July 12, 56-62.

Peck, Merton J. (1965) "Competitive Policy for Transportation?" in A. Phillips (ed.) *Perspectives on Antitrust Policy,* pp. 261-65 (Princeton, N.J.: Princeton University Press).

Peltzman, S. (1976) "Toward a More General Theory of Regulation" *Journal of Law and Economics* 19: Autumn, 211-40.

Pépin, Gilles (1968) "Les tribunaux administratifs" in Raoul-P. Barbe (ed.) *Droit administratif canadien et québécois,* pp. 551-620 (Ottawa: Editions de l'université d'Ottawa).

Phillips, A. (ed.) (1975) *Promoting Competition in Regulated Markets* (Washington, D.C.: Brookings).

Pickersgill, J.W. (1969) "Canada's National Transportation Policy" *Transportation Law Journal* 1: 79-86.

Polanyi, Karl (1957) *The Great Transformation* (Boston: Beacon Hill).

Posner, Richard A. (1969) "Natural Monopoly and Its Regulation" *Stanford Law Review* 21: February, 548-643.

Posner, Richard A. (1971) "Taxation by Regulation" *Bell Journal of Economics and Management Science 2*: Spring: 22-50.

Posner, Richard A. (1975) "The Social Costs of Monopoly and Regulation" *Journal of Political Economy* 83: 807-27.

President's Advisory Council on Executive Organization (Ash Council) (1971) *A New Regulatory Framework: Report on Selected Independent Regulatory Agencies* (Washington, D.C.: Government Printing Office).

Presthus, R. (1973) *Elite Accommodation in Canadian Politics* (Toronto: Macmillan).

Prichard, J.R.S., W.T. Stanbury and T.A. Wilson (eds.) (forthcoming) *Canadian Competition Policy: Essays in Law and Economics* (Toronto: Butterworth).

Purdy, H.L. (1972) *Transportation Competition and Public Policy in Canada* (Vancouver: University of British Columbia Press).

Reich, Charles (1966) "The Law of the Planned Society" *Yale Law Journal* 75: 1227-70.

Reschenthaler, G.B. (1972) *The Performance of Selected Independent Regulatory Commissions in Alberta, Saskatchewan and Manitoba* (Ottawa: Canadian Consumer Council).

Reschenthaler, G.B. (1976) "Regulatory Failure and Competition" *Canadian Public Administration* 19: 466-85.

Reschenthaler, G.B. (1977) "Bill C-13 and Regulated Industries" in W.T. Stanbury (ed.) *Papers on Bill C-13: The Proposed Competition Act* (Vancouver: University of British Columbia, Faculty of Commerce and Business Administration).

Reschenthaler, G.B. and B. Roberts (1978a) "A Re-examination of Canadian Airline Regulation" *Logistics and Transportation Review* 14: 3-27.

Reschenthaler, G.B. and B. Roberts (eds.) (1978b) *Perspectives on Canadian Airline Regulation* (Toronto: Butterworth for Institute for Research on Public Policy).

Reschenthaler, G.B. and C.C. Wulff (1977) "Regulation of the Dairy Industry in Alberta" (Edmonton: University of Alberta, Faculty of Business Administration).

Richardson, Ellen (1972) "Consumer Interest Representation, Three Case Studies: I. The Tariff Board; II. The Anti-Dumping Tribunal; III. The Textile and Clothing Board" (Ottawa: Canadian Consumer Council).

Ruppenthal, Karl M. and W.T. Stanbury (eds.) (1976) *Transportation Policy: Regulation, Competition and the Public Interest* (Vancouver: University of British Columbia, Centre for transportation Studies).

Sabatier, Paul (1975) "Social Movements and the Regulatory Agencies: Toward a More Adequate—and Less Pessimistic—Theory of 'Clientele Capture' " *Policy Sciences* 6: 301-42.

Sack, J.L. and Jeffrey Sack (1972) "Citizens' Advocates and Poverty Lawyers" *Canadian Forum* May, 35-40.

Scherer, F.M. (1970) *Industrial Market Structure and Economic Performance* (Chicago: Rand McNally).

Schultz, Richard (1977) "Regulatory Agencies and the Canadian Political System" in K. Kernaghan (ed.) *Public Administration in Canada,* 3d ed., pp. 333-43 (Toronto: Methuen).

Shaffer, E. (1972) "Energy Conservation Boards" in G.B. Reschenthaler *The Performance of Selected Independent Regulatory Commissions in Alberta, Saskatchewan and Manitoba,* pp. 146-81 (Ottawa: Canadian Consumer Council).

Shaffner, Richard (1977) *The Quest for Farm Income Stability in Canada* (Montreal: C.D. Howe Research Institute).

Shepherd, William G. (1973) "Entry as a Substitute for Regulation" *American Economic Review* 63: May, 98-105.

Sichel, Werner and Thomas G. Gies (1975) *Public Utility Regulation: Change and Scope* (Lexington, Mass.: D.C. Heath).

Silverman, Hugh W. (1973) "Government Regulation in Canadian Civil Aviation" *Transportation Law Journal* 5: 106-25.

Skeoch, L.A. (1966) *Restrictive Trade Practices in Canada* (Toronto: McClelland and Stewart).

Skeoch, Lawrence A. with Bruce C. McDonald (1976) *Dynamic Change and Accountability in a Canadian Market Economy* (Ottawa: Supply and Services).

Sloss, J. (1970) "Regulation of Motor Freight Transportation: A Quantitative Evaluation of Policy" *Bell Journal of Economics and Management Science* 1: Autumn, 327-66.

Smith, Adam (1937) *The Wealth of Nations* (New York: Random House, Modern Library Edition).

Stanbury, W.T. (1973) "The British Columbia Public Utilities Commission and the Consumer Interest" (Ottawa: Canadian Consumer Council).

Stanbury, W.T. (1976a) "The Consumer Interest and the Regulated Industries: Diagnosis and Prescription" in Karl M. Ruppenthal and W.T. Stanbury (eds.) *Transportation Policy: Regulation, Competition, and the Public Interest,* pp. 109-55 (Vancouver: University of British Columbia, Centre for Transportation Studies).

Stanbury, W.T. (1976b) "Penalties and Remedies under the Combines Investigation Act" *Osgoode Hall Law Journal* 14: December, 571-631.

Stanbury, W.T. (1977) *Business Interests and the Reform of Canadian Competition Policy, 1971-1975* (Toronto: Carswell/Methuen).

Stigler, G.T. (1971) "The Theory of Economic Regulation" *Bell Journal of Economics and Management Science* 2: Spring, 3-21.

Stigler, G.T. and C. Friedland (1962) "What Can Regulators Regulate? The

Case of Electricity" *Journal of Law and Economics* 5: 1-16.

Studnicki-Gizbert, K.W. (ed.) (1974) *Issues in Canadian Transport Policy* (Toronto: Macmillan).

Trebilcock, M.J. (1972) "The Case for a Consumer Advocate" (Ottawa: Canadian Consumer Council).

Trebilcock, M.J. (1975) "Winners and Losers in the Modern Regulatory State: Must the Consumer Always Lose?" *Osgoode Hall Law Journal* 13: December, 619-47.

Trebilcock, M.J. (1976) "Submission to the Royal Commission on Corporate Concentration" (Ottawa).

Trebilcock, M.S. (1977) "Regulators and the Consumer Interest: The Canadian Transport Commission's Costs Decision" *Canadian Business Law Journal* 2: March, 101-13.

Trebilcock, M.J. (1978) "The Consumer Interest and Regulatory Reform" in G. Bruce Doern (ed.) *The Regulatory Process in Canada*, pp. 94-127 (Toronto: Macmillan).

Trebilcock, M.J., L. Waverman and R.S. Prichard (1978) "Markets for Regulation: Implications for Performance Standards and Institutional Design" in Ontario Economic Council *Government Regulation: Issues and Alternatives*, pp. 11-66 (Toronto).

Trebing, Harry M. (1974) "Realism and Relevance in Public Utility Regulation" *Journal of Economic Issues* 8: June, 209-35.

Trebing, Harry M. (ed.) (1976a) *New Dimensions in Public Utility Pricing* (East Lansing, Mich.: Michigan State University Press).

Trebing, Harry M. (1976b) "The Chicago School versus Public Utility Regulation" *Journal of Economic Issues* 10: March, 97-126.

Trebing, Harry M. (1977) "Broadening the Objectives of Public Utility Regulation" *Land Economics* 53: February, 107-22.

Turner, Donald F. (1969) "The Scope of Antitrust and Other Economic Regulatory Policies" *Harvard Law Review* 82: April, 1207-44.

Warne, Colston E. (1972) "The Muted Voice of the Consumer in Regulatory Agencies" in W.J. Samuels and H.M. Trebing (eds.) *A Critique of Administrative Regulation of Public Utilities*, pp. 295-310 (East Lansing, Mich.: Michigan State University Press).

Waters, W.G. II (1976) "The Process of Evaluating Public Investments in Airports and Other Facilities" In Karl M. Ruppenthal and W.T Stanbury (eds.) *Transportation Policy: Regulation, Competition, and the Public Interest*, pp. 201-13 (Vancouver: University of British Columbia, Centre for Transportation Studies).

Waverman, Leonard (1975) "The Regulation of Intercity Telecommunications" in A. Phillips (ed.) *Promoting Competition in Regulated Markets*, pp. 201-39 (Washington, D.C.: Brookings).

Waverman, Leonard (forthcoming) "The New Competition Policy and Regulated Industry in Canada" in J.R.S. Prichard, W.T. Stanbury and T.A. Wilson (eds.) *Canadian Competition Policy: Essays in Law and Economics* (Toronto: Butterworth).

Weiss, Gary (1975) "End of Road for Free-Market Trucking in Alberta" *Financial Post* December 13, p. C-7.

Welch, Francis X. (1942) "The Effectiveness of State Regulatory Agencies" *Public Administration Service Bulletin* of R.R. Donnelly and Sons, no. 85, 8-9.

Westmacott, Martin, W. (1972) "The Canadian Transport Commission, Freight Rates and the Public Interest" (Ottawa: Canadian Consumer Council).

Westmacott, Martin W. (1976) "The Canadian Transport Commission, Freight Rates, and the Public Interest" in Karl M. Ruppenthal and W.T. Stanbury (eds.) *Transportation Policy: Regulation, Competition, and the Public Interest,* pp. 49-91 (Vancouver: University of British Columbia, Centre for Transportation Studies).

Willis, J. (ed.) (1941) *Canadian Boards at Work* (Toronto: Macmillan).

Willis, John (1968) "The McRuer Report: Lawyers' Values and Civil Servants' Values" *University of Toronto Law Journal* 18: 351-60.

Wilson, James Q. (1973) "The Dead Hand of Regulation" *Public Interest,* Spring, 39-58.

Chapter Three

Some Emerging Economic Issues
In Utility Regulation And Rate-Making

by *John F. Helliwell*
Department of Economics
University of British Columbia

INTRODUCTION

Regulated utilities, especially those producing and distributing energy products, are living in difficult times. They face rising costs of supply, high interest rates, and frequent rate hearings, each of which brings forth more widespread opposition.[1] Are these increasing frictions inevitable, or would it be possible to improve regulatory policies and procedures to make it easier for the utilities to satisfy their customers, their shareholders, their lenders, and their regulators? I shall argue below that much of the current friction is a consequence of inappropriate rate design, and I shall suggest changes. To set the stage, however, I shall first give a brief survey of the main elements of the existing economic analysis of regulation. This survey will illustrate that the literature has not been primarily concerned with the more important current issues. Then I shall give my interpretation of the causes of the current financial and social pressures on utilities and suggest what should be done to relieve them. In conclusion I shall raise briefly some of the other economic issues that are likely to require more attention in the next ten years.

ECONOMIC ANALYSIS OF REGULATION

I shall deal first with the economic theory of regulation as a whole, and then with the narrower literature that deals with the effects of rate of return regulation. There is a growing body of economic literature that goes under the heading of the "economic theory of regulation." Although it poaches liberally on territory that might more usually be considered the preserve of

[1] This is a revised version of a paper prepared for the McGill-Carleton Conference on Regulation in Canada: Process and Performance, Chateau Montebello, Quebec, March 3-5, 1977. In revising the paper, I have had the benefit of helpful comments from Ernst Berndt, Douglas Hartle, Milton Moore, Sanford Osler, Anthony Scott, Bill Stanbury, and Andrew Thompson.

students of political science, administration, and sociology, it avoids the need for interdisciplinary trappings by brandishing the economist's twin swords of supply and demand. (In the time of Alfred Marshall they were known as scissors, but everything is bigger now.) As originally formulated by Stigler (1971) and extended by Posner (1974), the economic theory of regulation states that regulatory laws and performance are the result of the interplay of the demand for and supply of regulation. Regulation itself is potentially worth demanding because "the coercive power of government can be used to give valuable benefits to particular individuals or groups" (Posner, 1974, p. 344). The demand for regulation comes sometimes from the supplying firms (who might consider regulation a means of establishing market control where other methods are more costly or not available), sometimes from one group of customers (who see the process as one that can be used to increase their market power relative to other customers, and the suppliers), and sometimes from a coalition of interests. The regulatory framework is supplied by governments for one or more of three reasons: a price is offered to the government, a coercive threat is made to the government, or the democratic process comes more directly into play when those demanding regulation corral enough votes to pass enabling legislation.

Posner distinguishes the economic theory from the well-known 'capture theory' (which states simply that the regulated firms effectively control the regulators) and the 'public interest' theory (which states that regulation is brought in to repair market imperfections, and that any failure to achieve the desired results is based on agency imcompetence). He prefers the economic theory to the former because he regards the 'capture theory' as lacking any explanation of the conditions under which 'capture' is likely to occur. He rejects the 'public interest' theory because it relies too much on incompetence (the world of economic theory is peopled with clear-eyed and self-interested calculators) being greater in regulatory agencies than elsewhere, but he does confess to being troubled (1974, pp. 352-55) by the public interest rhetoric in many discussions of regulation, and by the apparent fact that "many features of law and public policy designed to maintain a market system are more plausibly explained by reference to a broad social interest in efficiency than by reference to the designs of narrow interest groups" (1974, p. 350).

Stigler argues (1975, p. 137) that Posner is defining the economic theory too narrowly, and that the 'public interest' is a special interest like any other, the only difference being that the 'public interest' involves a larger group of supporters, each of whom has a less immediate interest in the outcome. If this seems to make the theory so broad and spongy that it cannot be refuted, that is just what Stigler has in mind. Aside from temporary accidents', the theory cannot be wrong; mediocre empirical results can only be due to bad measures of benefits and costs. Indeed, he argues, the theory is so robustly reliable that the "truly intended effects (of the legislation) should be deduced from the actual effects" (1975, p. 140). The main open issue, in his opinion, is to study the political process in a similar way, so as to be better able to deduce the power of a group to demand preferred treatment by the regulatory process.

Pushing forward with this invasion of political science, Albert Breton has recently suggested that the growth and nature of regulation, when viewed from the supply side, can best be understood in connection with the financing of the political process. In his explanation (1976, pp. 15-16), which can be regarded as an extension of his earlier economic analysis (Breton, 1974) of the political process, Breton argues that transferring the costs of democracy ("the orderly succession of one government by another") from individuals to political parties has not solved the problem of financing the costs. Political parties do this, he argues, by trading with the private sector, by exchanging beneficial laws and regulations for financial and other electoral support. This has the effect of encouraging regulation that completes the exchange and ensures the financing of the political parties, but ends up costing consumers and taxpayers more than would a more direct means of financing the democratic process.

All of the economic analysis of regulation described above relates to regulation defined much more broadly than the activities of the traditional regulated industries. Within the narrower definition of regulation the economic analysis has been generally more restricted, and more technical in its nature. Even in technical terms, the theories and results must be regarded as fairly primitive in nature. In view of the limited range and early stage of this research, we should not expect to find much that will help us to identify and resolve the major issues likely to confront the regulated industries in the next decade. Nevertheless, a tiny review of progress may help to fill out my description of the state of economic analysis of regulation.

One might sensibly ask several narrowly defined economic questions about regulatory performance. The one that has had the longest standing was first made well-known by Averch and Johnson (1962). They reasoned that a utility whose rate of return on capital was regulated to be less than some allowed rate would tend to use excessive amounts of capital (relative to the amounts that would minimize total costs for any given level of output) if the allowed rate of return was more than the marginal cost of funds to the firm. The discussion has since proceeded in several directions. Economists have rung the changes on the theoretical model with increasing fineness of detail. Still within the simple model of profit-maximization (with no uncertainty) subject to rate of return regulation, it was shown that the main increase in capital would be as a substitute for labour rather than 'padding the ratebase' (Bailey, 1973, p. 171), that the rate of return regulation will not induce the firm to expand past the point of maximum revenue (i.e., into an inelastic portion of the demand curve), and that regulatory lag can reduce the Averch-Johnson effect by, in effect, allowing the firm to maximize profits in an unrestrained way between hearings (Bailey, 1973). This latter result follows because the price is fixed between hearings, and the firm maximizes profits by minimizing costs; when a hearing is imminent, then the incentive grows for additional use of capital.

Another strand of the theoretical literature has dealt with assessing the welfare effects of the Averch-Johnson effect, starting with Klevorick (1971), and Sheshinski (1971), usually in the absence of any estimates of the cost consequences of the Averch-Johnson effect. Callen, Mathewson, and Mohring (1976) have recently extended this line of analysis by using the results of Dobell *et al.* (1972) on the demand for and cost of Canadian telephone services. Callen *et al.* calculate the total of consumer and producer benefits from an unrestrained monopoly and compare these benefits with, on the one hand, the benefits from systems subject to various degrees of rate-of-return regulation, and, on the other hand, from systems operated to minimize costs with price set equal to average or marginal costs. The calculation of the net benefits from rate-of-return regulation assumes a costless and continous regulation process, and suggests that the maximum attainable benefits from rate-of-return regulation are equal to 28 percent of the total revenues of an unconstrained monopolist, which would represent a somewhat smaller fraction of the total revenues of the regulated Canadian telephone industry. Those representing consumer interests will be unhappy to learn that the so-called "optimum" regulated rate of return is 1.26 times the cost of capital to the telephone system. This rate of return is much less than what an unregulated monopolist would earn in this situation, but is greater than the utility's cost of capital because the over use of capital gets worse as the regulatory constraint is tightened. Callen *et al.* argue, by reference to their example calculations, that rate-of-return regulation is much better than no regulation at all, but their calculations also show that it falls far short of the gains possible if utilities could be induced to minimize costs at all levels of output, and then to set price equal to marginal cost.

If, by some means, the prototype Canadian telephone industry represented by Dobell *et al.* (1972) followed the efficiency rules rather than the rules for profit-maximization subject to regulatory constraint, then the gains from regulation would be more than doubled (increased 2.3 times, according to Callen *et al.* 1976, p. 297), to an amount equal to 65 percent of the total revenues of an unregulated monopolist.[2] In many ways, this is the most striking feature of the Callen *et al.* results, and it suggests not only that departures from cost-minimization should be carefully watched for in any regulatory review, but also suggests potentially important lines for future empirical research. In the simplified world modelled by Callen *et al.*, the input choices and average costs depend importantly on whether a firm is minimizing costs (and setting price equal to marginal costs) or is maximizing profits subject to a regulatory constraint. Some direct tests of their hypothesis

---

[2] The multiple 2.3 would be even larger if the regulated rate of return were set at other than its "optimal" value, and the latter can only be roughly estimated by the regulatory authority. The quantitative effect of "non-optimal" rates of return is not very large, however. The multiple of 2.3 would increase to 2.44 if the allowed rate of return were set equal to 1.1 times the cost of capital and to 3.45 if the allowed rate of return were set equal to twice the cost of capital. Sherman (1976) has suggested that input taxes on capital and subsidies to other inputs should be used to offset the Averch-Johnson effect and thus obtain the minimum-cost results.

should be possible by comparing the behaviour of government-owned and investor-owned utilities in Canada, at least in those instances (e.g., Ontario Hydro) where the utility is instructed to minimize costs rather than to maximize profits. In many cases, it would be difficult to know how to distinguish the objectives of the managers of privately and publicly owned utilities in the same industry. In these cases, it would thus be impossible to use differences or similarity in utility costs or capital/labour ratios as a way of testing for the effects of cost-minimizing instead of profit-maximizing behaviour.

Another interesting and timely extension to the Averch-Johnson literature has been made by Atkinson and Halvorsen (1976), who explore the effects of automatic adjustment clauses, or 'tracking', on the input decisions made by regulated utilities. As you might expect, to introduce tracking for an input whose price is rising will increase the use of that input relative to others, to an extent that grows with the length of the regulatory lag. If fuel costs are tracked, and if there is a significant regulatory lag, then utilities will increase their use of fuel relative to other inputs whose cost increases are not tracked. One consequence of this is to partially offset the Averch-Johnson over-capitalization effect, by increasing the amount of fuel used per unit of capital. However, one would still expect to find excessive use of capital and fuel relative to labour. In their empirical estimation of input choices for fossil fuel steam-electric plants, Atkinson and Halvorsen find, in contrast to earlier studies by Courville (1974), Petersen (1975), and Spann (1974), that there is no significant departure from the relative factor usage that would minimize costs.[3] They explain their result as the consequence of the fuel adjustment clauses offsetting the Averch-Johnson over-capitalization effect, and note that the earlier findings made use of data relating to years before fuel costs started rising rapidly, and before fuel adjustment clauses came into widespread use.

Other recent extensions of the Averch-Johnson literature have involved assessing the effects of uncertainty, and have generally shown, in fairly abstract terms, that the introduction of various kinds of uncertainty makes precise theoretical conclusions more difficult to obtain. One example will help to give the flavour of this research, and also to illustrate the common tendency of economic theorizing to deal with further refinements of less and less substance, without enough concern for the realism of assumptions. This charge, which is often levelled by practioners against economists, has enough validity to explain why there is such a gulf between the economic literature on regulation and the literature, for example, in the *Public Utilities Fortnightly,* read by regulators and the regulated. For example, a recent article (Peles and

---

[3] However, they do note that *absolute* price efficiency is rejected at a very high level of significance, while relative price efficiency is only accepted at the .25 significance level. The rejection of absolute price efficiency implies that the level of output is not at the profit-maximizing level. Given the regulatory lag, rising input prices, and the requirement that utilities meet all demands in their service areas, it is no surprise that output is above the level that would maximize static monopoly profits.

Stein, 1976) in a leading economics journal showed that the introduction of uncertainty in the net revenue stream would *reverse* the Averch-Johnson over-capitalization effect if the uncertain net revenue were proportional to the captial stock, *and* if all revenues in excess of the regulated return are immediately refunded to users through lower prices. In these circumstances, where the shareholders take their lumps when uncertain profits are low and get nothing back when uncertain profits are above the regulated maximum, there is every incentive to reduce the incidence of uncertainty. In the special case where the uncertain element is proportional to the capital stock, the xdverse revenue effects of uncertainty can be lessened by cutting the capital stock, thus reducing and potentially reversing the Averch-Johnson effect.

The analysis is sophisticated and well presented, but I think it ignores too many important features of the regulatory process. In Canada, rate-of-return regulation usually involves 'test year' calculations, thus abstracting from any of the abnormal or random circumstances that cause random fluctuations in revenues. Once rate schedules are fixed on the basis of these test year calculations, they remain fixed (except for any automatic adjustment clauses) until the next rate case is initiated (almost always by the utility) *even if* events in the interim lead to sub-normal or super-normal profits. Thus, even if the uncertain elements in the net profit stream were proportional to the capital stock (and why should it be proportional to capital, rather than to output, to inputs, or to GNP?) the operation of rate-of-return regulation in Canada is such that random increases as well as decreases find their way to the shareholders, and hence do not provide any incentive for a risk-neutral firm to cut its capital stock.

Enough is enough. My intention in this section has been neither to survey all of a burgeoning literature nor to dissect or discredit the contents. I have tried to give only a representative sampling, to highlight a few points of special interest in the Canadian context, and to illustrate the tendency of economists to generate a perplexing array of theoretical conclusions based on rather special assumptions. In the course of doing all that, I hope that I have shown the need to do more than summarize the existing literature on the economics of regulation if I am to be of much use in spelling out the likely major issues for regulation in the 1980s.

I turn now to the broader tasks. First, I shall describe in very general terms the emerging situation, and then explain the four major factors that I think to be responsible. I shall then conclude with a brief discussion of several further aspects of regulation that are likely to be of concern over the next decade.

THE MAIN ISSUE FOR THE 1980S

Evidence has been accumulating that regulated utilities of several types are finding it increasingly difficult to satisfy their customers, their shareholders, their lenders, and the public at large. Utilities find themselves with rates that are not high enough, at least in the final segments of the rate structures, to cover the costs of building and operating additional capacity.[4] Four factors, of varying importance in different industries, have combined to produce this situation:

- rate structures with declining blocks;
- inflation combined with historic cost accounting;
- rate base accounting involving straight-line depreciation; and
- marginal costs, in real terms, that are above average real costs in some utilities, especially in energy supply.

Basically, the problem is that all the existing users and owners of a utility are undamaged by expansion only if price exceeds marginal cost, while the price structures of regulated utilities are established so that total revenues (volume times average price) should match average costs based (with some exceptions) on historic cost accounting. The four factors I have listed above have combined to produce a situation where this condition is far from being met. For example, B.C. Hydro's energy charge to large industrial users is 4 mills, while the anticipated energy cost of their next major hydro project (before taking direct account of environmental costs) is 12 mills and the opportunity cost of oil or gas used in thermal generation in the Burrard plant is equal to 18 mills per kilowatt hour.[5]

This discrepancy puts great pressure on both the utility and its customers. The utility knows that every incremental unit of demand is being sold at less than it costs, thus making the utility and its existing customers worse off than they would be without the extra demand. The customers are caught in a bind; they know that the situation is wasteful and is bound to be paid for by them in the long run, but they naturally resist any solution that involves increases in the costs of their existing power. New customers are less troubled by the current situation, especially if they are cutting themselves into a system with a substanial block of low-cost power, because the procedures automatically work so that the old customers subsidize the new ones. However, once they have been added to the system and have established their own claim to a share of the old low-cost power, their attitude is likely to change.

Another way of putting the matter is that rising inflation, rate base accounting, declining block rate structures, and rising real costs have together

---

[4] Joskow and MacAvoy (1976) have documented these circumstances for U.S. electric power companies, and the corresponding Canadian evidence has been surfacing in a number of regulatory hearings. Similar concerns have been expressed by M. & M. Systems (1975) in an energy regulation study sponsored by a group of Canadian electricity and natural gas utilities.

[5] These calculations are based on the research of Sanford Osler, who has established a framework within which to calculate, using B.C. Hydro's own planning cost estimates, the marginal costs of energy and capacity for each of the projects for the future as well as for various systems of interlocking projects. All costs are measured in terms of 1976 prices.

assured that the remaining unallocated historic costs of existing plant are much less than the current-dollar costs of new plant. The electric utility that has old hydro plants, largely written off, financed with old low-interest debt, has a valuable capital asset, one that grows more valuable with every increase in the costs of alternative energy sources. The crisis for regulation has come about because the rate structures now have to do two quite separate jobs, neither of which they were designed to do . On the one hand, the rates have to properly allocate the high costs of new facilities while on the other hand, they have to distribute the economic surpluses from the existing plant. In principle, there are ways of designing rate structures that make some attempt to perform both these functions, and I shall make some specific suggestions in due course. Before I do that, I ought to be more specific about the four factors that have produced the growing pressures on the regulated industries.

Rate Structures With Declining Blocks

If, as I have suggested, utilities are now in a situation where expansion of demand at existing rates does not come near to covering the costs of new capacity, then rate structures with declining blocks must be a contributing factor. Under a declining block structure, the price for the last unit purchased is less than the average price. For each customer, the decision about how much of a service to use is based on the price for additional units, so that a declining block structure increases any gap that might exist between marginal cost and marginal revenue.

If declining block rates are now part of the cause of a problem, how did they come to be established? The history is long and complicated, and the reasons are many. The basic reason, however, is quite simple; declining block rates were a recognition of the fact and perception that marginal costs were less than average costs. That is a sufficient explanation for a regulated utility whose rates are designed to cover its costs; for an unregulated monopoly the declining block structure can be an effective means of differential pricing, obtaining for the utility a share of what would otherwise be consumer surpluses in a system with a single price for all units purchased.[6] At one time the standard model of a regulated industry was of a 'natural monopoly', so called because it enjoyed substantial economies of scale, so substantial and pervasive that the larger firm could always produce more cheaply than the small one. In elementary economics textbooks, regulation is posed as the problem of ensuring that price equals marginal cost, and

---

[6] An extension of this point would suggest that a profit-maximizing monopolist would have different rate structures for each separable class of use, with the tailing rate in each class chosen to equate marginal cost equal to marginal revenue, and the intra-marginal rates set high enough to capture consumer surpluses. Since each class of customer would in general have different types of need for the utility's services, the utility would in general prefer a different rate structure for each. The ability of unregulated utilities to use this type of differential pricing in monopolistic situations presumably lay behind the initial demands for regulation of public utilities.

regulatory agencies are criticized for their use of a general rule that price should equal average cost. In the supposed conditions of declining cost, setting price equal to average costs means that price is too high and output too small (e.g., Samuelson and Scott, 1975, p. 459).

Declining block rates can thus be seen to be partially intended as a means of allocating the financial deficits that arise if price is set equal to marginal cost in a declining cost industry.[7] Other reasons for adapting declining block tariffs include the desire to allocate billing and other customer-related fixed costs, and sometimes a misguided attempt to take account of the fact that marginal costs are below average costs in all off-peak periods. I describe this attempt as misguided because the declining block rate structure cannot perform the function of peak-load pricing because it makes no distinction between peak and off-peak use, so that if it is right for the one it must be wrong for the other.

So much for the source of declining block rates. If, as I shall suggest below, the basic justification for them has gone, at least temporarily if not forever, what is happening to the declining block structure? At this stage, no one can tell, but there is clearly something happening. To some extent, it is being eroded as a by-product of fuel adjustment clauses being used to raise rates in tailing blocks only, or to increase energy charges rather than capacity charges in tariffs that make such a distinction. In addition, there has been much discussion, especially in U.S. regulatory agencies, of a variety of rate structure changes that have the effect of flattening the rate structure. The confusion that abounds in these discussions is largely due, I suspect, to the lack of realization that rate structures are now having to perform their traditional role of rationing use at the margin as well as distributing the benefits of existing low-cost plant. This situation is further complicated by judicial precedents, especially in the United States, and statutory decrees that utilities are to set rates on the basis of cost, with the usual presumption that the appropriate levels of cost are those coming from the utility's accounts.

In addition to the discussions about flattening rate structures, there has been a recent upsurge of interest in peak-load pricing.[8] This upsurge of interest is a natural result of the pressures I have already described. If new capacity costs much more than the existing plant, then one way of reducing the pressures is to cut the need for new capacity by cutting peak demands, since they are the ones that determine the need for capacity. Some of the discussion, both pro and con, about peak-load pricing makes it appear too large an element in the overall problem of matching future supply and de-

---

[7] The separation of capacity and energy charges for many customers of energy transportation and distribution utilities might also be thought of in this light, but is probably better considered as a means of splitting capacity costs and variable costs, which would be worth doing whatever the shape of the long-run total cost curve.

[8] For examples, see Grainger (1976) and Malko and Stipanuk (1976) in recent issues of *Public Utilities Fortnightly* and eight articles in the two 1976 issues of *The Bell Journal of Economics.*

mand in the regulated industries. It should be regarded as one element in a broader strategy of getting utility prices to reflect marginal social costs.

Let me explain how it could fit in. Suppose that a system had been established in which prices for the last units purchased were equated to the long-run marginal costs of the utility's service. Off-peak discounts (and peak-time premia) could then be used if their use reduced total costs by more than total revenues. The excess revenues thereby generated reflect the benefits of fuller average utilization of fixed plant, and hence, represent a reduction in long-run marginal costs that should be reflected in the level of utility rates. The same should be true for any set of price variations that promises to lower the total costs of the system, even if, as some critics of peak-load pricing have noted, the consequent reduction in prices could lead to more energy being used in total than if peak-load pricing had not been instituted. What peak-load pricing can do, if applied in the right places, and after prior experimentation to prove its efficiency, is lower the overall unit costs of energy. This lowering of costs *should* lead to more energy being used than in the absence of the system improvement, just as the recent increases in the costs of new capacity should lead to substantial cuts in energy use when they are properly reflected in utility rate structures.

Load management (i.e., non-price rationing at peak periods) by the utility can be viewed as a supplement to peak-load pricing, or sometimes as a replacement for it, with each having an edge in certain circumstances. Load management would seem to be the most effective way of smoothing very short-term fluctuations of demand or supply if the load management techniques are good enough that the standard of service does not materially decline. If the standard would decline materially and frequently, then the shortfall circumstances should be signalled to the customers by means of peak-load pricing, thus permitting the customers' own load management efforts to supplement or replace those of the utility.

From this lengthy excursion on rate structures, I return to consider the other three factors that, in addition to the declining block feature, led to the revenue, rate, and service pressures on regulated utilities.

Inflation Combined With Historic Cost Accounting

This aspect of the problem is not unique to regulated utilities, but is especially important in regulated industries that use historic cost accounting as the sole basis for price-setting. There are two issues here. One is an accounting problem, involving the appropriate allocation of expenses when the length of the measuring rod (i.e., the price of money, equal to the inverse of the general price level for goods and services) is changing. It would not be appropriate, in this general survey paper, to get into the intricacies of alternative methods of accounting for inflation. In broad terms, however, if cost recovery and allocation were done in real terms, so as to allocate the real value of initial expenditure, then general inflation would not create any difference between the accounting charges for the use of old and new plant.[9]

The second issue is concerned with the *rate* of inflation rather than the level of prices, and relates to interest rates. One of the major assests of old utilities is in fact to be found on the liability side of their balance sheets—old long-term debt issued at interest rates in some cases only one-half as high as current rates. The long-term interest rates of ten or fifteen years ago included an inflationary premium relating to the next ten or twenty years. That premium was, in retrospect, much too small, while today's may even be too large. The net effect of the old debt is to reduce the cost (net of interest and debt repayment charges) of old plant relative to new plant. This adds to the difference between the accounting cost of old plant and the marginal cost of new plant, thus making it harder to find rates that fulfill the double role of allocating marginal costs and distributing the benefits from old plant.

Rate Base Accounting Involving Straight-line Depreciation

The usual method of rate base accounting involves payment by users of a capital charge that comprises an allowed return on the established rate base plus straight-line depreciation of initial expenditure. Putting aside the effects of inflation, this method of charging users means that initial users pay the highest charge, with continually smaller payments as each year passes. To give an example, if a generating plant costs $1 million, is to be amortized over twenty years, and has an allowed rate of return of 5 percent (remember, I am excluding the effects of inflation at this point), then the return on rate base, plus depreciation, would be just under $100 thousand in the first year, dropping to about $55 thousand in the last year. If the conventional method were applied in times of inflation, the charge would decline even faster. At a 10 percent rate of return, the charge would drop from $150 thousand in the first year to $60 thousand in the last year. And if prices in general had been rising at 5 percent per year, as suggested by the high interest rate, then by the tenth year of the life of the generating station, the annual capital charge for the old station would be about $100 thousand compared to about $190 thousand for a plant purchased new in that year. Even abstracting from inflation, and using a 5 percent interest rate, the capital charge on a new generator would be one-third higher than on a ten-year old generator.

The net effect of the rate base method, when combined with straight-line depreciation, is, therefore, to increase the apparent cost of using new plant relative to old plant even when the two are of equivalent efficiency. By reducing the amount of charges on old plant, and correspondingly increasing the charges on new plant, this method creates an apparent difference between the average cost of old plant and the cost of new plant *even if* the cost of new plant is appropriately measured as the discounted present value of all

---

[9] The use of accounting methods that allocate the real cost of old assets is not the same as using replacement cost accounting, because of possible changes in relative prices.

costs over its lifetime.

Alternative methods are available. The simplest procedure would be to levy a capital charge (comprising both interest and principal) that was constant in each year of the asset's useful life. With this fairly minor adjustment, one fairly major source of discord between old and new users could be removed. Some utilities have used it in the past, and it may perhaps be used now in some jurisdictions.[10] To be even more effective, the annual charges should be set level in real terms, to avoid a similar problem reappearing through the effects of general inflation.[11]

Rising Real Costs of Supply

The three preceding factors related to factors that made the costs of using old facilities seem less than the costs of new facilities. This final factor raises the possibility that, even after all accounting and rate structure adjustments have been made, some regulated utilities may be operating under conditions of decreasing returns to scale. More precisely, the possibility is that the increasing real cost of renewable and non-renewable inputs may more than offset future increases in the efficiency with which these factors are combined. The prime candidates for this condition are the electrical utilities, which are facing simultaneously the increasing scarcity of low-cost hydro sites, increases in the perceived values of alternative uses for those sites, manyfold increases in the market value of fossil fuels, and widespread skepticism about the full costs and risks of nuclear generation. At the other end of the spectrum, telecommunications probably has a right to expect extensive technical developments, and extensive application of already known technology, that will reduce the real costs of telecommunications and also broaden the range of services that these utilities can provide.

I have now completed my description of the four factors that have jointly brought about some of the major current and future economic and political problems of the regulated utilities. I have hinted in passing at what I think to be the most promising methods of attacking these problems, but some reiteration may be useful.

ATTACKING THE PROBLEMS

The main pricing principle, for a utility that needs to maintain financial integrity and customer satisfaction, should be that increases in demand should be sold at prices (meaning, in effect, the tailing blocks of all rate schedules) that cover the full long-term marginal costs of that supply.[12] The

---

[10] Canadian Western Natural Gas used this method, with the approval of the Public Utilities Board, for many years prior to 1940.

[11] The details of the method have been worked out, and applied to data from a B.C. natural gas transmission and distribution company in Helliwell and Lester (1975).

[12] The implications of such a rule for long-run planning were first thoroughly explored for the electricity supplies of France (for example, Boiteux and Stasi, 1964) and Great Britain (Turvey, 1968).

adjective "full" is there to ensure that all environmental costs and values for alternative uses of resources should be explicitly included, and "long-term" emphasizes that so-called fixed as well as variable costs must be included. A recent major study submitted to the Ontario Energy Board by Ontario Hydro (1976) recommends rate structure revisions designed to be more consistent with the marginal cost principle. The 1977 hearings before the Ontario Energy Board are the first large-scale public assessment of these principles in a Canadian setting. One of the key open issues is how opportunity costs ought to be handled in the calculation of marginal costs. Using electricity as an example, the marginal costs of capacity and energy ought to comprise the highest costs for each within the grid network. Does that mean that every jurisdiction in Canada ought to charge the same price for energy? Subject to limitations of grid capacity, and taking account of power losses in transport, the answer from either an economic free-trader or a conservationist must be "yes." Doubts may be expressed by those who wish to use low-cost power as a spur to industrial growth, and would rather use it for a lower-valued purpose at home than export it at a higher price for use elsewhere in Canada or in the United States. These doubters must recognize that there may be substantial waste in this form of subsidy, as well as subsequent recriminations by firms when rates are eventually forced up by the more costly expansion required by the extra demand.

Another issue is posed by the links between energy trade and local self-sufficiency. If Ontario charges North America-wide prices for its power, and exports any power that is temporarily surplus to its needs, are dependencies thereby created that would make it difficult to reduce the flow when the surplus no longer existed? The speed with which the so-called 'Northern Tier' of the United States built up a dependence on Canadian crude oil provides a useful case in point.

To the extent that trading potential is excluded on one basis or another, then the area for defining marginal costs is reduced. Within a more fragmented set of jurisdictions, there will naturally be a range of marginal costs, one appropriate for each jurisdiction. If these differ very much, then they provide some measure of the possibilities for mutually advantageous trade. The full advantages of using larger areas to define marginal costs are only to be obtained, of course, if all jurisdictions adopt pricing rules that properly reflect the common marginal cost. If they do not, then there are efficiency losses which may be supplemented by resentment in a 'conserving' region that exports to a region with 'wasteful' rate making practices.

Turning from broad questions of principle to more practical considerations, it is unlikely that suitable pricing practices would be adopted even for all energy utilities within a province, let alone across all provinces. For this reason, and also because of the problems of coordinating change on a large-scale basis, regulated utilities and their regulatory agencies should work in the first instance to establish consistency between marginal rates and marginal costs within their own systems, taking into account prices outside their system only where trade links exist or where current prices within the system are improper measures of social cost. For example, the marginal cost of fuel that should be used by the Nova Scotia Power Corporation in establishing its marginal rates should be the cost of imported oil landed in Nova Scotia, even if, in the short term, the cash cost of oil to the corporation is less than that amount by dint of federal subsidy.

It is quite likely that if long-term marginal cost were used for pricing all units of output of Canadian regulated utilities, there would be a revenue surplus to be distributed. If this were so, then the utilities and their regulatory agencies will have to design some method for handling the surplus in a way that is consistent with both equity and efficiency. To maintain efficency, any payments back to customers must not influence marginal prices. What is required to achieve equity is less easy to define, as the issue was probably not in the minds of those establishing regulatory rules for utilities that were presumed to have marginal costs less than average costs, and hence to need, if anything, a subsidy to cover losses rather than some procedures for distributing surpluses.

The difficulty of establishing appropriate means for distribution will depend on how big the surplus is. If the surplus is not very large, a simple credit against each customer's bill, set so as to leave initial utility bills unchanged, would avoid any perverse effects on demand.

If the surplus is large, and is distributed to old customers according to initial usage levels, then new and old customers would pay different average bills for the same service. The disadvantaged position of the new customer is shared to some extent by any customer whose demands were small at the time when the initial claims to the surplus were established. On the other hand, if new or growing customers are permitted an increased share of the surplus as their demands grow, then to that extent they are paying less than marginal cost for their new or expanded service. Hence, it becomes apparent that changes in utility bills are likely, if the surplus is large, for at least some customers if the utility is to avoid restricting the benefits to initial users and also to avoid charging less than marginal cost for new demand.

In the longer term, the issue is perhaps best settled by gradually removing the surpluses from the direct customers of the utility, so that the surpluses may be distributed more broadly without damaging the efficiency of the utility's rate structure. If, in the process, large average as well as marginal rate increases are required for some classes of user, then the changes could be phased in and accompanied by some temporary relief. Economic analysis of these redistributive issues usually suggests (e.g., Berg and Roth, 1976) that cash subsidies are more efficient than tying relief to utility use, while equity is best served by defining need more broadly than in terms of payments for utility services.

There might also be some potential for using the surpluses to help finance the investment required to reduce energy consumption. For example, the payment of the rebate might require that the user meet certain minimum standards of energy efficiency. Some of the surplus might even be held back as an investment fund from which customers could borrow to upgrade insulation, etc., with the loan and interest to be repaid out of future rebates.

A final important but often ignored implication of marginal cost pricing is that customers should be encouraged to produce as well as to conserve utility services. Thus electric utilities should stand prepared to buy surplus power from their customer's self-generation projects, and at terms that reflect the utility's marginal cost of power. Too often, the existing arrangements reflect efforts by the utility to subvert or forestall self-generation by the customers. This can be done by refusing to pay a good price for surplus power, by charging a very low price to those with self-generation possibilities, or by being less than active in dealing with the technical problems of linking outside sources to the power grid. In the present financial circumstances of the power utilities, it is to be hoped and expected that utilities and their regulators will be much more aggressive in their efforts to tap the energy generation and saving possibilities that exist among their industrial, commercial, and residential customers.

OTHER ISSUES FOR CANADIAN REGULATION

Quality of Service in the Regulated Industries

It is frequently alleged that utilities and their regulators are overly concerned with the standard of reliability of their service, so that they can avoid public criticism. This takes the form of a criticism if the amount of extra investment and operating costs required to maintain the ultra-reliable service is so great as to make it a bad buy from the point of view of the customers. On the other hand, it is sometimes alleged that regulated utilities provide a lower standard of service than their customers deserve and pay for because reductions in the standard of service provide a means of cutting costs and increasing profits without openly courting a regulatory review.

The issue of overly expensive and excessive standards of reliability is most frequently raised in the case of electric utilities, perhaps because these utilities are facing the tightest financial bind and are hence most in need of new ways of cutting costs.

The Treatment of Social Costs in Utility Planning and Pricing

It is increasingly apparent that indirect and non-financial costs are important elements in regulatory consideration of new projects, particularly in the case of hydro, thermal, and nuclear electricity generation. It is important that these risks and alternative uses should be defined more precisely, paid for, where possible, by the utilities, and included in the prices charged to customers.

Government Versus Private Ownership of Regulated Utilities

Do government-owned and privately-owned utilities operate in similar ways and with similar objectives? Can the differences in behaviour be adequately explained by the differeces in objectives? How do their cost levels compare? Are firms of both types subjected to the same type of regulatory review? If not, why not?

Consistency Across Jurisdictions

In Canada, there is a complicated criss-crossing of federal and provincial jurisdictions. This would not matter much if the principles and procedures adopted were not so often at cross purposes. However, the variety of independent jurisdictions does have one important advantage, in that there is much more chance of encouraging experimentation with alternative procedures, and more chance of getting change started. I suspect that experiments with alternative utility rate structures have been much more active in the United States, and are much more likely in Canada, than they would be if there were unified national regulatory systems in each country. [13]

Links Between Investment and Pricing Decisions.

Most utility regulation involves the setting of prices, and some involves the approval of new projects. Seldom are the two brought together and handled consistently. This inconsistency makes worse the problems outlined in the previous section. For example, an exaggerated projection of future growth (perhaps based on current rate structures with excessively low marginal rates) can be used to justify a new investment project. The new investment project, when completed, raises the utility's "revenue requirements" so that price increases are subsequently permitted, leading to demand growth that falls below expectations. The failure of demand to grow as fast as forecast means that revenues once again fall below costs, and another rate increase follows. The final result of this sort of vicious circle is that the utility tends to have more plant than it should, and hence to have average costs that are needlessly high. To get out of the vicious circle, it is important that regulatory agencies should ensure that the demand growth forecasts used to justify new projects are consistent with well-designed rate structures that adequately reflect marginal costs.

The Scale, Costs, and Efficiency of Regulation

Regulation is increasing in scale and cost, yet there are few mechanisms whereby its efficiency and usefulness can be checked. Who regulates the regulators? How often is regulatory performance monitored, and procedures assessed to see if they meet current needs? Are there any procedures available to close down agencies that are no longer needed, to reform those that are doing the wrong things, and to spruce up those that are doing the right things in a slack or inefficient manner? Should there be? If so how should these reviews be established, and whose interests should be represented?

----

[13] For a survey of recent U.S. developments in electric rate structures, see Smith (1976).

REFERENCES

Atkinson, S.E. and R. Halvorsen (1976) "Automatic Adjustment Clauses and Input Choice in Regulated Utilities" Discussion Paper No. 76-9, June (Seattle: University of Washington, Institute for Economic Research).

Averch, J. and L.L. Johnson (1962) "Behavior of the Firm under Regulatory Constraint" *American Economic Review* 52, December 1053-69.

Bailey, Elizabeth E. (1973) *Economic Theory of Regulatory Constraint* (Lexington: D.C. Heath).

Berg, S.V. and W.E. Roth (1976) "Some Remarks on Residential Electricity Consumption and Social Rate Restructuring" *The Bell Journal Of Economics* 7: Autumn, 690-700.

Boiteux, M. and P. Stasi (1964) "The Determination of Costs of Expansion in an Interconnected System of Production and Distribution of Electricity" in J. Nelson (ed) *Marginal Cost Pricing in Practice* (Englewood Cliffs, N.J.: Prentice-Hall).

Breton, Albert (1974) *The Economic Theory Of Representative Government* (London: Macmillan).

Breton, Albert (1976) *The Regulation of Private Economic Activity* (Montreal: C.D. Howe Research Institute).

Callen, J., G.F. Mathewson and H. Mohring (1976) "The Benefits and Costs of Rate of Return Regulation" *American Economic Review* 66: June, 290-97.

Courville, L. (1974) "Regulation and Efficiency in the Electric Utility Industry" *The Bell Journal of Economics and Management Science* 5: Autumn, 53-74.

Dobell, A.R. *et al.* (1972) "Telephone Communications in Canada: Demand, Production, and Investment Demand" *The Bell Journal of Economics and Management Science* 3: Spring, 175-219.

Grainger, G.H. (1976) "A Practical Approach to Peak-load Pricing" *Public Utilities Fortnightly* September 9, 19-23.

Helliwell, J. and J. Lester (1975) "A New Approach to Price Setting for Regulated Pipelines" *The Logistics and Transportation Review* 11: 320-37.

Joskow, Paul L. and Paul W. MacAvoy (1976) "Regulation and the Financial Condition of the Electric Power Companies in the 1970s" *American Economic Review* 65: May, 295-301.

Klevorick, A.K. (1971) "The 'Optimal' Fair Rate of Return" *The Bell Journal of Economics and Management Science* 2: Spring, 122-53.

M. & M. Systems (1975) *Energy Regulation Study: Reports One and Two* (Edmonton: Energy Regulation Study).

Malko, J.R. and D. Stipanuk (1976) "Electric Peak-load Pricing: A Wisconson Framework" *Public Utilities Fortnightly* July 15, 33-37.

Ontario Hydro (1976) *Electricity Costing and Pricing Study* (Toronto: Ontario Hydro).

Peles, Y.C. and J.L. Stein (1976) "The Effect of Rate of Return Regulation Is Highly Sensitive to the Nature of the Uncertainty" *American Economic Review* 66: June, 278-89.

Peterson, H.C. (1975) "An Empirical Test of Regulatory Effects" *The Bell Journal of Economics and Management Science* 6: Spring, 111-26.

Posner, R.A. (1974) "Theories of Economic Regulation" *The Bell Journal of Economics and Management Science* 5: Autumn, 335-58.

Samuelson, P.A. and A.D. Scott (1975) *Economics* (Toronto: McGraw-Hill Ryerson).

Sherman, Roger (1976) "Curing Regulatory Bias in U.S. Public Utilities" *Journal of Economics and Business* 29: Fall, 1-9.

Sheshinski, E. (1971) "Welfare Aspects of a Regulatory Constraint: Note" *American Economic Review* 61: March, 175-78.

Smith, Robert (1976) "The Developing Direction of Electric Rate Structures" *Public Utilities Fortnightly* August 26, 28-32.

Spann, R.M. (1974) "Rate of Return Regulation and Efficiency in Production: An Empirical Test of the Averch-Johnson Thesis" *The Bell Journal of Economics and Management Science* 5: Autumn, 38-52.

Stigler, George J. (1971) "The Theory of Economic Regulation" *The Bell Journal of Economics and Management Science* 2: Spring, 3-21.

Stigler, George J. (1975) *The Citizen and the State: Essays on Regulation* (Chicago: University of Chicago Press).

Turvey, R. (1968) *Optimal Pricing and Investment in Electricity Supply* (Cambridge, Mass.: MIT Press).

Chapter Four

Self-Regulation and the Canadian Air Transportation Administration: The Case of Pickering Airport

by *Sandford F. Borins*
Graduate School of Management
Northwestern University

INTRODUCTION

When economists write about government regulation, they do it as the severest of critics. The basis of this criticism is the belief, grounded in welfare economics, that social welfare is maximized where freely competitive markets are allowed to operate, and that government intervention in specific markets is justified only because of natural monopolies or pervasive externalities. This belief is the basis for economists' criticisms of such regulatory bodies as marketing boards, the Canadian Transport Commission (CTC), rent control offices, and the Anti-Inflation Board.

Economists have been equally critical of the behaviour of self-regulated or Cabinet-regulated nationalized industries. This paper will deal with one such nationalized industry, the Canadian airports industry. All major Canadian airports are owned, constructed, and operated by the Canadian Air Transportation Administration (CATA), a powerful branch of Transport Canada.[1] The book value of CATA's portfolio of airports is 3 billion 1978 dollars. In fiscal year 1978-79, CATA will employ over 12,000 people and spend a total budgetary and non-budgetary allocation of over $600 million. CATA will take in revenues of $132 million for user fees and $60 million for the travel tax.

A measure of the opprobrium in which CATA is held by professional economists is seen in the result of a poll taken by Professor S.L. Warner in 1974, which asked a sample of Canadian economists whether they agreed or disagreed with the resolution that "A new Toronto International Airport (the

[1] This article is based in part on numerous conversations with CATA personnel in the course of the author's research on his dissertation (Borins, 1976) and his teaching at Carleton University. The author wishes to thank William Stanbury, John Baldwin, and Blair Baldwin for their comments on a draft of this article. Of course, the author alone is responsible for the views presented here.

Pickering Airport) should be built before the year 2000.'' Warner worded the resolution so as to increase its support since one could agree with the resolution, while nevertheless disagreeing with CATA, which wanted to build the airport as soon as possible. A sample of 159 economists who were given only the resolution *opposed* construction of Pickering by 50 to 18 percent, with 32 percent undecided. A larger sample of 567 economists, who were given briefs for and against the proposition sided overwhelmingly (68 to 24 percent) with the view that Pickering should not be built.[2]

The essence of economists' criticisms of nationalized industries is that they are inefficient. Two models which typify economic thinking about nationalized industries are the Averch-Johnson model of a regulated utility (Averch and Johnson, 1962) and Niskanen's (1971) model of a bureau. In the Averch-Johnson model a profit-maximizing utility is held by the regulator to a fair rate of return on capital: if that rate exceeds the firm's cost of capital, it will be excessively and wastefully capital-intensive. In the Niskanen model, the objective of the bureau is to maximize its budget subject to the constraint that the budget be equal to or greater than the minimum total cost of producing the output. Unfortunately, these models have inspired too little empirical work for us to draw definitive conclusions as to whether nationalized industries are less efficient than the same sort of industry lodged in the private sector. Furthermore, economists should accept the fact that few, if any, nationalized industries are going to be de-nationalized and should therefore devote their efforts to improving efficiency in those nationalized industries that *actually* are inefficient. In order to do this it is necessary to have better knowledge of how nationalized industries operate, so that we can identify and influence the key variables that determine their behaviour.

This article is an attempt to look at the decisions of the CATA, our nationalized airports industry, in the planning of the second Toronto International Airport at Pickering, and to ask why these decisions were made. My explanation looks at forces both external to CATA and emanating from within CATA. My objective is to use the Pickering story, as a case study, to understand how CATA operates.

The article begins with a history of the Pickering Airport proposal up to 1975, when the Province of Ontario vetoed the project by refusing to provide access roads. This is followed by a discussion of CATA's behaviour as an

---

[2] Professor Warner's study, which was supported by the Centre for Transportation Studies of the University of Toronto and York University, sampled from economics faculty members at Canadian universities and readers of the *Canadian Journal of Economics*. The poll was part of a study in advocacy planning, which is a method developed by Warner of providing information to decision-makers. In this study two teams of economists prepared briefs both for and against the airport. The part of the sample receiving briefs was divided into four groups, each group receiving a different combination of a pro and a con brief. This procedure allowed Warner to separate out the influence of the debating skills of the two teams from the basic distribution of opinion held by the sample. In this case, it was clear that the sample opposed Pickering, and that the information strengthened the opposition. The methodology is discussed in detail in Warner (1975).

organization, as exemplified by the Pickering story. Then a new set of external pressures which led to the Province's veto are discussed, and implications for CATA's future behaviour are explored.

THE HISTORY OF PICKERING[3]

In the mid-1960s the demand for air travel to and from Toronto was growing at rates greater than CATA[4] had anticipated; consequently airport facilities at Malton (the main Toronto airport) were approaching capacity before CATA had expected. In response to what was perceived as a capacity problem, CATA hired John B. Parkin Associates to prepare a study about expanding facilities at Malton. The answer Parkin Associates (1967) reported to CATA in November 1967 was that CATA should acquire some 3000 acres of land adjacent to the western edge of Malton to provide for new runways, terminals and ground access. This acquisition would bring Malton from its present 4200 acres to a size equivalent to O'Hare airport in Chicago, the world's busiest. This would provide ample room for the rest of the century. The report also counselled immediate coordination with the provincial and local governments to ensure land-use compatibility near the airport. The Cabinet approved the Parkin plan, subject to provincial and municipal agreement. This was announced by Paul Hellyer, then federal Minister of Transport, in August 1968.

The federal and Ontario governments were rather surprised to see that this innocuous proposal provoked heated opposition from local area residents, who organized the Society for Airport Noise Abatement (SANA), and from the area municipalities, whose development plans would be upset by the zoning changes required to accommodate the enlarged ariport. One would also expect that land developers who held parcels near the airport which could no longer be used residentially, or which would bring lower returns because of the noise, expressed their opposition quietly. Furthermore, the Cabinet had decided in July 1968 that Montreal would get a second airport (which later became known as Mirabel). It seems likely that the large contingent of Toronto area M.P.'s, casting their eyes on Montreal, which had been a recipient of so much federal largesse, demanded that Toronto also receive a new airport. The federal government in December 1968 reversed itself and decided not to expropriate additional land near Malton. Hellyer announced that CATA, with the co-operation of the Government of Ontario, would be seeking a site for a second airport, to be constructed as soon as possible.

---

[3] The official CATA version of the story can be found in TAAP (1974f, pp. 5-69). Opponent versions of the story are Godfrey and Massey (1972) and Budden and Ernst (1973).

[4] The Canadian Air Transportation Administration was not organized in its present structure until the early 1970s. This was done by pulling together various branches of the Ministry of Transport which were responsible for the air mode (for example, Airport Services, Civil Aeronautics). As these branches were the forerunners and component parts of CATA, I will refer to decisions and policies before the early 1970s as CATA decisions and policies.

What followed was a three-year search for a second airport site. CATA and its consultants did the actual searching. At the bureaucratic and political levels, representatives of the Government of Ontario expressed their reactions to the various sites CATA was examining. Throughout the search period, the CATA position was consistently that the new airport should be built on a large site, that it should be in a lightly populated area so as to minimize noise disruption, and that it should be as close to airport users as possible.[5] The Government of Ontario consistently evaluated airport sites in terms of the support they would provide for the Toronto-Centred Region Plan, which was first presented publicly by Premier Robarts in May 1970. The plan, entitled *Design for Development,* emphasized the importance of controlling the sprawling growth which was occurring to the west of Toronto, and stimulating planned growth to the east of Toronto (Government of Ontario, 1970). The report stated the Province's attitude to the airport in the following way:

> The location of a new international airport to serve Southwestern Ontario would be of most crucial significance to the future spatial pattern of the Toronto-Centred Region . . . The integrity of the Development Concept requires that a site be chosen which does not add a powerful magnet for development in a location which conflicts with the strategic components of the plan (Government of Ontario, 1970, p. 23).

Ultimately, the Pickering site emerged as something of a compromise between federal and provincial preferences. Of all the sites on the short list, the province most preferred the one farthest east, at Lake Scugog, some sixty miles east of downtown Toronto. CATA preferred the sites at Orangeville (northwest of Toronto), Campbellville (west of Toronto), and Beverly Township (southwest of Toronto) because they were all close to the future airport's users, referred to by CATA as the "travelling public." Each side preferred the other's favourite site or sites least. Pickering was the compromise. From the provincial point of view, it was slightly to the east of Toronto; from CATA's point of view, it was closer to the users than the Province's favourite. The ultimate compromise was worked out at the political level between Don Jamieson, then Minister of Transport, and Darcy McKeough, then Provincial Treasurer of Ontario.

When the choice of the Pickering site was publicly announced in March

---

[5] In 1970, part of the airport planning team investigated the possibility of constructing additional terminals and runways on the present Malton site. This part of the team produced two reports favourable to this option. The CATA version of the story makes it clear that this proposal was reviewed by outside consultants (Hans Blumenfeld, the firm of Kates, Peat, Marwick), sharply criticized, and ultimately rejected in August or September 1970. Following that, the names on the memoranda changed, and Kates, Peat, Marwick began to play an increasingly prominent role in the planning process. My hypothesis is that the rejection of this proposal led to a "purge" of the original project team, and its replacement with one dominated by Kates, Peat, Marwick personnel. In addition, there was a change in Deputy Ministers and a general reorganization of the Department of Transport into the Ministry of Transport. This turning to new advisors may have reflected the overall reorganization.

1972, an opposition group, People or Planes (POP), sprang up in Pickering to lead opposition to the planned expropriation of 17,000 acres for the airport. POP allied itself with numerous ratepayer, anti-pollution, and naturalist groups in opposition to the airport, and presented its position as one of opposition to "mindless growth," pollution, and the destruction of farm land.

In August 1972, just before the federal general election was called, (which was held on October 30 and resulted in a minority Liberal government), the federal government responded to its chorus of critics by agreeing to appoint a judicial inquiry to look at the need for the airport. The three-person Airport Inquiry Commission was finally appointed in October 1973 and hearings which involved a great deal of technical presentation by both CATA and POP were held between February and June 1974. The Commission reported to Cabinet in December 1974 and fundamentally accepted CATA's position (Airport Inquiry Commission, 1974). The Commission's Report was made public in January 1975. Following a few more weeks of debate both within and outside the government, Cabinet decided to approve CATA's plan to proceed with the land expropriation and begin construction of the new airport in the summer or fall of 1975.

In addition to the political story of the Pickering airport, there is also the bureaucratic story. CATA invested many man-years and dollars in airport planning, and it is important to look at what the foot-soldiers were doing day after day for six years when the politicians' interest in the issue was occasional and fleeting. This large investment in planning stands out as something of a contrast to the more cursory planning undertaken for most airport expansions in previous years, and is typical of the expansion in research and policy analysis activities which occurred throughout the entire federal bureaucracy in the early 1970s.

At first, work on the airport was done at CATA headquarters in Ottawa. After the "purge" of the original project team (see footnote 5 above), a new team was reconstituted in Toronto, and known as the Toronto Area Airports Project (TAAP). This team worked closely with the management consulting firm of Kates, Peat, Marwick, which was also located in Toronto, and many personnel from Kates, Peat, Marwick were simply seconded to TAAP.

The planning work done prior to the choice of the Pickering site dealt with some issues in detail, and others quite cursorily. Air travel demand forecasts were judgmental. The planners decided that air travel would continue to grow rapidly for the rest of the century, but less rapidly than during the 1960s. One forecast, which had the level of originating-terminating passenger traffic through Toronto growing from 5.2 million passengers per annum in 1970 to 48 million passengers per annum in 2000,[6] was used as the basis for all facility planning. The impact of aircraft noise was also not examined at length. Sites were simply constrained to be in unpopulated areas,

---

[6] This implies an average annual rate of increase of 10 percent.

and this was measured by counting the present population within a five-mile radius of the site.

More detailed work was done on physical planning, to ensure that airports could be built at each site examined. Also the costs of building at the different sites were estimated. The issue that mattered most to the project team, users' ground access cost, was examined in detail at this stage in the analysis (TAAP, 1972). Based on studies of the urban origination and destination points of the flying public, the planning team estimated passengers' ground access dollar and time costs for each site through to the year 2000. Given the variety of airport locations, there were substantial differences among the various sites.

Later work by the planning team shifted to a number of other areas. A 6etailed air travel propensity model was constructed, to predict travel demand scientifically (TAAP, 1974c). Noise contours for a myriad of patterns of aircraft operations were generated to examine the impact of aircraft noise for alternative assignments of traffic to the two airports (TAAP, 1974a). The facility planning work was carried on in more detail. This involved estimation of peak-hour flows through various parts of the new airport, and planning the facilities required to handle these flows (TAAP, 1974b). This exercise also involved detailed work on which types of flights would be assigned to each airport (TAAP, 1974e). Finally, the costing of facilities was treated in much greater detail (TAAP, 1973b). All of this work was scrutinized by the opponents of Pickering and defended by the Project team throughout the hearings of the Airport Inquiry Commission.

To understand the behaviour of CATA and the Toronto Area Airports Project group throughout this period, it is necessary to look at the pressures acting on the organization.

CATA'S ENVIRONMENT

It must be understood that the business of building airports is one that is fraught with great uncertainty. There are uncertainties about the future demand for air travel, about the sizes and noise-generating characteristics of future aircraft, and about future technology for handling aircraft. Decisions to choose a certain site for an airport, or to build a certain type of terminal are far-reaching decisions, and their consequences will be felt for a long time. Such decisions are irreversible—for example, tearing up a poorly designed terminal is impossible. Also, the lead times for such decisions are very long; for example, it is difficult to plan and build a major terminal in less than five years. Lead times themselves are uncertain, due to the delays which might be encountered in getting Treasury Board and Cabinet approval and in managing the construction of major projects. As a result, airport planners constantly run the risks of either building too soon, and providing excess capacity, or building too late, and causing congestion. As discussed above, in the mid-1960s, CATA underestimated demand at Toronto, built too late, and experienced several years of unexpectedly long queues in Terminal 1 before Terminal 2 was ready.

We will now examine a number of external sources of influence upon CATA. These sources, by their pressure, set the implicit prices to CATA of building too soon or too late and of adding to old airports or starting new ones.

To begin with, CATA is a federal Crown agency, and as such is responsible to the Minister of Transport. Those who are dissatisfied with CATA's performance can complain to the Minister privately, or attempt to embarrass him publicly. The Minister must appear to be responsive to groups who can harm his image in the press or on the floor of the House of Commons. Some of the groups with which CATA must deal are people who live near existing airports and complain about aircraft noise, airlines which can complain about the facilities provided by CATA and the fees charged, the general aviation lobby (small planes owned by individuals and corporations) which can also complain about the fees it is paying and the service it is receiving, and the "travelling public," who, while not formally organized, can write angry letters about facilities and service at Canadian airports. Unlike private corporations, whose effectiveness is primarily measured in terms of their profitability, CATA's effectiveness is probably measured by the Minister in terms of the absence of complaints by airport users and neighbours and in terms of his public (and political) image as a competent manager of his portfolio. [7]

One reason we might expect CATA to be very responsive to the "gripes" of the air transport industry is that so many CATA people have been involved in it. For pilots, both civilian and military, air traffic controllers, radar operators and others, a job with CATA is seen as the logical next step after one's years of active duty. Furthermore, a great proportion of CATA people have pilots' licences, and continue to fly as a hobby, and therefore understand first-hand many of the concerns of the general aviation lobby.

Any government agency's ability to satisfy the demands of its clients is constrained by its budget. Unlike the private corporation, CATA's capital expenditures are not funded through accumulated profits or capital market borrowing. CATA stands in a bureau-sponsor relationship with the Treasury Board, the alleged protector of the public purse. If CATA (through its Minister) can convince the Treasury Board that tax revenues should be invested in airports, then the monies will be forthcoming. The task of persuading the Treasury Board involves demonstrating to it that greater expenditures are the answer to the complaints made by airport users, and that responding to these complaints is politically more important than responding to the pressures of other groups in society.

In the 1960s and early 1970s, CATA was very successful in getting funds

---

[7] A similar concept is Neustadt's observation that two major elements of Presidential power are a President's professional reputation and public prestige (Neustadt, 1960).

from the Treasury Board. This was partially because air travel, as a mass consumption good, came of age in Canada during that period, partially because massive airports were perceived by most cities as a source of considerable civic pride, and partially because CATA was able to convince the politicians that congested airports were an affront to the federal government.

One budgetary reform in recent years has been the creation in 1970 of an Airports Revolving Fund for Montreal, Toronto, and Vancouver International Airports, which are supposed to be self-financing in accordance with the "user pay" principle. This fund, however, provides the appearance of budgetary change, but not the reality. To begin with, the Fund was not required to pay the substantial capital cost of the facilities which had been put in place prior to its establishment; thus it was, at first, a user pay policy limited to operating cost. For new facilities such as Mirabel or Pickering, Treasury Board approval is still necessary before any money can be spent. If approval is given, the Treasury Board charges the Fund interest at a rate of 8 percent regardless of the market rate. However, since it is an intra-governmental charge, interest need not be paid in real dollars. Whether or not the users ever will pay for the capital cost of Mirabel (or Pickering) is still an unresolved question since the government can always decide to forgive the interest charges.[8] This financial structure is very different from that of airport authorities in the U.S. (such as the Port Authority of New York and New Jersey) which are free to go to the capital market whenever they choose, but are obligated to pay off their debts in real dollars.

Economists would think that the proper way to trade off the desires of CATA's "clients" (which ultimately are demands for resources) and the cost of capital is through benefit-cost analysis. CATA's policy is not made that way. Decisions about when to add new capital are based on a set of physical standards that define the minimum acceptable performance of the airport system in terms of such things as the speed with which traffic (which, in different contexts, means people or automobiles or aircraft) flows through a given facility. These standards have taken on the sanctity of Standard Operating Procedures (SOPs), and very infrequently are questioned. They are the preserve of the civil engineers who plan and build airports, and whose education has been in terms of design standards, not resource tradeoffs. Technical, not economic, efficiency is the objective, within the broad political parameters.

In order to apply their standards, CATA planners must make predictions about the uncertain future, attempting to guess how decisions taken today will look in five, ten or even more years, depending on which alternative future comes about. To do this, they must anticipate the responses of the travelling public, the airlines, the general aviation lobby, the environmen-

---

[8] Feldman and Milch (1977, pp. 38-39) report an interview with Walter McLeish, Administrator of CATA, in which McLeish says that the small steps taken in the direction of cost-recovery have generated considerable tension within CATA and that CATA does not expect to recover all costs in the foreseeable future.

talists, the anti-noise lobby, and the Treasury Board. This awareness of future consequences is probably heightened by the tendency of CATA people, unlike the generalists who staff many other ministries, to stay in CATA for most of their careers. Therefore, they *can* be held responsible for yesterday's errors (in theory at least).

EXPLAINING CATA'S BEHAVIOUR

This section applies the themes developed in the previous section—uncertainty, pressure group influence, financial control, and the professional background of CATA staff—to explain several aspects of CATA's behaviour in the Pickering story. Each aspect is posed as a question which our hypothetical economist might ask. Why didn't CATA attack the Malton capacity problem with peak-load pricing, rather than a new airport? Why did CATA planners approach their analytical task in the particular way they did? Why didn't CATA attempt to get full use out of the Malton site before recommending a new airport?

Why is There No Peak-load Pricing of Airports?

For an economist, the obvious solution to the problem of facilities which, like airports, are crowded at some times of the day and empty at others is the imposition of peak-load pricing, to spread demand throughout the day and thereby reduce and delay the requirements for additional capacity. At present, the two major airport fees CATA charges are the passenger ticket tax (8 percent of the ticket price up to a maximum of $8) and the landing fees charged the aircraft. Each of these could be assessed on a time-of-day basis without too much administrative difficulty by using the scheduled arrival and/or departure time of the flight. If the airport congestion is a matter of congestion on the access roads and in the parking lots at the airport, parking fees could also be based on the time of day. In short, CATA seems to have at its disposal enough policy instruments that it could launch an attack on the peaking problem through pricing.

Landing fees are presently charged on the basis of the weight of the aircraft and type of flight. They can vary from $1.30 for a small Cessna to $600 for a Boeing 747 on a transoceanic flight (CATA, 1976). Though a small plane uses the runway for half the time a commercial airliner uses it, the small plane pays a landing fee which is a minute fraction of that paid by the airliner. This landing fee schedule therefore does nothing to discourage the small aircraft from using the airport during the times of day when commercial aircraft traffic is busiest.

The landing fee schedule in use is basically a "value-of-service" pricing system. Among common carriers, domestic traffic is charged the least, transborder traffic more, and international traffic the most. Culley (1972, p. 19) calculated cost margins for various types of commercial flights, and found, as expected, that direct aircraft operating costs are 50 percent of revenue for domestic flights, 47 percent for transborder flights, and 38 percent for international flights. I would interpret this landing fee schedule as an attempt by CATA to raise a given amount of revenue while at the same time minimizing the "griping" from its client groups. Griping can be expected when a client group can no longer make use of the airport because it has been priced away from it. Conversely, as long as a group can still afford to use the airport after a fee increase, the legitimacy of its gripe is diminished. A policy of gripe minimization is, of course, identical to a policy of value-of-service pricing. Those to whom the use of the airport is worth most pay the most. An example of how this policy has worked was the response to the Treasury Board's mandate to CATA to bring in an extra $22 million in airport fees as part of the economic restraint program announced by then Treasury Board President Jean Chrétien on December 18, 1975 (Treasury Board, 1975). Landing fees were simply raised by 30 percent across the board.

Another consideration in landing fee policy is that landing fees for domestic flights must be kept low because poor financial performance of the domestic industry, particularly the federally owned Air Canada, is an embarrassment to the federal government, and especially to CATA. Since there are foreign competitors to Air Canada and Canadian Pacific on all transborder and international but on no domestic routes, the most efficient way to aid the domestic industry is by keeping fees low on domestic flights.

What would peak-load pricing do that CATA's clients wouldn't like? First of all, prices based on the time required to take off or land ("a second is a second" for any user) would completely discourage general aviation from Toronto airport at busy times of day, because these fees would rise from their present miniscule level to over $100.[9] Needless to say, this would have the general aviation lobby up in arms. When talking about the general aviation problem with CATA people, their answer is that they are aware of the peaking problem and general aviation's contribution to it. Nevertheless, they say that they would prefer not to deal with it by pricing, but rather to handle it by discretion, namely with the air traffic controller either permitting the plane to land, or discouraging it from landing. I would interpret this as an example of regulator's general preference for discretion rather than rules. Peak-load pricing is seen as a hard-and-fast rule which upsets the relationship between controller and pilot; CATA people would rather work out the peaking problem "within the family." On February 6, 1978, Walter McLeish, Administrator of CATA, informed the Parliamentary Committee on Transport and Communications that CATA does not intend to charge peak-period landing fees for general aviation at Malton. At the same time, CATA gave regional air traffic controllers discretionary power to restrict or prohibit aircraft flying under visual flight rules (that is, most general aviation) from using seven major Canadian airports (Dorval, Mirabel, Vancouver, Ed-

---

[9] Rose and Hamilton (1976, p. 49) simulated a marginal cost pricing scheme for Malton airport and found that a general aviation aircraft using the airport during the busy period should be charged $134 to land or $117 to take off. This is only slightly less than the charges they would assess commercial aircraft, $156 to land and $134 to take off.

monton, Calgary, Winnipeg, and Toronto). These restrictions, which were justified for safety reasons, may be defined quite broadly—in terms of the time of day, communications equipment on the aircraft, and/or qualifications of the pilot.

If peak-load pricing were adopted for Toronto and other busy Canadian airports such as Dorval (Montreal) and Vancouver, airlines would undoubtedly have to bear some transition costs as they adjust their schedules and aircraft utilization patterns. The airlines could find the transition costs great if it forces them to mothball some aircraft and acquire others. We can expect that CATA would be hesitant to impose these transition costs which disturb the quiet lives and present standard operating procedures of the airlines. This hesitancy is probably reinforced at the present time by the poor financial health of the Canadian carriers.[10]

Another problem with peak-load pricing is expressed in a typically Canadian way. Much of Malton's peaking problem comes about because of the aircraft departure-arrival cycle for transatlantic flights. These flights leave Canada between early evening and midnight, arriving in western Europe in the morning; they stay on the ground in Europe for several hours, then leave in the early afternoon, arriving in North America in the afternoon, and leave again a few hours later. It is felt by CATA that this cycle is price-inelastic, although there is not enough evidence on cross-elasticities demand throughout the day for an economist to draw this conclusion. In addition, it is felt that pricing congestion out of Toronto would simply exacerbate congestion in London, Paris, and Amsterdam. The preference expressed is to recognize peaking as a global problem and deal with it internationally. However, the British have not been willing to wait for an international agreement, and have imposed peak period surcharges at Heathrow and Gatwick since 1972.[11] The CATA response is typical of the attitude that sees Canada as a small power in international diplomatic or economic relations, and that prefers seeking international agreements to acting unilaterally.

A final reason for not having peak-load pricing is CATA's policy of building large, uncongested airports. If an airport is built to accommodate the busiest peaks, then airport capacity is not scarce and does not need to be rationed by a peak-load pricing scheme.

---

[10] Very recently their financial health has improved. Bagnall (1978, p. 16) states: " following swiftly on the heels of the worst slump in aviation history, in 1977 CP Air and Air Canada made after-tax profits of $3.3 million and $20 million, respectively, on revenue of $394 million and $1,188 million. Since each airline lost $10 million in 1976, this represents a collective turn-around of $43 million. . . . First-quarter results for 1978 indicate the airlines are still improving—Air Canada announced an $8.2-million after-tax profit vs an $8.1- million loss in 1977; CP Air lost about $1 million but this also compares favorably with an $8-million loss in first-quarter 1977 (the first quarter is traditionally a losing quarter for both airlines)." See also *Business Week* (1978) for a story on Air Canada's recovery under its new president Claude I. Taylor.

[11] Payne (1975) found that small peak-hour surcharges (£20 initially and later £50) shifted some commercial traffic out of the peak. This, however, is very limited evidence, and the British Airports Authority has reserved judgment as to whether surcharges were a success.

Why Do CATA Planners Do What They Do?

CATA planners face the uncerain future by assessing the risks of being wrong in one direction or another, determine the type of error which would be hardest to tolerate, and then plan so as to minimize the chance of making that error. To be more specific, given the previous problems CATA encountered when it provided too little capacity at Malton and the relatively loose financial constraints it faced, it was clear that the risk (to CATA personnel) of under-building was worse than the risk of over-building. As a consequence, CATA used a very high demand forecast for its planning. In the initial demand forecasts, originating-terminating travel to and from Toronto, after the 14 percent annual growth rate experienced in the 1960s, was predicted to grow at about 10 percent per annum in the 1970s, 7.5 percent per annum in the 1980s, and 6.7 percent per annum in the 1990s. Despite the deceleration, these are still very high long-term growth rates. The later demand study, which attempted to use a propensity model, predicted travel to and from Toronto airport to grow at 9.2 percent per annum in the 1970s, 7.0 percent per annum in the 1980s, and 5.8 percent per annum in the 1990s, which implies that any predicted number of trips will be reached two to three years later than in the initial back-of-the-envelope predictions. Even the propensity model study has been criticized for estimating on the high side (Abouchar, 1977 and Borins, 1976).

The predictions of aircraft noise at Malton and Pickering were approached in a similar way. After the opposition to Malton expansion manifested in 1968, CATA planners operated on the assumption that the consequences of under-estimating future aircraft noise at Malton would be worse than the consequences of over-estimating it.

In preparing their noise forecasts, CATA planners had to make assumptions about three uncertain areas: whether or not airlines would be required by government to retrofit the noisy engines of their present fleet, whether or not the Concorde (by far the noisiest plane in the air) would be in commercial operation, and whether or not the Boeing 707 and Douglas DC-8 (the worst noise offenders presently in widespread use) would be phased out rapidly or slowly. In all cases, CATA planners made the most pessimistic assumption for the Pickering airport: no retrofitting, long-lived 707s and DC-8s, and six to eight Concorde landings or takeoffs per day by 1980, eighteen Concorde or SST landings or takeoffs per day by 1985, twenty-four by 1990, and forty by the year 2000 (TAAP, 1973a). Under these assumptions, the moving of international and long-haul flights (and thus the 707s, DC-8s, and Concordes) from Malton to Pickering dramatically reduces noise at Malton while, so long as the Pickering area is appropriately zoned, not creating much new noise at Pickering. The CATA study predicted that the number of people, at the 1973 population level, annoyed by noise (that is, within the 28 NEF footprint)[12] at Malton would increase from 85,000 in 1973 to 139,000 in 1985, if Malton was used alone. On the other hand, if international and transborder long-haul traffic is moved to Pickering, by 1982 the number of people within the 28 NEF footprint at Malton would be reduced to 21,000, while increased from zero in 1973 to only 2000 in 1982 at Pickering (TAAP, 1974a). To show how critical these assumptions are, De Havilland Aircraft, the most technically competent opponent of Pickering, used the same computer program as did CATA to calculate noise levels, but made different assumptions. In 1980, if Malton were used alone and if the aircraft mix were that predicted by Air Canada in its testimony to the Airport Inquiry Commission (which includes no Concorde's and fewer DC-8s and 707s than predicted by CATA, but assumes no retrofitting), then 55,000 people would be in the 28 NEF footprint, rather than CATA's predicted 119,000. Using the Air Canada fleet mix prediction for 1985, and assuming/that all operations stay at Malton and that there is still no retrofitting, the number of people within the 28 NEF footprint would fall to 49,000, rather than increase to/the 139,000 predicted by CATA. If, in addition, one assumes that the noisy aircraft have been retrofitted, then the noise level at Malton falls still farther, and the noise reduction due to opening Pickering is still smaller.[13]

The opponents of Pickering claimed that CATA's noise forecasts were simply "cooked" to justify a pre-ordained decision. My interpretation is less sinister. The pessimistic noise forecasts were the "worst case" that a reasonable man, *with the information available in 1973,* might have expected to occur. In 1973, even though the Federal Aviation Administration had proposed to require aircraft flying into the U.S. to retrofit (a regulation which

---

[12] Noise annoyance is currently measured in Canada and the U.S. by means of Noise Exposure Forecast (NEF) contours. 28 NEF is the contour at which aircraft noise is first perceived as a problem. At that level, the federal Central Mortgage and Housing Corporation recommends sound insulation for buildings and sociological studies (Kryter, 1970) find that 25 percent of the population feel that the area is unacceptable for residential living. At a more severe level, 35 NEF, over 40 percent feel the area is unacceptable for residential living. CMHC defines 35 NEF as the upper limit for residential land use near airports.

[13] De Havilland (1974) made some very optimistic predictions about the benefits of retrofitting. For example, they predicted that if Malton were used alone in 1980 according to CATA's predicted fleet mix, but with all noisy aircraft retrofitted, the number of people within 28 NEF would be reduced to 21,000—due solely to the retrofit! In the Airport Inquiry Commission hearings, De Havilland's work was criticized by CATA because they made excessively optimistic assumptions about the amount of noise reduction retrofitting would actually bring about. The critics of Pickering also seemed prone to making assumptions which supported their case. One problem inherent in the adversary nature of the Airport Inquiry Commission's hearings is that they established upper and lower bounds on the probability distribution of future noise levels at Malton, but did little to elucidate the nature of the distribution between those two points. The curious might wonder why De Havilland went to all this trouble. The reason is that they perceived that a defeat of Pickering would lead CATA to take more seriously the option of moving short-haul traffic to Toronto Island Airport, which would be served by De Havilland-built Stolcraft.

CATA would also apply to Canadian aircraft[14]), the Republican Administration had not given the proposal its endorsement, and Congress had not acted. Other U.S. environmental regulations, such as automobile emissions standards, had been softened or rolled back. The Concorde had no track record, so widespread adoption was unlikely. Given the hindsight of 1977, it is clear that history has unfolded somewhat differently. The Ford Administration, in its last days, finally endorsed retrofitting (U.S. Dept. of Transportation, 1976), and in 1978 Congress is in the process of enacting legislation earmarking some of the present airline ticket tax to pay for it. Even if the Concorde is given permanent U.S. landing rights, it does not appear that the project will be sufficiently profitable for the British and French to produce any beyond the initial sixteen. However, the planners of 1973 were not blessed with our hindsight.

In the area of facility planning, the CATA studies display a great unwillingness to modify present practices. The daily peaking pattern is assumed to remain fundamentally unchanged for the rest of the century (TAAP, 1974b). Passengers' modal choices for ground access to the airport are expected to remain the same as at present, with 58 percent of all passengers using cars, 24 percent using taxis or limousines, and only 18 percent using the bus, (TAAP, 1974e, p. II-15). Finally, CATA expects greeters and well-wishers to continue to use the airport, with an average of seven greeters or well-wishers per ten arriving or departing passengers (TAAP, 1974e, p. II-23). In short, the facility planning studies are based on CATA policies/assumptions which take a passive approach to peaking and ground transit modal choice.

Why Pickering? Why Not Improve Malton?

Even after the 1968 rejection of the Parkin plan to acquire 3000 acres of land to expand Malton, and after the 1970 rejection of the plan to build another runway and terminal on the vacant west side of the present Malton site, the proposal to modify Malton has still been the subject of discussion. The recent versions of the proposal include the adoption of peak-load pricing, a toleration of lower design standards and hence longer queues throughout the airport, construction of off-site terminals, measures to discourage greeters and senders, and measures to encourage greater use of the bus to obtain access to the airport. All these proposals have in common the notion that CATA has not utilized its capital stock at Malton fully, and that it should do so before providing new capital at Pickering (or elsewhere).

An initial reason for CATA preferring Pickering is the uncertain question of noise. If it builds Pickering, it risks finding that the aircraft noise situation improves sufficiently that Pickering is unnecessary as an answer to

---

[14] Since most Canadian-owned commercial aircraft fly into the U.S., they would have to be retrofitted if the U.S. enacted the proposed regulation. CATA could not act unilaterally to require Canadian aircraft to retrofit because the U.S. aircraft manufacturers would not tool up to manufacture retrofit kits unless the large U.S. fleet was required to retrofit.

the Malton noise problem. If it stays at Malton, it risks finding that the aircraft noise situation worsens, thereby raising the ire of Malton area residents. The balance of pressures made the former risk much easier to accept than the latter.

Futhermore, the Malton proposal would antagonize airport users, because it would imply a lowering of the present standards for airport facilities, and because it would make Malton a more difficult airport to manage. The feeling in CATA was that the practice of the whole family driving out to the airport to meet or bid adieu to any of its members is an unassailable element of our Canadian lifestyle, particularly among ethnic Canadians who tend to embrace this practice most fervently. CATA seems to fear that attempts to price away congestion in the parking lots or the international arrivals lounge would incense the ethnic community, and their M.P.'s, all of whom happen to be members of the party in power since 1963.

On the other hand, the virtue of Pickering is that it will not disrupt this habit, because its access roads will be uncongested. The feeling within CATA is that it is a much smaller imposition on passengers to make them drive ten or fifteen miles further to Pickering than to make them take the bus to Malton. This assumption that current behaviour in travelling to the airport is immutable was a major reason for the construction of Mirabel Airport a full thirty-five miles from downtown Montreal. (By comparison, Dorval is but twelve miles from downtown and, to the chagrin of the connecting passenger, twenty-eight miles from Mirabel.)

CATA personnel take their amenity standards seriously. To allow them to deteriorate, or to see Malton too heavily used would be a failure to provide the service expected by the travelling public. On one occasion, a senior consultant to CATA told me that CATA would not tolerate the same conditions at Malton as at LaGuardia and National Airports in the U.S. As he put it, "Those airports are so busy there aren't any peaks. Why, they're operating at full capacity all day!" This statement suggests that excess capacity is good, not bad. In fact, many managers would make precisely that argument because they view excess capacity as organizational slack (Cyert and March, 1963, pp. 36-38). One virtue of slack is that there is something extra available for use in time of emergency. Another virtue is that in normal times there are more resources available than are absolutely necessary to do the job, which means that no one need work at top efficiency. In short, X-inefficiency is present (Leibenstein, 1966). To take an example, if the traffic flow at Malton increases, air traffic controllers will have to cope with the situation by positioning planes closer together, at the legally permitted minimum separations. With a slower traffic flow it is not necessary to work with that much precision. The same would probably be true of many other jobs at the airport.

Ultimately, one can think of Pickering airport as a way of providing a great deal of slack for the two Toronto airports. Pickering would be so big that the land could be used for additional runways, taxiways, access roads, freight handling facilities, and terminals. The airport system would not run out of land for the foreseeable future, and all this land would give CATA space in which facilities meeting the highest standards could be provided. For CATA, Pickering was seen as a relatively easy acquisition; initially, all that would be involved was expropriating land from a few hundred people. Given Canada's *Expropriation Act,*[15] which does not erect any great legal barriers to the federal government, this was seen as a much less painful course than fighting Malton area residents and antagonizing the travelling public.

Finally, the cost-unconscious civil engineer may just respond to the proposal to prolong the life of Malton by saying something that anyone teaching economics to engineers has heard more than once: "Look, we're going to build Pickering sooner or later. So what difference does it make if we start it sooner?"

CHANGE COMES TO CATA

Of course, CATA did not get Pickering Airport. In 1975, the opponents of Pickering shifted their pressure from the federal govenment (by then a lost cause) to the government of Ontario. When both the provincial Liberals and the New Democratic Party came out against the airport, the Conservatives were backed into a corner; they could no longer disclaim responsibility. It is not at all coincidental that the first action the Conservatives took after being returned with a minority was to veto Pickering, thereby deriving the opposition parties of what was probably the one issue on which they were in agreement.

Ontario's "no" is not an everlasting "no." The Province said that it would not build access roads to Pickering at this time. The federal government still holds the land at Pickering, and has no intention of giving it up. Some day the Province might consent to build the access roads, especially if Ottawa pays the bill, or makes some other concession. In the meanwhile, the game has moved back to Malton, and CATA has now been forced to look seriously at what can be done to make better use of Malton until the now more distant day when Pickering will be opened.

Besides Pickering, CATA has suffered a number of other reverses in recent years. It has been completely unsuccessful in its attempt to persuade the community in Vancouver to accept another runway or an extension of the major runway at Vancouver International Airport (Roger, 1977). Mirabel is a Pyrrhic victory, because it is widely viewed as being unnecessary and inconveniently located.

A major change in CATA's environment is that the Treasury Board is asserting tighter control now. Since CATA had been a big winner in the budgetary battles of previous years, the Cabinet may be more inclined to let it be a loser for a few years. The change in priorities that has put national unity

---

[15] R.S.C., c. 106 s.l.

at the top of the list is something of which smart bureaucrats (who, as Allison (1971, pp. 175-76) said, always have answers in search of a problem) are aware, and which they undoubtedly are using to justify many dubious expenditures. Despite this, ti may lie beyond human ingenuity convincingly to portray big airport projects in Vancouver or Toronto as the best way to keep Quebec in Confederation.

How has CATA responded to its defeats and to the changes in its environment? On the Toronto airport question, one can observe two rather inconsistent patterns of behaviour. On the one hand, CATA people are doing studies about how to live with a more congested Malton. On the other hand, Transport Minister Otto Lang has given dire warnings of a coming congestion crisis at Malton, and has announced that no additional overseas carriers will be granted landing rights in Toronto until 1980 (Romain, 1976, p. 10). Lang's position may simply be that of a Cabinet Minister "covering his ass," and shifting the blame for future problems which might occur at Malton onto the shoulders of the Province of Ontario.

In general, it appears that CATA people are responding to the changes in the environment in two different ways. Some "hawks, or hardliners" within CATA see the defeats as temporary victories for ecologists, anti-growth groups, and opponents of progress, and are sure that this too will pass, and airports will be built in the way they always have been built. Others in CATA admit that its opponents may be right that the tradeoff between the convenience of the travelling public and other societal values has hitherto been a trifle one-sided and see the need for using more sophisticated methodologies, such as benefit-cost analysis, in the evaluation of transportation investments.[16] One possible indication that the latter view is gaining ground is the increasing use within all of Transport Canada, including CATA, of standardized approval-in-principle and program approval documents for all kinds of capital expenditures. These documents are to be filled out by project managers and approved by Ministry-level personnel before capital expenditure proposals go into the Program Forecast submitted to Treasury Board. Teh documents require the project manager to specify the objectives of the project and provide detail about the costs and benefits of alternative ways of achieving the objectives. The forms also mandate the inclusion of a benefit-cost analysis, environmental considerations, and energy conservation analysis. Another indication of the course CATA will take in the future is the backgrounds of the people brought into the organization priorities and procedures are to change, the organization will ultimately need more economists and community planners. The economists will be necessary if CATA is to undertake a cost-benefit analysis of current standards and re-examine its pricing policies. Community planners will be necessary if community groups are to be given a real voice in airport planning. If these profes-

---

[16] The use of such methodologies as benefit-cost analysis and decision analysis in airports and other transportation facilities is discussed in Waters (1976).

sionals do join the organization in numbers, and if they begin to rise through it, then we will have a strong indication that a process of change is underway.

In order for CATA to change, continued outside pressure is necessary. The position the Treasury Board takes is crucial. Simply saying "no" to proposed capital budgets is not enough; a full scale review of CATA, as well as its parent ministry, is in order. Interested parties should argue for more public review of CATA decisions. If CATA were required to hold hearings, like the CTC hearings in which the Consumers' Association of Canada has been intervening frequently, this would be a small step in the right direction.[17] A further step would be the use of CATA funds to finance these interventions.

In conclusion, I would express the cautiously optimistic observation that the balance of external pressures and internal dynamics which led to CATA's decisions on Pickering might be changing in the direction of policies which are both more economically efficient and responsive. This process of change is worth watching (Langford, 1975) and assisting where possible.

---

[17] For discussions of the problems with consumer intervention in general and with the Canadian Transport Commission in particular see Stanbury (1976) and Brown-John (1976).

REFERENCES

Abouchar, A. (1977) "Traffic Forecasts for the Pickering (Second Toronto International) Airport: A Critical Examination" *Canadian Public Policy* 3: Winter, 14-22.

Airport Inquiry Commission (1974) *Report* (Ottawa: Information Canada).

Allison, Graham T. (1971) *Essence of Decision: Explaining the Cuban Missile Crisis* (Boston: Little, Brown).

Averch, H. and L. Johnson (1962) "Behaviour of the Firm under Regulatory Constraint" *American Economic Review* 52: December, 1052-69.

Bagnall, James (1978) "Up, Up and Away Go Canada's Flag-Carriers" *The Financial Post* May 27, p. 16.

Borins, Sandford F. (1976) "The Economics of Airport Planning: The Case of Toronto" Ph.D. dissertation, Harvard University, Department of Economics.

Brown-John, C.L. (1976) "Up against a Regulatory Wall: A Professor and the C.T.C." in K.M. Ruppenthal and W.T. Stanbury (eds) *Transportation Policy: Regulation, Competition and the Public Interest,* pp. 157-70 (Vancouver: University of British Columbia, Centre for Transportation Studies).

Budden, S, and J. Ernst (1973) *The Movable Airport* (Toronto: Hakkert).

Business Week (1978) "Cutting the Cord at Air Canada" March 20, pp. 116, 118.

CATA (1976) Airports and Field Operations Branch, *Air Services Fees Regulations* (Ottawa: Supply and Services Canada).

Culley, E.K. (1972) *Airline Impact of Airport Facility Charges,* Canadian Transport Commission Research Study No. 35 (Ottawa: CTC).

Cyert, R.M. and J.G. March (1963) *A Behavioral Theory of the Firm* (Englewood Cliffs, N. J.: Prentice-Hall).

de Havilland Aircraft of Canada Ltd. (1974) *Statement of Evidence to Airport Inquiry Commission: Presentation Material and Concluding Argument* (Toronto: de Havilland).

Feldman, E. and J. Milch (1977) "Options on the Metropolitan Fringe: Strategies of Airport Development" paper presented to the Cornell University Conference on Urban Choice and State Power, June.

Godfrey, C. and H. Massey (1972) *People or Planes* (Toronto: Copp Clark).

Government of Ontario (1970) *Design for Development: The Toronto-Centred Region* (Toronto: Queen's Printer).

Kryter, K.D. (1970) *The Effects of Noise on Man* (New York: Academic Press).

Langford, J.W. (1975) *Transport in Transition: The Reorganization of the Federal Transport Portfolio:* (Montreal: McGill-Queen's University Press).

Leibenstein, Harvey (1966) "Allocative Efficiency vs. X-Efficiency" *American Economic Review* 56: June, 392-415.

Neustadt, R.E. (1960) *Presidential Power* (New York: Wiley).

Niskanen, W.A. Jr. (1971) *Bureaucracy and Representative Government* (Chicago: Aldine).

Parkin Associates, John B. (1967) *Master Plan for the Toronto International Airport*, Report prepared for the Department of Transport, Ottawa (Toronto: John B. Parkin Associates).

Payne, N.J. (1975) "Experiences with Peak Hour Surcharges at Heathrow" paper presented at the Western European Airport Authorities Conference, June.

Rodger, Ruth (1977) "The Vancouver Airport Planning Committee: Some Glimmers of Air Transportation Policy" (Ottawa: Carleton University).

Romain, Ken (1976) "Toronto Airport Study Launched to Ease Expected Congestion" *Globe and Mail* October 29, p. 10.

Rose, K. and G. Hamilton (1976) "Airport Landing Fees and Congestion—A Systems Analysis" paper presented at the Transportation Research Board annual meeting, Washington, D.C.

Stanbury, W.T. (1976) "The Consumer Interest and Regulated Industries: Diagnosis and Prescription" in K.M. Ruppenthal and W.T. Stanbury (eds) *Transportation Policy: Regulation, Competition, and the Public Interest*, pp. 109-56 (Vancouver: University of British Columbia, Centre for Transportation Studies).

Toronto Area Airports Project (1972) *Ground Transportation Cost Analysis—Alternative Airport Systems* (Toronto: TAAP).

Toronto Area Airports Project (1973a) *Aircraft Movements Forecasts— Update* (Toronto: TAAP).

Toronto Area Airports Project (1973b) *Cost Projections to the Year 2000— TIA Malton and NTIA Pickering* (Toronto: TAAP).

Toronto Area Airports Project (1973c) *Summary of Forecasts* (Toronto: TAAP).

Toronto Area Airports Project (1974a) *Noise Exposure Forecasts for Toronto International Airport (Malton) and New Toronto International Airport (Pickering), 1971-1985* (Toronto: TAAP).

Toronto Area Airports Project (1974b) *Peak Hour Analysis and Forecast for the Toronto Airports System* (Toronto: TAAP).

Toronto Area Airports Project (1974c) *Originating—Terminating Passenger Forecasts for the Toronto Airports System*, 2 vols. (Toronto: TAAP).

Toronto Area Airports Project (1974d) *1972 Passenger Survey and Measurement Project at Toronto International Airport (Malton)* (Toronto: TAAP).

Toronto Area Airports Project (1974e) *Summary of Airport Roles and Traffic Assignments—Toronto Area Airports* (Toronto: TAAP).

Toronto Area Airports Project (1974f) *New Toronto International Airport (Pickering): Written Summary* (Toronto: CATA).

Treasury Board (1975) "Notes on the Expenditure Reductions" (Ottawa: Treasury Board News Release, December 18).

United States Department of Transportation (1976) *Aviation Noise Abatement Policy* (Washington, D.C.: U.S. Dept. of Transportation).

Warner, S.L. (1975) "Advocate Scoring for Unbiased Information" *Journal of the American Statistical Association* 70: March, 15-22.

Waters, W.G. II (1976). "The Process of Evaluating Public Investments in Airports and Other Facilities" in K.M. Ruppenthal and W.T. Stanbury (eds) *Transportation Policy: Regulation, Competition, and the Public Interest,* pp. 201-13 (Vancouver: University of British Columbia, Centre for Transportation Studies).

Chapter Five

Technical and Organizational Change in a Regulated Industry: The Case of Canadian Grain Transport*

by *David H. Maister*
Faculty of Commerce and Business Administration
University of British Columbia

INTRODUCTION

The physical system for the handling and transportation of Canadian grain from farm to seaport was, in the early 1970s, basically unchanged in nature from that which existed in the early years of this century. Primary collection of the grain was accomplished by farm-truck deliveries (averaging 5 to 10 miles) to an extensive network of small, often wooden, country elevators located primarily on rail *branch* lines (as opposed to main track). Individual rail cars were loaded at these elevators, and to the railways was left the task of assembling sufficient cars to create a train for the long-haul (800 miles) movement from Prairie province to export position (Vancouver or Thunder Bay).

By way of contrast, the U.S. system had long ago abandoned the "country" system for one based on large-scale "subterminals" (or "inland terminals" as they came to be known in Canada). In this system, primary collection of farm output was accomplished by relatively long-haul (50 to 100 miles) trucking (either by the farmer or by for-hire carriers) so that sufficient volumes could be accumulated at one location to load a whole train prior to long-haul rail movement. This system developed both because of economics of scale in elevator operation and the inherent cost advantage held by trucks over rail for movements below 100 miles (i.e., primary collection). (For a description and discussion of the U.S. grain transportation system, see Goldberg, 1968.)

In 1971, a Canadian federal government research body published an

---

* This article is based upon Maister (1976). Support for the author's dissertation was received from the 1907 Foundation and the Centre for Transportation Studies at the University of British Columbia.

analysis (Ross, 1971) which demonstrated that an "inland terminal system" had (and probably had had for some time) significant cost advantages over the existing Canadian system, *on a system-wide basis*. However, the development of such a system was inhibited by a variety of barriers, regulatory and other, and a vigorous debate resulted in the industry (and in government) as to whether, and how, such a system should be adopted in Canada. Participating in this debate were a wide variety of individuals, groups, and institutions, all affected by or with the power to affect the possibility of change in the industry: farmers and their organizations, owners of elevators (both private industry and farmers' cooperatives), the railways, municipal, provincial, and federal governments (including various government agencies such as the Canadian Wheat Board and Canada Grains Council).

Due to the actions of various of these participants, some of the regulatory barriers to inland terminals were modified in 1974, and by 1976, the first inland terminal in Canada[1] was opened. The rapid introduction of the new "technology" after the regulatory change appears to constitute *prima facie* evidence in support of the well-known hypothesis that economic regulation of an industry inhibits the rate of technological change (see, for example, Capron, 1971). While this may indeed be the case, it is equally clear that this basic hypothesis begs many additional questions we may wish to ask about the experience of the Canadian grain industry. For example: if the inland terminal system offered significant cost advantages, why was there not a force for change before the 1970s? (The equivalent system in the U.S. had begun developing in the 1950s: Goldberg, 1968, p. 23.) What exactly were the barriers to the introduction of the new system, and why did they exist? What forces led to their removal? How can we explain the behaviour and attitudes of the various participants?

In posing these questions, we are suggesting that the familiar basic hypothesis ("regulation inhibits change") is too simple: our understanding of *how* and *why* regulation may inhibit change requires more sophisticated hypotheses and a closer examination of the facts. In brief, we need to study the *dynamics* of regulatory change.

The purpose of this paper is to study such *dynamics* by a close examination of the events in the Canadian grain industry during (and prior to) the 1970s. We shall see that there is currently no single, unified theory that can answer the broad range of questions posed above: economic, political, and sociological factors all have a major role to play in explaining what occurred. However, the analysis presented below leans heavily on the body of research known as "channel theory," the study of relations between a firm, its suppliers, and its customers, taken from the literature of marketing (see Stern and El-Ansary, 1977). This choice was not arbitrary. It is sometimes

---

[1] In fact, the federal government, through the Canadian Grain Commission, had operated five facilities since the 1930s which were known as inland terminals. However, neither in conception nor operation did these correspond to the modern concept of inland terminals.

overlooked that regulation is often (if not usually) a process of adjudication between the regulated firm and its suppliers or customers, and hence the principles of channel theory should provide some insight into the behaviour of regulated industries. An important secondary purpose of this paper, therefore, is to explore the efficacy of channel theory in explaining change in regulated industries.

The structure of this paper is as follows: first, we shall briefly review various theories of change in regulated industries, in an attempt to sketch out a preliminary "model" of the dynamics of change. Second, we provide a brief description of the physical and institutional structure of the Canadian grain transportation industry. Third, the model is then "tested" by examining in detail the events in the industry during the 1970s. Fourth, we conclude with an assessment of the model and suggestions for future research on change in regulated industries.

THEORIES OF CHANGE IN REGULATED INDUSTRIES

In his review of research on change in regulated industries, Capron notes that "regulation is widely held to have had an adverse effect on technological change," but goes on to observe that "this view lacks an accepted analytical and empirical base" (Capron, 1971, pp. 2-3). In large part, this is because of the extreme generality of the proposition as stated. Certain more specific propositions can, however, be identified. It can be argued that regulatory *lag* (i.e., delay in reaching decisions) must *de facto* reduce the speed of introduction of new technology or other change, although this effect is likely to be small, if we consider only the lag created by the regulatory agency itself. Of more consequence is *extended* regulatory lag created by the opportunity for "vested interests" to prevent change by exploiting the full panoply of the regulatory process of hearings, submissions and the like (Capron, 1971, p. 5). A similar proposition, widely reported, is that regulatory bodies are "captured" by the organizations they regulate and tend to preserve monopolistic positions in the face of change that would introduce competition. (For examples often cited in support of his proposition, see Adams and Dirlam, 1968.) A separate approach is contained in the proposition that, by limiting allowable profitability, regulation may inhibit innovation (which, because of the risks involved, requires the opportunity for high profit), and hence change. Against this, however, can be made the counter-proposition that, in multi-firm regulated industries, regulation of rates related to industry-wide average costs preserves the incentive for cost-cutting innovations.[2]

It will be noted that these criticisms of regulation fall into two general

---

[2] Of course, there are those who would argue that some forms of regulation, such as rate of return regulation, lead to high capital intensity and hence relatively rapid rates of technological innovation. This debate was commenced by Averch and Johnson (1962). For a discussion of some aspects of this debate, see Westfield (1970).

categories: (i) those that argue that specific regulatory tools (such as rate-of-return regulation) constitute a barrier to change and (ii) those that point the finger at the very fact of regulation. Our concern in this analysis is primarily with the former category. Within this category, the propositions concerning regulation and barriers to technological change, there is little that helps us explain how and why the regulations themselves might change. Mechanisms for the removal of regulatory barriers such as those described above tend to stress *deregulation,* since the central proposition is that rigidity (i.e., a slow response to changes in market and other environmental conditions) is an inherent tendency of regulatory (and other bureaucratic) institutions (see, for example, Braybrooke and Lindblom, 1963). However, it should be noted that change in regulations can come about as a result of direct policy initiatives by the political sector (i.e., government) to the regulatory body (see Schultz, 1978). Where such directives are not permissible, by law or custom, the *threat* of deregulation may lead the regulatory body to act in self-preservation and be more receptive to change (see Baldwin, 1975).

Such reflections remind us that there do exist various well-developed theories of the behaviour of bureaucracies. No attempt will be made here to review these theories in all their glory, since government bodies (and bureaucracies in general) constitute but one sector within the network of institutions that comprise the industry under review. In addition, as noted above, there is a relative emphasis in this paper on an alternative body of theory: that of channel relationships. However, some acknowledgement of the contributions of the study of policy formation in bureaucracies must be made here. One of the most influential of these contributions is that of Braybrooke and Lindblom which describes public policy-making activities as exhibiting the basic characteristics of "disjointed incremental" decisions: that is, that there is an inherent conservatism in the policy-making process which militates against sweeping changes (Braybrooke and Lindblom, 1963). Such a process, if correct, would constitute an important factor in our understanding of the structure of regulatory barriers to change, as would other propositions from political science such as hypotheses concerning the preference on the part of governments (and other bureaucracies) for "solutions" that involve the least capital expenditure and the least change in administrative procedure (see Mitchell and Mitchell, 1969, chapter 7). As we shall see, these propositions have analogs within the theory of channel relationships (i.e., the relationships between manufacturers, wholesalers, and retailers and others involved in the distribution of products).

A transition between the fields of political theory and the study of distribution channels is provided for us in the work of Assael (1968) who examined the role of trade associations in conflicts arising in a distributive industry. Assael distinguished between "self-resolution" (appeals to members for cooperation) and "political action" as means of resolving such conflicts, and provided evidence to support the proposition that (a) political action is a last resort, employed only when self-resolution fails, and (b) the greater the homogeneity within an industrial sector, the more successful will be its attempts to conduct political activity.

Conflict and Power

Such propositions, while clearly in the realm of political theory, also belong to the modern theory of relationships between institutions in a distribution channel. This body of research derives primarily from the work of Palamountain (1955, p. 57) who noted that such relationships were "so directly a power conflict," in which "power has come to rival economic factors as the dominant element." Palamountain's stimulus led to the sudy of marketing channels as "organized behavior systems" (Alderson, 1957, p. 32) in which attention is focused upon two key concepts: conflict and power. (It should be noted that much of modern channel theory is derived from concepts and developments in the fields of sociology and psychology. For a discussion of these antecedents, see Stern (1969).)

Conflict has been defined as a situation in which "(one) component (of a system) perceives the behavior of another component to be impeding the attainment of its goals" (Stern and Gorman, 1969, p. 156). Varying goals among members of a distribution channel are not, however, the only source of conflict, which may also be caused by the following factors: (a) *Role Deviance* (in which one or more of the institutions in a system does not act within its rights or obligations as perceived by other member institutions); (b) *Conflicting Perceptions of Reality;* (c) *Conflicting Forecasts or Expectations;* (d) *Zero-Sum Competition for Scarce Resources;* (e) *Breakdown in Communications* (whereby the information necessary for interorganizational coordination and problem-solving is not communicated); (f) *Conflicts of Values* (e.g., some members of the system valuing stability more than growth); (g) *Conflict of Status Aspirations* (whereby some members may resist change even if it will produce economic benefits, if it alters their relative status in their perceived community); and (h) *Conflicts of Domain* (whereby members of a system may oppose an otherwise beneficial change if it involves loss of some decision-making power) (Stern and Gorman, 1969; McCammon and Little, 1965).

This list of conflict sources is neither mutually exclusive nor exhaustive: it does, however, serve to remind us that opposition to change may arise in various forms, and thus contributes to our understanding of the structure of barriers to change. The obvious question, however, is what this taxonomy has to tell us about the mechanisms for overcoming these barriers. In part, the answer to this question is contained in the taxonomy itself. Stern and Heskett (1968, p. 294), after identifying differing goals, domain conceptions, and perceptions as the primary sources of conflict, go on to observe "conflicts in interorganizational systems are expected to be resolved by setting superordinate goals, obtaining domain consensus among channel members, and absorbing uncertainty (i.e., unifying perceptions)." In other words, the appropriate behaviour required to overcome conflict (and, specifically, barriers to change) depends upon the conflict source. The first step towards conflict resolution is the proper identification of the causes of conflict.

Such a conclusion, however, ignores the question of exactly how, for example, differing perceptions are to be changed to a common one. Who is to take on this task? The almost universal answer within channel theory literature to this question is "the channel captain": the member of the system that has the dominant power. This leads us to consideration of the second key concept of channel theory: the bases of power.

According to Heskett, Stern, and Beier (1970), the bases of power in a channel of distribution may be summarized into four categories: (a) *Reward (or Coercive) Power,* whereby one member of a system has the ability to reward or punish another member(s); (b) *Expert Power,* whereby one member has power because of *other* members' belief that he (or it) has some special knowledge or expertness; (c) *Legitimacy Power,* whereby one member of the system has power because of other members' belief that he (or it) has a legitimate right to influence them and that they are obligated to accept this influence; and (d) *Identification (or Referent) Power,* which accrues to a member of a system to the extent that other members' "identify," or accept the fact that similar goals and values to theirs are held by the original member.

To summarize briefly: we have in this (cursory) review of channel theory concepts identified some of the major causes of conflict in an interorganizational system, suggested how we might identify the entity with the power to remove the conflict. We have noted that the first step in the resolution of the conflict is to identify the source, and must thus ask: what mechanisms can the channel captain employ to resolve conflict? The literature is remarkably sparse on this topic, but some guidelines are provided by Heskett *et al.* (1970, pp. 85-89); the "constructive" use of leadership is marked by (a) non-zero-sum bargaining (such as the sharing between participants of gains from any proposed change); (b) the assumption of system risk deriving from the proposed change; and (c) transmission of information in order to remove (or reduce) differences in perception and expectations for the future. (It is important to note that if the channel captain's power derives from sources *other* than "expert power," his attempts to remove conflict by transmission of information will fail: the success of dissemination of information will depend upon the credibility of the source.)

Will the channel captain act? Alderson (1965, pp. 37-45) suggests that this will depend upon the channel captain's "stake" in the sytem, that is, its need for the channel to "survive" to achieve its own ends. With a high stake, an entity is more likely to act to resolve conflict.

We have now completed our brief review of what might be termed "modern classical" or "mainstream" channel theory concepts. However, we must still introduce one or two perspectives that shall prove useful in our analysis. An important research tradition in the exploration of change is that employed by Rogers and Beal (1958) which examines the diffusion of innovations among individuals. One of the major analytical tools of this research is the categorization (and socio-differentiation) of participants into "innovators," "early adopters," "majority adopters," and "laggards." The application of this taxonomy to institutions, as performed by McCammon (1965), is capable of generating certain propositions of interest to the present enquiry. First, he notes that channel captains, by very virtue of their power, tend to be well-established firms, and hence have the most to lose by an innovation that involves a restructuring of the firm's relationship with its suppliers or customers. For this, and other, reasons he accepts the (Schumpeteran) view that innovative activity is likely to come from outside the existing power structure (Schumpeter, 1947). A further consequence of this organizational rigidity (cf. the discussion of bureaucratic theory above) is that "most firms absorb innovation gradually, or react to innovative competition through a series of incremental adjustments (McCammon, 1965, pp. 88-89).

A Theory of Change

It will be recalled that the questions we are attemping to address in this paper are of the form "why was there not a force for change to inland terminals in the Canadian grain transportation industry prior to the 1970s? Why did the barriers to change (regulatory and other) exist and why did some of them fall when they did?" While we shall not attempt the mammoth task of constructing a full-blown "model" of change in regulated industries, it will prove useful to sketch the outlines of such a theory in order to structure some of the hypotheses alluded to above.

The process of change may be viewed as a transition from one equilibrium to another, divided into three stages: (i) a "disequilibrating stage" wherein pressure for change arises; (ii) an "initiation stage;" and, (iii) in many situations, what has been termed an "intertype competition stage" (Palamountain, 1955), in which the new and old systems compete until a new equilibrium is reached. The focus of this paper is on the first two stages.

The definition of "equilibrium" employed here is derived from the channel theory considerations discussed above. We must first distinguish between the equilibrium of an individual participant in a system, and the equilibrium of the system as a whole. An individual participant's attitude to a particular potential change in the system will be a function of (minimally) three variables: the priorities he places upon various goals, the degree to which the current system satisfies each of these goals, and his perceptions of the benefits of the new system. The net dissatisfaction (or "disequilibrium") of an individual participant is hypothesized to be insufficient to lead to change (or even proposed change) in the system: this will be dependent upon the dissatisfaction of individual participants weighed by their *power*. System disequilibrium may thus come about by changes in either goals or power, the objective performance of the current system, or changes in perceptions about the current and potential systems. A preliminary flow model of the "disequilibrating stage" is presented in Figure 1.

Figure 1

THE DISEQUILIBRATING STAGE OF PROCESS CHANGE

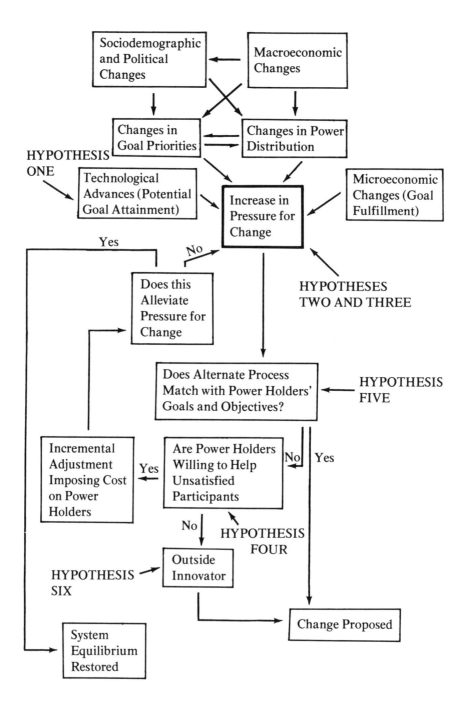

The hypotheses of interest are as follows:

Hypothesis 1: The existence of a potential change that will reduce total interorganizational system cost is not, in itself, sufficient to cause the adoption of that change by an industry, if the change does not match with the *dominant* goals of the industry.

Hypothesis 2: Change will be opposed by system participants if it creates a conflict with respect to (a) their domain consensus, (b) their goals, or (c) their perceptions of reality.

Hypothesis 3: Pressure for change will be greater if (a) there is a dominant power holder (a "channel captain") *and* (b) the change matches with his goals and perceptions.

Hypothesis 4: Established organizations will respond initially to pressure for change by adopting short-term (incremental) decisions with a minimum of capital investment and/or adjustments in interorganizational patterns of behaviour.

Hypothesis 5: The higher the cost to the channel captain of supporting the existing system, the more likely he is to support change.

Hypothesis 6: If established organizations fail to deal with the dissatisfaction of individual participants, then innovative activity is likely to come from organizations outside the existing power structure.

The process described in Figure 1 takes us to the point where change in the system is proposed due to net system disequilibrium. We must now address the topic of the "initiation stage" whereby proposals for change are transformed into initiation. The outlines of such a process are described in Figure 2 below. Hypotheses of interest related to this process are:

Hypothesis 7: A change proposal will be followed by attempts to remove differences in perceptions of reality by the dissemination of information.

Hypothesis 8: The success of this will be dependent upon the credibility of the information source.

Hypothesis 9: The struggle to remove opposition to change will be conducted in the economic, power, and political arenas, with the latter employed only as a last resort.

Hypothesis 10: The political success of any group to remove (or preserve) barriers to change will be dependent upon the homogeneity of interests of the group.

We have now completed our review of the conceptual framework upon which this analysis shall draw. We next turn to a brief description of the dimensions and basic institutional structure of the Canadian grain transportation industry, and then return to test the hypotheses given here.

Figure 2

THE INITIATION STAGE

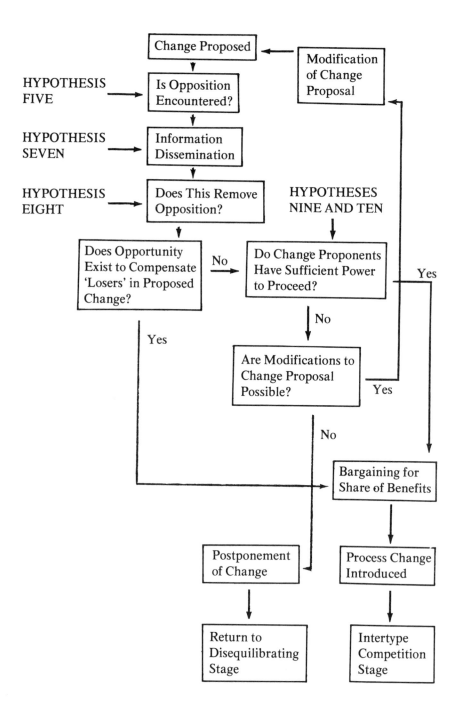

THE STRUCTURE OF THE CANADIAN GRAIN TRANSPORTATION INDUSTRY

The bulk of Canadian grain in the early and mid-1970s was grown on approximately 170,000 farms (down from 288,000 in 1931) located in the three Prairie provinces. The volume of grain marketed per year fluctuates widely, averaging 600 to 700 million bushels with occasional peaks of up to 1 billion bushels. The predominant grain crop are wheat, barley and oats, accounting for approximately 40 percent, 33 percent and 16 percent of total production. These crops (known as "Board grains") are all marketed (for export sales and, until 1975, for all interprovincial sales) by the Canadian Wheat Board (CWB) to whom the farmer is required to sell his crop. The remaining 10 percent of grain production (grown from virtually zero in 1950) is accounted for by coarse grains and feedgrains such as rye, flaxseed and rapeseed which are subject to an open (free) marketing system (and are known as "off-Board grains). All production of Board grains (i.e., wheat, barley and oats for export) are marketed on a "pool basis," the profits being distributed by the CWB back to the producer in proportion to the volume delivered.[3]

The farmer is at complete liberty to grow whatever crops he desires. However, he must, at the beginning of each crop year, "assign" his land to various crops. Upon this assignment is based the total number of bushels of each grain that the farmer will be allowed to deliver to the Canadian Wheat Board in the ensuing year. The number of "bushels per assigned acre" (known as the "quota") is determined by the Board after it has received all the assignment information and can compare totals with projected sales requirements. This is usually accomplished well in advance of the sowing season. Once the quota has been announced, the farmer may deliver any amount up to his assigned limit at any time during the crop year. It should be noted that the farmer is not required to actually deliver *any* quantity of grain because of his assignment (he can, for example, sell his crop in the open market for interprovincial sales and, since 1975, for other domestic sales). Neither is he required to actually grow the crops named in his assignment: if he has, for example, a large carryover of wheat from a previous crop year, he may "assign" some of his land merely to be allowed to deliver the wheat in his possession. He may actually grow some other crop. The assignment system applies to *all* crops, since the Board has the power (*Canadian Wheat Board Act,* R.S.C., c.44) to establish quotas for all crops.

Delivery to Elevators

Delivery of grain from the farm to the country elevator is almost

---

[3] Statistics on the Canadian grain industry may be found in the Canada Grains Council's Statistical Handbook, published annually. Financial statistics on the operations of the Canadian Wheat Board appear in the Board's annual report. A comprehensive discussion of the grain transportation system, together with relevant statistics, is given in Candlish. (1973).

universally conducted by the farmer himself, with an average haul of 10 miles and a payload per trip of 200 bushels (Canada Grains Council, 1974, p.155). The farmer must, at the beginning of the crop year, have designated two alternative delivery points to which his deliveries for the coming year are restricted. (This rule exists to facilitate transportation planning by the Canadian Wheat Board.) In 1976, the country (or "primary") elevator network was composed of 3964 elevators with a total storage capacity of 344 million bushels, located at 1495 distinct points (Canada, 1977, p. 134).

When the producer delivers his crop to the primary elevator, he sells his crop to the elevator company's agent. When the agent buys the grain, he may be doing so in one of two capacities: either he is acting as an agent of his employer, the elevator owner, or else he is acting as an agent of the Canadian Wheat Board. If the former (i.e., for grains not marketed by the Board), the elevator agent pays the farmer for his grain. (The agent has, in general, little personal discretion on prices paid which are set by the parent company. However, the agent must agree with the farmer on the grade of the grain, since this affects payment.)

If the agent is acting for the Canadian Wheat Board (i.e., for wheat, barley and oats sold for export), then he gives the farmer a "cash ticket" in the amount of an "initial payment" (set and announced by the CWB before the commencement of the crop year), *less* the country elevator handling tariff and *less* the rail freight rate.

Movement of all grains (Board and off-Board) out of country elevators is under the control of the Canadian Wheat Board. Grain companies must report weekly their stocks to the Board, who after consultation with the two major railways (the state-owned Canadian National Railway and the privately owned CP Rail) and grain companies, issues shipping orders to the railways to move grain from country elevator to port. The procedure by which this was done in the years 1958-1976, known as the "Block Shipping System," is of more than passing interest. The Canadian Wheat Board has divided the Canadian grain-growing region into 48 "blocks." Available rail cars (as reported by the railways) are allocated to each block according to grades of grain available (as reported by the elevator owners) and required (by the CWB's own sales activities). It is important to note that even though the Board does not control the marketing of off-Board grain, it *does* control their shipment by rail out of the country elevators. In making its assignment of rail cars, therefore, the Board must balance its own requirements with principles of equity in making cars available for the movement of off-Board grains.[4]

Having assigned cars to blocks, the Board then proceeds to allocate cars within each block to specific companies. Prior to 1976, the principle employed (known as the "Bracken Formula") was such that each company

---

[4] Standard 40-foot boxcars average 2000 bushels capacity. The new grain hopper cars have about 3000 bushels capacity.

received a proportion of available cars equal to its receipts of grain from producers in the previous crop year (Candlish, 1973, pp. 53-55). The final step in the chain is that the grain companies allocate their allotted cars among the various elevators that they control within the block. For some of the cars, the elevator companies will be loading Board grain according to Canadian Wheat Board instructions; for others they will be loading their own (off-Board) grain.

All but a minute portion of grain moving off the Prairies moves by rail, primarily because of the long distances, but also because of the cheapness of the rail rate. Rail rates on export grain (to Vancouver or the Lakehead) or on grain for domestic sales moved to the Lakehead are held at 1899 levels (approximately 0.5 cents per ton-mile, compared to the railways' overall average rate of approximately 1.3 cents per ton-mile) according to a statutory agreement known as the Crow's Nest Pass Agreement. These rates (known variously as "the grain rate," "the Crow rate," etc.) may only be changed by an act of the federal Parliament. The origins of this Agreement have been well summarized by Mason (1978, p. 242) as follows:

> The Crow or Statutory rates are the result of the Crowsnest [sic] Pass Agreement of 1897 between the federal government and the Canadian Pacific Railway. In exchange for a $3 million subsidy from the federal government to construct a rail line from Lethbridge, Alberta to the mineral rich Kootenay Valley of British Columbia, the CPR agreed to lower, by three cents per hundredweight, the rate on moving grain to the Lakehead. In addition, the rate on certain settler's effects incoming to the prairies was lowered. In 1903 the CPR further reduced the rate on grain transport in response to competition from the many independent branch line operations emerging especially in the Winnipeg vicinity. Between 1903 and 1925 the rates on grain transport fluctuated widely and in 1925 the 1899 rate was legislated to include all export destined grain and all grain moving through Thunder Bay; these rates have been substantially in effect until the present.[5]

The main ports of export for the grain are via the Lakehead (approximately 65 percent in the mid-1970s), the West Coast ports of Vancouver and Prince Rupert (33 percent) and the Hudson Bay port of Churchill (2 percent) (see Figure 3). The latter port is only open for two months of the year, and regional development considerations are an important factor in the exploitation of this route.

Grain delivered to Vancouver, Prince Rupert and Churchill is either loaded direct to export, or processed and consumed locally. Grain delivered to the Lakehead may go through a variety of routes before being loaded to export or delivered to domestic processors. The bulk of the grain is sent by lake vessel to a "transfer elevator" in the lower St. Lawrence, where it is stored and loaded into ocean-going vessels. The primary reasons for this transfer are the early freezing of the lakes in the winter months and the problems of

---

[5] Additional discussion of the statutory rate (by which name it will be referred to in the remainder of this paper) may be found in Purdy (1972).

TABLE 1

Major Grain Flows in Eastern Canada, 1972-1973

(million bushels)

From / To	Thunder Bay R	Thunder Bay W	Georgian Bay R	Georgian Bay W	Lower Lake R	Lower Lake W	Lower St. Lawrence R	Lower St. Lawrence W	Maritime R	Maritime W	Overseas	Domestic (R)	Total
Western Canada (R)	533.2						1.3						534.5
Thunder Bay R							10.5						10.5
Thunder Bay W				51.9		31.8		369.2		2.4	36.7		492.0
Georgian Bay R									32.0			25.9	57.9
Georgian Bay W								5.1					5.1
Lower Lake R												24.8	24.8
Lower Lake W								15.5			1.1		16.6
Lower St. Lawrence R												75.5	75.5
Lower St. Lawrence W										4.2	335.2		339.4
Maritime R												3.8	3.8
Maritime W											34.8		34.8
Local (Eastern) Production (R)			4.0		3.1		1.8						8.9
Total	533.2		4.0	51.9	3.1	31.8	13.6	389.8	32.0	6.6	507.8	130.0	

Source: R.G. Menzies, *Eastern Grain Movement Report* (Winnipeg: Canada Grains Council, 1975), p. 11.

ocean vessels negotiating the Seaway. The various routes used to transfer grain from Thunder Bay to Eastern positions, and typical volumes, are shown in Table 1.

Flow of Payments

Since it will play an important role in our exposition, we shall review here the flow of financial transactions in the system described above. (These are summarized in Table 2.) The first step in the process is the trucking of grain by the farmer to the country elevator. These costs are borne by the farmer. Upon delivery, as noted above, the farmer is paid (by he grain company) the "initial payment," (set by the Canadian Wheat Board), *less* the (statutory) rail freight charge and *less* a handling charge. This latter charge is subject to regulation by the Canadian Grain Commission (CGC) (19 Elizabeth II, c.7), a body within the federal Department of Agriculture, who establish *maximum* handling charges.

On Board grains, storage fees as well as the financing charges on grain inventory are paid by the Board to the elevator company. Storage fees, like handling charges, are subject to regulation by the Canadian Grain Commission. When the grain is delivered to the terminals, the railways are paid by the elevator companies the (statutory) freight charges withheld by them from the producers' initial payment. The Canadian Wheat Board reimburses the elevator companies for the purchase of the grain, paying them the full initial price. The terminal elevator company (as we shall see, often the same as the primary elevator company) receives from the Canadian Wheat Board a payment for terminal elevation charge and for cleaning. These payments are also subject to regulation by the Canadian Grain Commission which establishes maxima.

For grain transferred to eastern elevators, the Canadian Wheat Board employs the grain companies as agents to deal with the lake vessel owners for the transportation, reimbursing the grain companies for transportation charges plus an "agency commission."

At the end of the crop year (July 31), the Board closes the "pool account" and distributes the profits to the farmers in the form of a final payment.

Table 2

THE TIMING OF PAYMENTS: CANADIAN GRAIN TRANSPORT SYSTEM

ACTION	PRODUCER	GRAIN COMPANIES	RAILWAYS	CANADIAN WHEAT BOARD
1. Trucking of Grain to Primary Elevator	- Trucking Costs			
2. Grain Delivered to Primary Elevator	+ Initial Payment - Elevation Tariff - Rail Charge	- Initial Payment + Elevation Tariff + Rail Rate		
3. Storage		+ Storage Tariff + Financing Charges		- Storage Tariff - Financing Charges
4. Transport to Terminal				
5. Arrival at Terminal		- Rail Charge + Initial Payment + Terminal Tariff	+ Rail Charge	- Initial Payment - Terminal Tariff
6. Transfer to Eastern Elevator		- Payment to Lake Vessel Owner		
7. Arrival at Eastern Elevator		+ Payment to Lake Vessel Owner + Agency Fee		- Payment to Lake Vessel Owner - Agency Fee
8. Sale to Buyer				+ Sale Price
9. Closure of Pool (end of crop year)	+ Sale Price - Initial Payment - CWB costs			- Sale Price + Initial Price + CWB costs

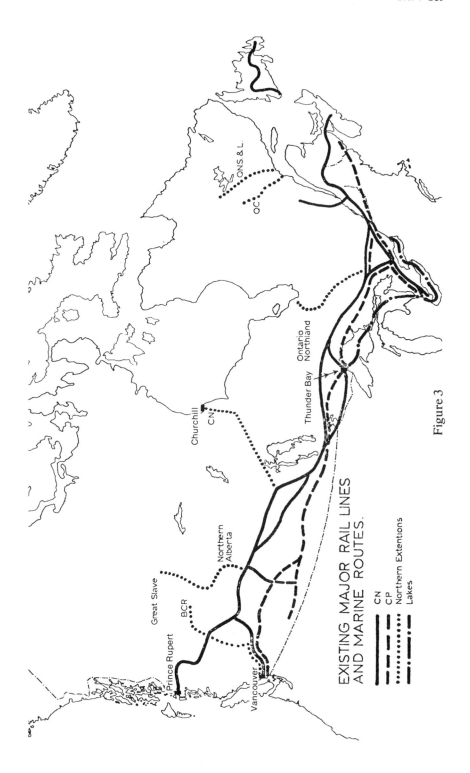

EXISTING MAJOR RAIL LINES
AND MARINE ROUTES.

CN
CP
Northern Extentions
Lakes

Figure 3

Institutional Structure of the Industry

A functional classification of grain transport reveals six basic types of operators: producers, country elevator operators, railways, port terminal operators, lake shippers, and transfer elevator operators. To this list must be added the various government agencies. Companies in the railway and lake shipper sectors differ from the others in that they are not vertically integrated. In all other sectors, while some single sector operators exist, the predominant form of organization is vertical integration of ownership and operations. This is primarily true of the four farmer cooperatives.

The primary elevator sector in 1976 was composed of eight companies, four of which were entirely owned by farmers in the form of cooperatives: Alberta Wheat Pool, Saskatchewan Wheat Pool, Manitoba Pool Elevators and United Grain Growers (UGG). The first three named (each operating in a single province) were formed in the 1920s prior to the establishment of the Canadian Wheat Board, with the purpose of acting (on a voluntary basis) as marketing pools. It was largely their failure in this capacity during the Depression of the 1930s that led to compulsory, Prairie-wide pooling in the form of the Canadian Wheat Board. Since that time, these companies have continued to operate primary and terminal elevators, and trade in off-Board grains.

The remaining four grain companies in the primary elevator sector are known as "the private trade," to indicate that they are not producer-owned. Since World War II, there has been a significant withdrawal of the private trade from the primary elevator sector, largely by selling out to the Pools. Between 1964 and 1974, the three Pools increased their percentage ownership of country elevators from 42 percent to 61 percent, and together with United Grain Growers, owned 75 percent of the 1976 licensed storage capacity in country elevators (Canadian Grain Commission, 1976).

In broad outline, the explanation of this movement of private capital from the primary elevator sector is as follows. As noted above, the tariffs that may be charged for handling and storage of grain are regulated by the CGC who establish maximum allowable tariffs. There is freedom to price at any level below this, but until 1974, maximum tariffs were set so low that all companies charged the maximum. While an additional source of revenue for elevator operators was available from the Canadian Wheat Board, in the form of an "agents' fee" for services rendered in handling Board grain (thus, in effect, side-stepping the CGC's regulatory power!), primary elevator operation remained by common agreement, very unprofitable (Candlish, 1973). The Pools were able to cross-subsidize primary elevator operations from profits earned in the terminal elevator sector, or from profit nargins on the trading of off-Board grains, but both of these activities imply a significant degree of vertical integration. By and large, it was the non-integrated private companies that disappeared from the primary sector in the pool-war years.

TERMINAL ELEVATORS

In 1976, there were twenty-four port terminal elevators operated at the four major export ports: one in Churchill, one in Prince Rupert, five in Vancouver and seventeen in Thunder Bay (Canadian Grain Commission, 1976, p.x.). The Churchill and Prince Rupert terminal elevators were owned and operated by the federal government, but accounted only for a very small portion of grain movement. In Vancouver, the farmers' cooperatives (the three Pools and United Grain Growers) accounted for three of the five terminal elevators, and 65 percent of the storage capacity. In Thunder Bay, they owned thirteen of the seventeen terminals, and 80 percent of storage capacity. Terminal operations have traditionally been considered profitable (Candlish, 1973, p. 164), since the Canadian Grain Commission has allowed a more rapid rise in terminal tariffs than at country installations.

Competition among terminal operators is very limited, with a variety of cooperative arrangements in force. Grain loaded at country elevators is consigned to an individual terminal elevator (usually the company's own), although since 1971 an arrangement has existed so that to balance the work load, cars may be reconsigned from a busy terminal to an idle terminal. (This coordination is performed by an official of the Canadian Transport Commission.) At Thunder Bay, all terminal elevator operators belong to the Lakehead Terminal Elevator Association, which acts jointly on their behalf on such matters as labour agreements, negotiation with the port authorities, grain movements, tariffs and regulations.

THE RAILWAYS

There are two railway companies involved in the transport of grain from the Prairies: the Canadian National Railway (CN) and CP Rail (CP). The Canadian National Railway is publicly owned, while CP Rail is a subsidiary of the giant Canadian Pacific Ltd., a conglomerate with operations in trucking, real estate, shipping, mining and other areas. Together, these two railways account for 95 percent of all rail transport in Canada. A third, Northern Alberta Railway, is jointly owned by CN and CP. Grain moving at (federal) statutory rates accounts for over 20 percent of the railways' tonnage, and over 30 percent of total ton-mile output (Canada, 1976). However, because of the low statutory rate only 12 percent of rail revenue is derived from this traffic. The railways have long claimed that transporting grain at statutory rates was non-compensatory, but few, if any, western interests conceded this. The decades-old debate was brought to a head in 1977 by the investigations of the Snavely Commission (Canada, 1976) which found that railway losses on grains in the mid-1970s totalled $90 million per year.

Apart from the requirement to transport grain, the railways are constrained from abandoning service to light density branch lines. Abandonment of service may only take place with the permission of the federal Canadian Transport Commission (CTC), a multi-modal regulatory agency created in 1967 to succeed, among other bodies, the Board of Transport Commissioners. As part of the *National Transportation Act* of 1967 (R.S.C. 1966 - 67, c. 69) which created the CTC, the railways were granted subsidies to cover their losses on unprofitable branch lines that the Canadian Transport Commission required them to continue (but *not*, it should be noticed, on grain traffic originating from main track elevators).[6]

GOVERNMENT AGENCIES

In this review of the industry structure, we have had cause to introduce a number of government agencies. One of the most striking facts about this industry is the number of separate government bodies with responsibility for some aspect of the system. These relationships are summarized in Figure 4. Unindicated, but of crucial importance to the future of the grain delivery system, are the provincial governments of the three Prairie provinces, whose functional role in this system is to provide and maintain the local roads between farm and elevator. If the physical configuration of the country elevator network were to change, the provincial governments might be called upon to make significant investments.

Problems with the System

OLD ELEVATORS / EXCESS CAPACITY

Among the primary problems of the grain industry in the late 1960s was the fact that the existing country elevator system was old and overbuilt (Candlish, 1973, p. 141). A large proportion of these elevators were small wooden structures with highly labour intensive modes of operation, and low average throughput relative to capacity. Low throughput elevator construction had been encouraged by the federal government through tax concessions on elevator construction, and by the *Temporary Wheat Reserves Act* (TWRA) of 1956. This Act provided for the federal government to pay, out of the federal treasury, the storage and interest charges on all stocks of wheat above a prescribed level. The object of this policy was to support producers' income by allowing them to deliver wheat (and hence receive payment for it) during a period of low world demand. There was a consequent need for storage facilities, and the proliferation of low handling capacity, high storage capacity elevators was a result. These facilities depended for their profitability upon storage revenues (rather than handling revenues) and were thus exposed in a situation when the need for storage (i.e., high world demand) declined. This reliance on storage revenues was heightened by the Canadian Grain Commission policy of restraining increases in handling tariffs, so that these tariffs were in many cases below handling costs. The consequence of these policies was that the country elevator sector became predominantly

---

[6] For a discussion of this and other transportation subsidies see Ruppenthal (1974) and Ruppenthal and Stanbury (1976).

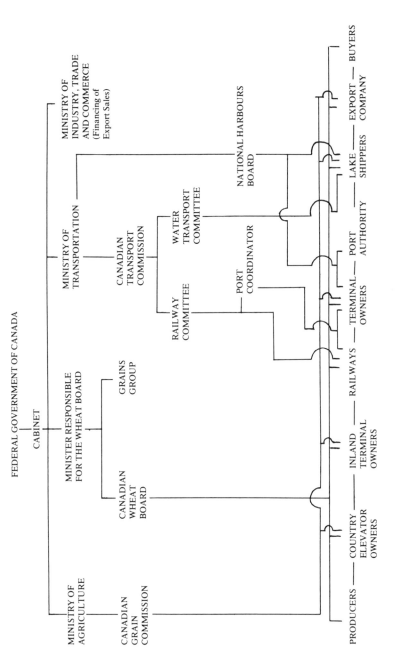

Figure 4 Government Entities in the Grain Delivery System

dependent on storage revenues, which might disappear if the market for grain turned up and stocks depleted.

INEFFICIENT BRANCH LINES

Related to this problem of widely scattered, small country elevators was the fact that the majority of them were located on light density rail branch lines. The low volumes of grain emanating from many country elevators meant that these branch lines did not generate the volume of traffic necessary for efficient rail operations. This problem was accentuated by the existence of the Crow's Nest Pass rate on grain. Because this rate was considered by the railways to be well below the cost of transporting grain, their maintenance of these branch lines had been such that many of them were in poor states of repair.

Pressure by the railways for abandonment of light density branch lines grew up particularly during the 1950s (largely because rising truck competition had diverted most other traffic from these lines, leaving them predominantly dependent upon grain traffic). The *Report* of the MacPherson Royal Commission on Transportation in 1961 (Canada, 1961) recommended substantial abandonment, but due to fears of social problems that this would cause in country communities, the federal government did not act on this recommendation. Instead, it imposed a "freeze" on abandonments in 1967, while incorporating a subsidy for losses incurred on branch line traffic into the 1967 *National Transportation Act* (Candlish, 1973, p. 167). This subsidy attempted to cover the costs of the total movement of grain originating on branch lines, that is, not just the branch line movement.

SHORTAGE OF GRAIN CARS

A second major effect of the non-compensatory statutory rate was that the railways had not invested in any grain box-cars since the 1950s. The box-car fleet in use in the early 1970s were cars retired from service with other commodities.[7] With the trend in other commodities increasingly to the use of specialized cars, even these inefficient general purpose box-cars were becoming in short supply. This created capacity problems, to which a tentative step towards a solution had been taken by the Canadian Wheat Board which purchased an initial 6,000 modern grain hopper cars in the early 1970s.

PORT CAPACITY

Additional capacity problems existed in the port areas, particularly at Vancouver. In part, these problems were due to the congestion of the rail switching yards, which were said to be in need of modernization. Although

---

[7] No citation could be found for this assertion, but it was reported to me by a wide variety of people interviewed in the course of this research, including railway personnel.

these yards are not solely dedicated to grain traffic, the railways did not wish to encourage the use of Vancouver as a grain export port, under *current statutory grain rates*. Since the westbound route over the Rockies was more costly than the eastbound route to Thunder Bay, the railways' losses were reduced (given that the revenue they receive is the same to each destination) by the use of Thunder Bay.

The capacity problems of the West Coast were accentuated (and this was becoming increasingly true also of Thunder Bay) by the lack of *cleaning* capacity in the port terminals. The throughput of grain through a terminal is significantly slowed by having to clean the grain, and part of the terminal's storage capacity is tied up by the screenings resulting from the cleaning process. The West Coast port operators had not significantly expanded their cleaning capacity in the late 1960s and early 1970s largely because of the switching yard congestion problems. In 1974, the Canadian Wheat Board announced that sales commitments were not being met, due to the inability of the system to deliver the grain, primarily to Vancouver. It should be stressed that at both Vancouver and Thunder Bay, the total (all commodities) volume of traffic had become of increasing concern as the landside capacity of these ports was being reached. In 1976, the Canadian Wheat Board announced an incentive program to encourage expansion of terminal facilities in Vancouver, and a number of companies indicated plans to so expand (Canadian Wheat Board Weekly News Review, April 15, 1976).

SUMMARY: MULTIPLE PROBLEMS

The problems of the grain delivery system clearly possessed two major interrelated dimensions. On the one hand, the physical structure of the system was such that it was poorly suited to speedy, reliable throughput. This was a result of the branch line collection process, the inefficient low-throughput elevators, the lack of hopper cars and the capacity problems at the port. The other dimension of the industry's problem was financial. The country elevator sector was in need of substantial investment to replace outmoded facilities, and the railways' losses on carrying grain at statutory rates were claimed to be substantial.

Underlying both of these problems had been the use of the grain delivery system by the federal government to protect the incomes of the producer. It may be seen from Table 3 that the combined effects of maximum elevator tariffs, statutory rail rates and *Temporary Wheat Reserves Act* payments had been to keep the costs to the producer low; indeed, the producers cost declined from 40 cents per bushel in 1967-1968 to 32.4 cents per bushel in 1971-1972. It is clear that these charges were "disconnected" from the variations in per bushel costs that had taken place over the corresponding period.

ALTERNATIVE SYSTEMS

We now turn to consideration of some alternative systems that would solve some of the problems outlined above. The predominant alternative

Table 3

Average Grain Delivery Charges to Producer, 1967-1972
(cents per bushel)

	1967/8	1968/9	1969/70	1970/1	1971/2
Farm Trucking Costs	3.2	3.2	3.2	3.2	3.2
Country Elevator					
Handling Charges	5.3	5.5	5.8	5.8	5.8
Storage and Interest Charges	15.2	13.8	12.0	7.6	4.9
Total	20.5	19.3	17.8	13.4	10.7
Railway Freight	13.8	13.8	13.8	13.8	13.8
Terminal					
Storage Charges	3.5	3.9	3.1	1.6	1.7
Lakehead	4.4	4.6	4.9	4.9	4.9
Total	7.9	8.5	8.0	6.5	6.6
CWB Marketing Charges	5.7	9.1	5.1	2.4	2.5
Total	51.1	53.9	47.9	39.3	36.8
Less TWRA Payments	11.1	15.5	13.5	7.9	4.4
Net Charge to Producer	40.0	38.4	34.4	31.4	32.4

Source: Fact Sheet No. 2, (Canada Grains Council, Winnipeg: 1975)

system is that of "inland terminals," a concept consisting of three major elements: bulk accumulation of grain by road prior to rail shipment; inland cleaning of grain; and the use of "unit trains" (complete trains in which all cars are filled with grain, so that the expensive railyard operations of forming the complete train is avoided).

Such a system, it is argued, would have the following benefits. First, system costs could be reduced by the substitution of truck movement for rail in the primary collection process. Second, inefficient small country elevators would be replaced by high volume "inland terminal" facilities. Since most elevator expenses are fixed, clear economies of scale exist. Inland cleaning of grain would greatly reduce capacity limitations in the port terminal sector. Indeed, the need for port terminals at all would be greatly reduced, since cleaned grain could be loaded direct to ships. A final, not inconsequential advantage would be the increased flexibility of the system. In the winter season, when the St. Lawrence Seaway is closed, grain has been routed from Thunder Bay (by lake vessel) to Georgian Bay, and thence by rail to Maritime ports. (The reason for not routing direct by rail from Thunder Bay is that a special rail rate category, "At and East" rates provided for substantially lower rates for grain shipments originating from Georgian Bay and Upper Lake ports. The railways received a subsidy to compensate for this CTC-enforced lower rate. See Menzies, 1975.)

This routing involves the elevation of grain four times—in the country, at Thunder Bay, at Georgian Bay and in the Maritimes. The quantity of grain involved is of the order of 32 million bushels (Menzies, 1975, p. 11). If a full inland terminal system existed, it would be possible to move grain in a unit train direct from the inland terminal to the Maritimes, thus avoiding two elevations. Since Maritime port elevators do not have cleaning facilities, the use of this direct route is only made possible with inland cleaning. Otherwise, the grain would still have to be routed through Thunder Bay.

Costs

It was no simple task in the 1960s to translate these notional "advantages" into "hard-data" cost comparisons, due to the lack of available data and the disputes that existed over the appropriate methodology for costing rail operations. Indeed, the assembly and publication of system-wide cost comparisons is *endogenous* to the process of change that we are attempting to explain. The cost comparisons compiled by the Grains Group, a federal research team reporting to the Minister responsible for the Canadian Wheat Board (Ross, 1971), are therefore of more than passing interest.

The Grains Group attempted to compare the system costs of four "benchmark" systems: (a) the (then) current (1971) system of 5000 country elevators; (b) a "rationalized" country elevator system of 3600 country elevators involving abandonment of 5,525 miles of light-density rail branch lines; (c) a "high-throughput" country elevator system of 389 elevators (with no inland cleaning or unit trains); and (d) a full inland terminal system with 80 facilities, inland cleaning and unit trains. The estimates of costs were

Table 4

Cost Matrix of Alternative Systems,[1]
1968/9 Levels Grains Group 1971 Study
(cents per bushel)

Cost Component	"Present" System	Rationalized System	Hi-Through put System	Inland Terminal System
Farm Trucking Costs	3.2	3.9	5.6	7.0
Country Elevator	12.4	10.1	15.0[8]	
Inland Terminal				11.5[8]
Rail Cost	29.9[2]	24.2[3]	21.0[4]	17.7[5]
Terminal Cost[6]	6.9	6.9	6.9	5.7
Total System Cost To West Coast or Thunder Bay	52.4	45.1	42.5	41.9
Seaway Rates to St. Lawrence Ports	11.1	11.1	11.1	11.1[7]
Lower St. Lawrence Terminal Costs	6.6	6.6	6.6	6.6
Total System Cost To St. Lawrence Ports	70.1	62.8	66.2	59.6
Storage Capacity Provided (million bushels)	399	302	274	200

NOTES:

1. Handling volumes: Country Locations - 675 million bushels.
2. Rail Costs: Long-Term Variable Costs 16.8¢ (0.7 ¢ per ton mile)
    (per bushel) Constant Cost Allocation 7.4 (0.3 ¢ per ton mile)
    Total Retrievable Cost for
    "Uneconomic Branch Lines: 5.7 (0.24¢ per ton mile)
    _____
    29.9¢
    Source: Railways.
3. Rail costs in rationalized system equal those of current system *less* retrievable costs from abandoned branch lines. (Source: Railways.)
4. Rail costs for hi-throughput estimated (by Grains Group) as being average of unit-train rate and existing cost levels.
5. Unit train rate estimated (by railways) at 7.5 mills per ton mile.
6. Includes cost of cleaning (except for inland terminal alternative). Revenues from screenings not taken into account.
7. Opportunity to by-pass Thunder Bay not taken into account.
8. Includes amortization of original investment at 8 percent per year over 40 years (for basic structure).

Source: P.S. Ross, *Grain Handling and Transportation Costs in Canada* (Ottawa: Grains Group, 1971).

Table 5

Total Cost Matrix of Alternate Systems, 1968/9
($ million)

Cost Component	Present System	Rationalized System	Hi-Throughput System	Inland Terminal System	1968/9 Charges
Farm Trucking	21.6	26.3	37.8	47.3	21.6
Country Terminal	83.7	68.2	101.3		37.1
Inland Terminal				77.6	
Rail	201.8	163.4	41.8	119.5	93.2
Terminal	46.6	46.6	46.6	38.5	31.1
Total System Handling and Transportation Cost	353.7	304.5	327.5	282.9	183.0
CWB Marketing Changes	53.1*	53.1*	53.1*	53.1*	53.1*
Total	415.1	365.9	388.9	344.3	244.4
Storage Charges (Country)					80.4*
Storage Charges (Terminal)					22.7*
Less TWRA Payments					90.4*
Net Charge to Producers					257.1

*See comments in Source statement

Source: Derived from Tables 3 and 4 by multiplying per bushel rate by assumed volume by 675 million bushels, except for items marked with an asterisk, which are actual figures calculated from Table 3 at 1968/9 volume of 583 million bushels.

derived from thirteen separate sector studies commissioned by the Grains Group, based on detailed specification (including exact location) of each of the benchmark systems. The results of this analysis, as published in 1971 (based on 1968/9 cost levels) are shown in Table 4. The Grains Group concluded "the existing system is competitive only if one ignores the costs of the rail system and then, only if the present elevator system goes through a drastic and continuing reduction. The least cost alternative . . . appears to be a system of 80 or so inland terminals" (Ross, 1971, p. 26).

It is of interest to compare the total dollar costs that these results imply with the actual charges to the producers in 1968-1969. This is done in Table 5. It may be seen that of the $415 million total cost of the system, the producer paid only $257 million in 1968-1969.

The Grains Group analysis was not without fault. Their estimate of total cost savings of $70.8 million annually if the inland terminal alternative was adopted (a reduction of 18 percent from the then current system costs) is crucially dependent upon their assumption of throughput volumes of 675 million bushels. At one billion bushels, the cost savings can be shown to be in the region of $100 million (Maister, 1976), and such volumes on a regular basis are clearly within view. Secondly, they failed to take into account port terminal investments required to expand capacity that could be *avoided* if an inland terminal system was built. Next, they neglected to include the costs of maintaining and replacing country elevators as they deteriorated (a potential cost of $30 million per year). Questions can also be raised about the estimates of rail costs and trucking costs, and the omission of potential savings from exploitation of the "winter route."

A detailed revision of the Grains Group analysis of costs has been presented by the author elsewhere (Maister, 1976), suggesting that total savings with an inland terminal system may be as much as *twice* that suggested by the Grains Group. However, the purpose of this article is not to derive precise estimates: the point is, that the Grains Group's analysis seemed to provide a substantial case for the development of an inland terminal system. Indeed, the size of the potential savings would seem to imply that the economic benefit of an inland terminal system had been in existence for some years, as suggested by the development of an equivalent system in the United States some years before (Goldberg, 1968). We are now in a position to explore the forces that prevented the development of such a system in Canada, to explain why interest in such a system arose when it did, and to explain why change was possible in the mid-1970s. We shall begin our answering of these questions by focusing upon the regulatory forces that inhibited the introduction of inland terminals in Canada.

REGULATORY BARRIERS TO INLAND TERMINALS

In order to introduce the bulk accumulation of grain by road that is implied by the inland terminal system, it would be necessary to persuade farmers to drive a greater distance to deliver their grain, or to use for-hire truckers. Only by obtaining high utilization of capacity through attracting deliveries from a wide catchment area could a large inland terminal hope to be a success. However, prior to 1971, the *Canada Grain Act* (19 Elizabeth II, c.7) (the Act governing the Canadian Grain Commission, and hence its regulatory activities) required that elevator owners charge exactly the same handling tariff (per bushel) at all elevators they owned. Thus it was not possible for an elevator company to offer a "discount" to producers to encourage them to use the more efficient facilities.

Compounding this problem was a second regulatory barrier to inland terminals: the Canadian Grain Commission (as noted above) had held country elevator handling tariffs at extremely low levels, so that even if a company wished to attempt the device of sharing the benefits of an efficient installation, the fact that virtually all elevators were loss-making propositions discouraged them from the attempt.[8]

The case of the cleaning tariff provides an even better (and third) example of a regulatory barrier to inland terminals. As noted in the description of the industry given above, all grain passing through a terminal elevator was charged a handling tariff and a cleaning charge. However, prior to 1975, the cleaning charge had not been changed from its low level of 1 cent per bushel since the early 1920s. This low level clearly established sufficient incentive for grain companies to have their grain cleaned at the ports rather than invest in inland cleaning equipment themselves. Until such time as port cleaning tariffs reflected true costs (which were commonly agreed to be above 1 cent per bushel), a regulatory barrier to inland cleaning, and hence inland terminals would exist.

A fourth regulatory barrier was, of course, the statutory (Crow's Nest Pass Agreement) rates on rail transport of grain. The fact that these rates were low, relative to costs and more importantly the same for all shipments regardless of whether they originated from a small country elevator on a branch line or from an inland terminal on main track, meant that the potential inland terminal operator could not capture any of the cost savings that would fall to the railways by the introduction of unit trains. This situation corresponds to that reported above for the farmer/elevator company interface: due to the fixity and low level of the relevant tariffs, no capability existed for the beneficiary of a change in the transport system to compensate the loser.

Institutional Barriers

Apart from these four regulatory barriers to change, a number of other institutional arrangements involving government agencies would make the initiation of an inland terminal difficult, if not impossible. First, there was the rail-car allocation system. As noted above, the railways, because of low

---

[8] In pure economic theory, a company that took decisions based on marginal costs and revenues could justify differential pricing even where revenues did not exceed costs. In practice, however, the prospect of unprofitable operations dissuaded the grain companies from so doing.

net revenues on grain transport, had not invested in grain hopper cars. Yet the operational efficiency of inland terminals would, in part, be due to their ability to load hopper cars efficiently. The rail-car allocation system under the control of the Canadian Wheat Board did not allow for distinctions to be made in which elevators received which type of car. Hence, in spite of the existence of grain hopper cars purchased by the Board (and used free of charge by the railways), there would have been no guarantee that an inland terminal would receive the type of car to which it was best suited. A similar problem would appear at the port. As noted above, reconsignment of cars from one terminal to another in order to balance port area workloads had been introduced in 1971. This system depended upon the homogeneous treatment of cars containing Board grains as they arrived in port positions. If an inland terminal were to clean grain inland and hence some cars arrive with cleaned grain, and others with uncleaned grain, this procedure would be compromised. A further example is provided by the system for determining the number of cars allocated to a given country elevator. As noted above, this was based on the proportion of producer deliveries to that elevator in previous crop years ("the Bracken Formula"). While the Canadian Wheat Board did have a procedure whereby a new entrant could develop a "Bracken base," that is, receive an initial allocation of rail cars, an entrant the size of an inland terminal might well have caused problems for the Canadian Wheat Board in making a "fair" allocation of cars. A second aspect of the rail-car allocation procedure was potentially more problematical. The allocation of cars to companies took place *after* an allocation of cars to each of the Board's forty-eight geographical "blocks." Since the drawing area of an inland terminal would be so wide (on the order of 50 to 75 miles radius), there existed the possibility that this would cover more than one block, and hence would threaten the whole basis of the car allocation system.

While these non-regulatory arrangements may not be perceived as *major* barriers to inland terminals, they do illustrate the need for resolution of interorganizational problems before change could take place, as well as the key role in allowing change played by the Canadian Wheat Board, a government body.

The Causes of Regulatory Barriers

In the investigation of the causes of regulatory barriers to inland terminals, we must be careful to distinguish between the original genesis of the specific regulations that constituted barriers to change, and the forces that kept the regulations intact. As we shall see, the regulations and tariff structures were originally introduced for reasons far removed from the possible consideration of inland terminals. As is often the case with government regulations and edicts, however, the regulations and their effects have tended to live on far beyond the purposes for which they were originally introduced.

The first of the regulatory barriers, the inability of a company to charge different handling tariffs at different locations, grew out of the fears of producers at the turn of the century that such a power on the part of elevator operators would allow these companies to take advantage of monopoly positions at some delivery points, while meeting competition at others. The bar on this "monopolistic discrimination" was built into the original *Canada Grain Act* of 1912. The underlying principle was one of *equity*: that each producer should be treated equally with respect to handling tariffs, regardless of geographic location. In the early 1900s, when the elevator network was not as widespread as it later became and fewer and poorer roads existed, this issue was a substantial one.

The second element creating a barrier to the initiation of bulk accumulation had been the low level of the handling tariff (relative to costs), which would have discouraged differential tariffs even if they had been permitted. A number of considerations are important in understanding why this situation persisted into the 1970s.

The world price for wheat had remained between $1.00 and $2.00 for the forty-year period from the 1930s to the 1970s (Candlish, 1973, Exhibit 15). In consequence, any rise in the handling tariffs would have had a substantial adverse effect upon the producer's income (in the absence of any compensation), and significant producer pressure existed to keep these handling tariffs low. (See, for example, the handling tariffs given in Table 3).

Such pressure does not constitute a full explanation, since other forces existed which kept handling tariffs low. A country elevator operator received revenues from three basic sources: (a) handling tariffs received from the producer; (b) storage revenues; and (c) "agency fees" from the Canadian Wheat Board in payment for services rendered in handling Board grains.

Ultimately, the producer bore all of these charges, since expenses incurred by the Canadian Wheat Board were deducted from the profits of the pool before calculation of the final payment. However, of these charges, only the first was a direct charge on the producer. The others were "hidden" in the sense that they affected the producer by reducing the amount of his final payment. While he could, with detailed examination of the Canadian Wheat Board annual report, discover the extent of these other charges, they were (and are, according to industry sources) not as "real" as the immediate deduction of the handling tariff from his initial payment.

In consequence, as may be expected, the grain companies sought to obtain relief from low handling tariffs by increasing their revenues from other sources, primarily the Canadian Wheat Board agency fee. (It should be noted that the Board agency fee, calculated on a per-bushel basis, was also not variable between companies or locations. The "equity" principle of equal treatment of grain companies by the Board was an important element of the Board's charter, the *Canadian Wheat Board Act*.)

The third source of elevator revenues, storage charges, did not need any increase in tariffs to provide a substantial income to elevator operators. Since there are virtually no variable costs in storing grain, and because the regulated storage charge of 1/30 cent per bushel per day was generally considered adequate compensation given that the elevator company did not bear interest charges on stored grain (these were paid by the Canadian Wheat

Board), the degree to which storage revenues were an important source of income was determined by the extent of storage. Since this remained high throughout the 1950s and 1960s, an additional explanation of the lack of elevator company pressure to raise handling tariffs may be found here.

The third regulatory barrier to the introduction of inland terminals was the perceived unavoidability of cleaning charges on grain as it passed through port terminals. The terminal tariff was widely viewed as a single tariff for all services provided. However, this was not so. It was composed of tariffs for the two main services—elevation and the cleaning of grain. The impression of a single tariff had come about because the charge for cleaning grain had not been changed from 1 cent per bushel since the early 1920s. That the companies were able to maintain these low levels in spite of rising costs (cleaning being a labour-intensive operation) is explained, first, by their sale of "screenings" resulting from the cleaning process; and second, by their ability to offset costs by applying for raises in the (regulated) terminal handling tariff.

The fourth, and potentially most significant of the barriers to the establishment of inland terminals was the level of the statutory rate on grain transport, which discouraged the introduction of unit trains (plus the fact that the statutory rate could not be varied, thus preventing differential rail rates being used as an incentive). A large variety of considerations are necessary to understand why this barrier to change persisted. As noted above, the statutory rate could only be changed by an Act of Parliament. For such a change to take place, the federal government would require both the power and the desire to initiate the change. Considerations of power are discussed below; here we shall focus attention upon the goals of the federal government in establishing and maintaining the statutory rate.

The Crow's Nest Pass Agreement of 1897 was entered into by the federal government with clear policy objectives: the populating of the Prairies and the development of Prairie agriculture (Fowke, 1957), in particular the development of the "Wheat Economy" of the Prairie provinces. That the federal government accepted the responsibility for this act of policy is evidenced by the words of Prime Minister John Diefenbaker in the House of Commons in May of 1959: "The Crow's Nest Pass rates are a part of a bargain that was made between the railways and the Government on one hand, and the settlers who went West on the other hand" (Canada, 1959). It is clear from this that a key objective of federal policy was the expansion and maintenance of the rural economy. In the 1930s, the industrialization of the Prairies had not yet begun, and wheat remained the predominant crop. The statutory rate, which was in effect a subsidy to the western farmer, was clearly used as an instrument of social and national policy to advance the interests of western grain farmers.

While a fuller explanation of why the statutory rate remained in force through the mid-1970s is given below, we may note in passing that, like the primary elevator handling tariff, the railway tariff had been deducted immediately from the producers' initial payment. The clear incentive to keep such tariffs low applied in this case as well as that described above.

The Perpetuation of Regulatory Barriers: Attitudes of the Participants

The question to which we must now turn is why these proximate regulatory barriers to inland terminals did not fall prior to the 1970s, when the economic advantages of inland terminals had probably existed well before that date. It is at this point that we shall turn to channel theory for guidance in exploring the power and attitudes toward inland terminals of the various participants in the system. We shall begin our discussion with the farmer/producers.

FARMER/PRODUCERS

If inland terminals were to develop, most grain producers would be required to deliver their grain a greater distance: from a 1976 average of 10 miles to a possible 50 - 75 miles. The basic economic consequence would be that many producers would be required to purchase larger trucks, since the greater distance would usually imply fewer trips. The impact of truck purchase costs is, however, only one aspect of the problem. In most cases, the greater hauling distance would imply that the producer could no longer afford the time (or investment) to truck his own grain, and would require the services of a commercial (for-hire) trucker. Our theoretical model warns us that such a change in "role" or "domain" would act as a prime source of opposition to change (Hypothesis Two specified above). Other sociological factors of this nature may also be identified.

Under the inland terminal system (consisting of eighty such terminals), it is likely that there would be only one terminal within reasonable reach of a given producer. Thus he would have little (if any) choice in his delivery point, or, more importantly, of elevator company. While this would not be a new occurrence, since the Canadian Wheat Board had enforced a single delivery point requirement on producers in 1968, it should be noted that pressure from producers had led, in 1971, to a modification of the policy to allow for a choice of two delivery points (see Canadian Wheat Board Annual Report, 1971). Thus, choice of delivery point is clearly an important element of the producer's perception of his "proper" decision-making authority, that is, his "domain." Again, our theory identifies this as a potential conflict source (Hypothesis Two).[9]

A final aspect of the inland terminal system that would affect the producer's operation is that commercial trucking would remove the producers' opportunity to develop a personal interface with the elevator agents. The importance of this to the producer has been demonstrated repeatedly (see, for example, Canadian Transport Commission, (1972)). Finally, we must recognize the threat that an inland terminal system, and hence the closure of

[9] Public attitudes towards choice are discussed in relation to air transportation in Canada by Hardin (1975).

country elevators, would pose to the small rural communities around the elevators. To the extent that elevator closure is *perceived* to threaten these communities, and to the extent that preservation of such communities is held to be a primary goal of farmers, then another basis for opposition exists.

THE GRAIN COMPANIES

We now turn our attention to the impact that inland terminals will have upon the grain companies, and begin with their role as primary elevator operators. We have noted above that the primary elevator network had proven expensive, and in general, unprofitable. However, this is not to be interpreted to mean that grain companies would be in full support of the inland terminal concept.

First we note that the central concept of inland terminals is one of fewer, widely spread, large-scale units. This implies that some control or collusion needs to be exercised by some controlling authority to direct the location of these elevators. If this is not the case, then an *ad hoc* development (in the absence of collusion) would perhaps lead to over-capacity in the primary collection network. Since the economics of both inland terminals and "conventional" country elevators are characterized by high fixed costs (relative to total costs), there is a need for high utilization of capacity to break even. Whereas the investment necessary to establish a country elevator is small enough that a company may risk building close to another country elevator in the hope of diverting business, the start-up investment of an inland terminal (approximately $8 million) is such that few companies would be prepared to take such a risk. Two alternatives thus result: either the development of an inland terminal system will be centrally directed, or else a vigorous (and possibly wasteful) competition for locations will occur.

This first alternative (public control of the location of inland terminals) would significantly impinge on the decision-making authority of the grain companies—affect their "perceived domain." As we predicted above, such a solution would lead to opposition from all grain companies. The second alternative, in which location competition would result, would similarly be somewhat of a departure from normal competitive practice, in which inter-company agreements on location are common. For example, United Grain Growers long honoured its agreement with Saskatchewan Wheat Pool not to build competitively at the same location (this agreement ended in 1961).[10] Similarly, all sectors of the elevator sector of the industry (Pools, UGG and Private Trade) have engaged in "saw-offs" whereby agreement is reached between two competing companies on paired shutdown of elevator operations in order to leave each the "monopsonist" at one point.[11]

Inland terminals development would thus appear as a disruption of the normal practices of the grain companies, and has been resisted because of

---

[10] Personal interview with United Grain Growers' officers.
[11] *Ibid.*

that. Such a conclusion is consistent with Hypothesis Two, specified above.

The resistance to inland terminal development is not uniform among grain companies, however. By and large, the Pools have been opposed, with United Grain Growers and the private trade more favourable. In part, this difference may be explained with reference to the ownership of these different sectors.

As shown above, the Pools are owned by farmers, and may thus be expected to oppose the development of inland terminals on the grounds of the disruption of the rural community. Indeed, various public statements to this effect have been made by Pool officials. The private trade, not being owned by farmers, might be less committed to this concern and hence less opposed to change.

For a more detailed explanation, we must return to our examination of the change in operations that would result among the grain companies from the introduction of an inland terminal decision. The first element that warrants examination is the capital investment that would be required, and the relative losses of the various grain companies for "sunken investment" in existing elevators. The Pools, as noted above, had the largest investment among grain companies in country elevators (over 60 percent of all country elevators) (Canadian Grain Commission, 1976,p. xiv). To a large extent, their power in the industry was based on this factor (as well as the "identification" with the interests of the producer, as discussed above). To this extent, therefore, we might have predicted that the Pools would be the most reluctant to support the inland terminal concept, because of their vested interest in protecting the base of their power. A further nuance of this argument should be noted. The transitional effects between the current system and a "high-throughput system" (described above) are likely to be less severe than those occurring with the introduction of an inland terminal system, in the senses that (a) less investment per unit is required, allowing the risks to be goegraphically spread out, and (b) the "catchment area" of a high throughput elevator would be smaller, and hence not threaten as many country elevators. Eventually, of course, nearly all existing country elevators would disappear, but the transitional effects would be lessened. As our conceptual framework predicted, the most favoured solution by "established" organizations is the one involving the least investment and the least disruptive effects on current practices.

This element is shown nowhere so dramatically as in the impact on grain companies of inland cleaning. The full debate over inland cleaning is further discussed below, but a number of aspects deserve attention here. First, we must note that inland cleaning would compromise the existing investment in port cleaning equipment possessed by the grain companies operating port terminals. As indicated above, the investment of the Pools in port terminals is greater than any other producer group.

It will be seen that, once again, the Pools have the most to "protect," and their opposition to inland cleaning (as expressed on many occasions), confirms our hypothesis concerning the actions of dominant institutions.

Similarly, the attitudes of the private trade (with less investment in either country elevators or port cleaning) towards bulk accumulation and inland cleaning support the "outside innovator" theory outlined above.

Another aspect of inland cleaning needs to be examined. Under the system used in 1975, screenings resulting from the cleaning process were normally treated as the property of the port terminal operator, largely due to the impossibility of returning screenings to the producer.[12] Should cleaning be done on the Prairies, there would be strong pressures for the producer either to claim the screenings or to receive payment in lieu. This would involve a significant change in the grain company-producer relationship ("role perceptions") as well as being a potential loss of income to the grain company.

THE RAILWAYS

In terms of effects upon *costs* (if not necessarily income) the railways would potentially be the prime beneficiaries of a change to an inland terminal system. With such a system they could cease virtually all branch line activities and utilize unit trains. While this does involve a change in operating procedures, and an alteration of the railway-grain company relationship, the fact that unit trains have been utilized by the railways for other commodities implies that we should not expect opposition on this ground even though change in operations has been used as a "source of conflict" argument above.

A "high-throughput" elevator system (of, say, 300 elevators), although not supporting unit trains, would permit abandonment of substantial portions of the branch line network.[13] However, by itself, such a system would not match with railway goals. Since 1967, the railways had received subsidies for branch line operation, which, as noted above, partially offset their losses due to the statutory rate. If abandonment took place, with no corresponding financial adjustment, the railways would be financially worse off.

The railways' goals during the entire inland terminal debate remained some modification to the financial burdens of the statutory rail rate. If they appeared to favour a unit train (inland terminal) system, then this was primarily the result of the fact that to institute such a system, changes in the statutory rail rate provisions would be required.

---

[12] It would, of course, have been possible for grain companies to return to, or share with, the producer the revenues from the sale of screenings. However, this practice had not developed in Canada and grain company personnel indicated that there would be a variety of "operational difficulties" in so doing. No conclusion on this point may be reached on the basis of available evidence.

[13] For a discussion of the dimensions of potential abandonment with a "high-throughput" system, see Ross (1971). A more detailed analysis of abandonment potentials (and problems) will be found in the Hall Report (Canada, 1977).

THE PROVINCES

We must, in this discussion, acknowledge the role of the provincial governments in the inland terminal debate. Apart from their functional role to provide and maintain roads, the provinces' major interest in the debate has been the preservation of the small rural community, and on these grounds they have opposed inland terminals.[14] This opposition is important in that it points out a major conflict in goals: the conflict between the goal of cost minimization in grain transport versus the goal of preservation of the rural communities.

SUMMARY OF PARTICIPANTS' POSITIONS

We may summarize the preceding discussion in the following manner. The attitudes of most participants in the grain transportation industry have been against inland terminals, on the grounds of threats that it poses to role and domain perceptions and differing goals. As we shall see, there also existed in the 1960s and early 1970s a conflict in the perceptions of reality: that is, the cost benefits of the inland terminal system. To explain the lack of change in the industry, or the forces that perpetuated the regulatory barriers, we need only demonstrate that the opponents of change had sufficient power to influence the regulatory decision makers. To explain the changes in regulations that did occur, we need to demonstrate how either the goals or distribution of power in the system changed. It is to these tasks that we now turn.

The Perpetuation of Regulatory Barriers: Considerations of Power

THE FEDERAL GOVERNMENT

In the preceding discussion we failed to analyse the attitudes of the federal government, and its various agencies, towards the inland terminal question. This omission derives from the fact that a true analysis of the federal government position can only be performed after a discussion of its power position in the industry.

The power of the federal government with respect to the grain industry is very complex. As a central government, it clearly has a variety of coercive powers, in that it has the legal authority to enforce cooperation of the other institutions in the industry. Through its various agencies (the Canadian Wheat Board, the Canadian Grain Commission and the Canadian Transport Commission), or by its own direct action, it has the legal authority to deal with many of the barriers to the introduction of inland terminals. Reinforcing these legal authorities is the government's preeminent position with

---

[14] Examples of statements of opposition by the provincial governments to inland terminals may be found repeatedly in numerous issues of the Canadian Wheat Board's Weekly News Review during the period 1973 - 1977.

respect to the generation of funds. As Heskett, Stern, and Beier (1970, p. 83) note: "Financial capacity and capabilities are important indicators of reward and coercive power."

This latter consideration, the role of the federal government as a provider of funds, forces us to consider changes that have taken place in this regard. Prior to 1950, the federal government did not directly inject funds into the grain transport industry. However, with the establishment of the *Temporary Wheat Reserves Act* (TWRA), direct financial involvement of the federal government in the grain delivery system was established—its "stake" had increased. This direct financial involvement was increased in 1967 by the establishment of branch line subsidies to the railways, which transferred (some) losses from the railways to the federal treasury. (For the extent of these subsidies, see the Annual Reports of the Canadian Transport Commission.) The postwar period was thereafter clearly marked by a growth in the federal government's power position with respect to the grain industry.

However, in a constitutional democracy, the powers of a federal government are not unlimited, but are constrained by social and political realities. A prime example is provided by the attempt to grant to the Canadian Grain Commission the explicit power to direct the construction (and location) of elevators, a power that would have enabled a government agency to coordinate the orderly construction of an inland terminal network. Provisions in the 1970 *Canada Grain Act* that would have accomplished this were removed from the bill during parliamentary debate. Similarly, any suggestion of federal attempts to "tamper" with the statutory rail rate, even with provisions for cooperation to producers so that they would be no worse off, have been received in the past with vigorous (and successful) opposition, both in Parliament and in the West generally.

The key to understanding the federal government's power base is to recognize that while it does possess extensive coercive powers, these have not been reinforced, with respect to the grain industry, with the other bases of power outlined above. For example, *qua* federal government, it does not possess *referent* or *identification* power. It is clear that from many public statements made by individuals and organizations in the West that the grain industry (including grain farmers) does not perceive a matching of interests between themselves and the federal government.

Expertness as a basis of power is also lacking, in that most grain industry participants do not perceive the federal government as possessing any expertise in matters relating to the industry. The experience of the Grains Group is perhaps the best evidence of this. In the formation of this body, the government felt constrained to draw its membership from grain industry participants. This is evidence either of real lack of expertise within the federal government, or the government's awareness of its *perceived* lack of expertise. The hostile reception afforded to the Grains Group research output forced the federal government into transferring the task of "information collection and distribution" with respect to the cost impacts of alternate system structures (a channel captain's role), to the Canada Grains Council, an industry association formed under federal government prompting (and financing) in 1970.

Apart from these omissions of identification and expert power, there is some question about the federal government's perceived legitimate power. The attitudes of the western producer towards the federal government's *right* to take decisions with respect to the grain industry is best expressed by the farmer who, in referring to the Grains Group study conclusion that inland terminals were the most cost efficient system, voiced the fear that "an inland terminal system was going to be forced upon the West by Ottawa" (Yonge, 1973, p. 2).

The long-standing "East-West problem," (stemming from the National Policy of high tariff protection to domestic manufacturing since 1879), is the foundation of virtually all the constraints upon the federal government's power.[15] Such considerations also explain the federal government's actions with respect to the Canadian Transport Commission. As noted above, the CTC has legal responsibilities (under the 1967 *National Transportation Act)* to prescribe costing procedures for the railways, and to consider branch line abandonments (*Railway Act,* R.S. c. 234, s.1).

The authority of the CTC with respect to abandonments has been repeatedly superseded by federal government action. In 1967, a freeze in abandonment proceedings was imposed for the majority of the loss-making branch lines, and in 1972 a further freeze halted consideration of all abandonment hearings (Candlish, 1973, discusses these actions). Upon the expiration of these abandonment rulings, the federal government created a Royal Commission of Inquiry to make recommendations upon abandonments, once again superceding the CTC's authority (Canada, 1977). These actions give evidence of the lack of perceived expert or legitimate power possessed by the CTC, a lack clearly due to the CTC's role as a federal agency based in Ottawa. Further evidence of this is provided with respect to the CTC's responsibilities for railway costing. In spite of two major investigations of costing procedures conducted since 1967 (See Canadian Transport Commission, 1969), acceptance by western interests of railway cost data has not been complete. In one of the Canada Grains Council's investigations of the railway network, a minority position was filed by the provincial government representatives, based largely on dispute over rail costing procedures (Sardy, 1974, Appendix). The failure of the Canadian Transport Commission in this respect to develop perceived expert power culminated in the

---

[15] It is interesting to note in this regard that in 1970 (the beginning of the period under study in this paper) the party affiliation of members of the House of Commons representing constituencies in the Prairie provinces was as follows: Progressive Conservative (25), Liberal (10) and New Democratic Party (9). By 1974, these figures had changed to Progressive Conservative (36), Liberal (5) and New Democratic Party (4). Given that the Liberal party formed the national government with only a slim majority (and in some years acted as a minority government), the crucial role played by the Prairie vote in national politics may clearly be seen. (Data is taken from the *Canada Year Book* for 1971 and 1975.)

establishment of a second Commission of Inquiry, the Snavely Commission (Canada, 1976) to investigate railway costing practices in relation to grain.

In spite of the limitations expressed above, it would be a mistake to underestimate the federal government's power. The limitations are largely of the form of constraining the range of actions that are *acceptable* to other power holders, that is, are largely constraints upon the forms in which the federal government's power may be used. Our discussion would appear to lead to the conclusion that the federal government may be forced to channel its power through its agencies located in the West—the Canadian Wheat Board and the Canadian Grain Commission.

CANADIAN WHEAT BOARD

The power of the Canadian Wheat Board over the producers is extensive, and is founded on three distinct authorities: its position as monopoly purchaser (monopsonist) for Board grains; its authority to restrict the delivery points to which the producer may deliver his grain (applicable to all grains, Board and non-Board); and its authority to establish quotas on all grains, thus affecting the quantities of grain that the producer may deliver. These authorities find their expression as coercive powers, according to the classification established above, but other bases of power are of importance in understanding Board-producer relationships.

Perhaps the most important of these are *referent* and *identification* power. Fowke (1958) in a study of the events in the grain industry during the 1920s and 1930s establishes conclusively that the Canadian Wheat Board was instituted very reluctantly by the federal government, and only after the collapse of the provincially based (but privately operated) pools which had been formed because of the government's resistance to earlier producer pressure to establish Prairie-wide pooling. The Canadian Wheat Board may be viewed therefore, not solely as a creation of the federal government, but also of the farmer/producers. Because of this, the Board may be said to possess an *identification* base of power that flows from the producers.

The nature of this power source can only be understood by consideration of the principles embodied in the establishment and operation of the Canadian Wheat Board. Most of these principles relate to consideration of equity. The pooling of returns from the sale of grain, the keystone of the Board's existence, is based on the equity principle that all producers should receive the same return (per unit) for grain of an equivalent quality. The quota system is an expression of the desire for equality of opportunity to deliver grain. Even the rail-car allocation system of the Canadian Wheat Board (the "Bracken Formula") is an attempt to provide equality of opportunity to grain companies to move their grain. The acceptance of the Board's authority, that is, its perceived legitimate power, is thus largely constrained with respect to specific actions to the extent that these actions match with equity principles. Such considerations may be seen to place constraints upon the federal use of the Board to promote changes in the grain collection system. For example, the favourable treatment of inland terminals by the Board (perhaps in delivery point actions or rail-car allocation) would clearly violate equity principles and thus weaken its identification power.

The Canadian Wheat Board's relations with the grain companies, in their role as elevator operators, is also marked by the possession of significant authority by the Board over the activities of the grain companies. No grain (Board or non-Board) may be moved out of a country elevator without the permission of the Canadian Wheat Board. It should be noted, however, that this authority to control all grain movements was obtained by the Canadian Wheat Board in 1957 from the Canadian Grain Commission. The legislative basis for this authority is contained in the *Canada Grain Act* (*not* the *Canadian Wheat Board Act*) which grants to the Cabinet the ability to delegate this authority to any federal agency. The grain companies, therefore, have a *dependence for the attainment of their goals* (i.e., profitability) upon the Canadian Wheat Board.

The acceptance by the grain companies of the Board's power was not complete. The provincial Pools, like the producers, had been among the prime forces for the establishment of the Board, and an *identification* power source for the Board existed among these companies. However, no such identification existed among the private trade. The legitimacy of the Board's authority to control the movement of Board grains was accepted, but conflicts existed because of the Board's control of the movement of non-Board grains.[16]

We have dwelt at some length on the power position of the Canadian Wheat Board, distinct from its role as an arm of the federal government. This is because the Board is an independent agency: its employees are *not* employees of the federal government, their salaries being paid from the trading profits on grain. The same is not true of the Canadian Grain Commission, which is far from being an *independent* regulatory agency, as the Minister for Agriculture plays an important role in its major decisions. It is therefore not necessary to analyse the power of the Canadian Grain Commission independently of that of the federal government.

SUMMARY OF PARTICIPANTS' POWER

In this review of the federal government's power, we have seen that its power has grown along with its financial stake in the system, but that its freedom of action is constrained severely by the attitudes and power of others: primarily the producers and the grain companies.

Because of the extensive control of their operations exercised (primarily) by the Canadian Wheat Board, there may exist a tendency to underestimate

---

[16] These conflicts arose because, in a time of rail-car shortage, the Board had the power to decide whether to move its own (Board) grain, or to provide cars for the movement of the grain companies' (off-Board) grain.

the power of the producers. However, the fact that virtually all participants in the grain industry feel constrained to justify their positions and actions as being "in the best interests of the producer" reveals that, in theory, at least, the producer is a prime power holder in this industry. The basis of producer power is primarily political, and when mobilized, it can be a strong force.[17]

That this is so is evidenced by the success of producer pressure in forcing the establishment of the Canadian Wheat Board in the 1930s and in capturing various other gains for themselves in the form of the *Temporary Wheat Reserves Act,* the *Prairie Grain Advance Payments Act* (a system whereby producers received payment for grain in advance of delivery to an elevator), Two-Price Wheat and various other federal programs for the support of the producers' income. (For a discussion of these programs, see Candlish (1973), Fowke (1958) and Canada (1977)).

The grain companies also have substantial degrees of power, part of which is derived from their independent authority to close down or open elevators of any type. While, in principle, this power is mitigated by the possible loss of the producers' business, in fact, due to the increasing concentration of elevators in the hands of the Pools, many producers would be forced to deliver their grain to the same company at an alternate point. The Pools and UGG are also the beneficiaries of an *identification* power source conferred on them by their status as farmer-owned cooperatives: thus the power of the producers is transferred to the Pools. The concentration of ownership of port terminals in the hands of the Pools also gives them a strong power base.

The railways' power in this system, though potentially great, has been largely circumscribed by the legal limitations imposed on their freedom of action. They do not have discretion over abandonments, the rate to be charged for transporting grain or the allocation of rail cars.

In summary, therefore, the lack of change in tariffs and regulations of the Canadian Grain Commission preventing inland terminals prior to the 1970s is readily understandable by consideration of the fact that the attitudes and goals of powerful interests were sufficiently strong to influence the key decision maker, the federal government. The goals of the federal government during the postwar period (financial support of the farmer/producer population, equity in its dealings with the industry) inhibited it from providing leadership in the initiation of inland terminals. We now turn to the question of what happened to change this situation: why did the most of the regulations barring inland terminals fall during the early 1970s?

The Timing of Change in the Grain Transportation System

As may be expected, a full explanation of the timing of change involves shifts in power, in goals, and in perceptions. We have already referred, obli-

---

[17] See footnote 15.

quely, to one of the major shifts: the *National Transportation Act* of 1967 which introduced grain branch line subsidies. In contrast to its earlier financial assistance to the grain industry (*the Temporary Wheat Reserves Act* of 1956), the new program, for the first time, placed some of the burden of the inefficiency of the system on the shoulders of the federal government. Thus, as their stake increased, the federal government goals underwent a change of emphasis. Whereas before they had been observers of the system, they now became involved participants.

At the same time, the goals and powers of the grain producers (as a group) had evidenced a shift. In 1931, over 40 percent of farms were less than 200 acres, while by 1971 only 17 percent of farms were this small. The percentage of farms over 640 acres grew from 17 percent to 43 percent in the same period. (Canada Grains Council, 1974, pp. 227-229). The significance of this is that virtually all of the bases of producer opposition to inland terminals (trucking longer distances, dependence on small communities, need for personal interface with elevator agents) are more characteristic of the small farmer than of the large. The goals of the producer population were shifting.

The increasing concentration in the ownership of country elevators mitigated another of the bases of opposition to inland terminals: the lack of choice in delivery points. Of more significance was the changing position of the grain producer in Prairie society. With increasing development of livestock farming (and, indeed, of off-Board grain production), and with increasing urbanization (the rural population of the Prairies declined from 69 percent to 37 percent between 1941 and 1961) (Canada Grains Council, 1974, pp. 227-229), the "homogeneity" of western interests declined. As predicted by our theory, a loss of political power followed.

The increasing concentration of both the primary and terminal elevator sectors in the hands of the Pools also led, paradoxically, to a decline in their power in that, as they grew to the multi-sector conglomerates they are today, the Pools lost some of the "identification" power they derived from being farmer-owned. The increasing size of farms, and the lessened need of the individual farmers on the Pools for collective action also contributed to this.

Of all the changes that accumulated in the late 1960s, the change in the demand for wheat was the most profound. In 1963 - 1964, Russia began buying wheat from Canada, requesting all that Canada could supply. The high volumes to be transported placed severe strain on the system.[18] By 1967, after repeated years of high movement, the faults of the systems were revealed: as a result of such actions as the *Temporary Wheat Reserves Act*, the system was designed to store grain, not to transport it efficiently. It was in this

---

[18] Exact data on the flows of grain in the 1960s (and the Russian purchases) may be found in Canadian Wheat Board annual reports. The problems that resulted in the grain transportation system are discussed in Candlish (1973).

period that the federal ministers of Transport and Industry, Trade and Commerce visited Winnipeg to create an inter-industry "Grain Transportation Committee" which led to the development of the Block Shipping System and other coordinating mechanisms for the efficient transportation of grain (Grain Transportation Committee, 1967). This action coinciding with the 1967 introduction of branch line subsidies reveals the beginnings of real federal power in the industry. The exercise of this power is illustrated by the formation of the Grains Group to publish and disseminate information concerning the comparative costs of alternate systems: a key function of the "channel-captain" position.

The changes in goals and power described here set the scene for the regulatory changes to follow. However, the power of the federal government was still in its early stages. That its goals had shifted is illustrated by the proposed amendments to the *Canada Grain Act* of 1971. In the original bill, the government had sought to give the Canadian Grain Commission the power to explicitly direct the construction of elevators: this provision was removed in parliamentary debate. However, the new Act did remove one of the regulatory barriers to inland terminals: elevator companies were now able to charge different tariffs at different locations.

However, this change in the legislative provisions was not sufficient to induce a change in the system. In 1971, the maximum handling tariff was 3.75 cents per bushel (for wheat), a level too low to allow flexible pricing. With the world price of wheat at $2.00 per bushel, a rise in the tariff would have been a politically unpopular, and perhaps impossible, action.

The final change we wish to stress began to occur in 1972. The price of wheat on world markets began to rise, reaching over $5.00 per bushel by the 1973-1974 crop year. Under such circumstances, the second of the regulatory barriers could now fall: the Canadian Grain Commission raised the maximum primary elevator tariff in 1974 to 10.5 cents per bushel (from 3.75 cents per bushel, a level established in 1967). The Canadian Grain Commission next turned its attention to the third regulatory barrier: the low port cleaning tariff. In response to grain company requests for an increase of 2 cents per bushel in the existing 4.875 cents per bushel terminal *elevation* tariff, the Canadian Grain Commission responded by raising, over the objections of the Pools, the elevation tariff by only one-half cent,[19] but also by rais-

---

[19] Effective August 1, 1978 the Canadian Grain Commission raised "country-elevator maximums for a metric ton of wheat from $5.30 to $5.80 and terminal charges from $2.25 to $4. The Commission says it hopes grain companies will be able to set competitive handling charges below the maximums allowed." The *Financial Post* story (May 13, 1978, p. 2) continues, "industry officials clearly think the new maximums, while good news in the short run, will be adequate for only a few years at most. By then, they argue, capital requirements will be acute enough that the Grain Commission will have to consider raising the maximums again.

"I hope that maximums will be reviewed very soon, maybe even 12 months from now," says John Wachal, general manager of United Grain Growers Ltd. of Winnipeg. "It all depends on what happens to inflation. I don't think it's under control yet. . . .

Spokesmen for the Palliser Wheat Growers Association complain that tariff increases at the

ing the maximum *cleaning* tariff from 1 cent per bushel to 5 cents per bushel. In order to raise their total revenue, port terminal operators would be forced to impose "realistic" cleaning charges. At this level, an inland terminal operator could profitably invest in his own cleaning equipment. This decision was announced by the Minister for Agriculture, who also gave notice of his intention to deduct the cleaning charge directly from the producer's initial payment. The cost of cleaning was no longer to be hidden, and the third regulatory barrier to inland terminal had fallen.

It is important to note that the three regulatory barriers that had fallen were all removed by the federal government acting through the Canadian Grain Commission, its agency in the West. The fourth regulatory barrier, the statutory rail rate, was *not* acted upon: a fact that can best be explained by noting that any such change would have to be taken in the East, in Parliament. The statutory rail rate had long been a symbol of the rights of the West: in this respect the West still retained its traditional advantages.

As a final note of change, we should recognize that, not entirely coincidentally, one of the "procedural" barriers to inland terminals also fell in 1976. The Canadian Wheat Board announced that the allocation of rail cars would henceforth take into acount the congestion of the elevator, and not just the receipts from producers in the previous year (see Canadian Wheat Board Annual Report, 1976). This change would allow a new elevator operator to receive an allocation of rail cars corresponding to the amount of grain available.

THE INITIATION OF CHANGE

The actions of the federal government in raising maximum tariffs were followed quickly by the announcement of plans in late 1974 for the construction of an inland terminal at Weyburn, Saskatchewan. A group of producers, all members of the "progressive" Palliser Wheat Growers' Association, funded, *with a contribution from the federal government,* a feasibility study for the installation. They proceeded to sell shares to other producers, financing the remainder with a bank loan. The Weyburn inland terminal opened in November 1976. One of the world's largest grain companies, Cargill, which had entered the primary elevator sector in 1974, announced that it was commencing construction of three large scale facilities with handling capacities of 10 million bushels per year, (compared to Weyburn's 20 million). Similar announcements by other private grain companies (e.g., Bunge) followed in early 1976. It is, of course, of more than passing interest to note that these

---

terminal level are "hidden costs" not readily evident to farmers, although farmers end up paying for them through lower final Canadian Wheat Board payments. They would have been happier had the increased charges been levied at the country level, where farmers pay them directly and can see the cost of the system.

National Farmers Union spokesmen argue that new maximums are too high and will allow grain companies to manipulate charges to favor concentration of services at larger elevators at the expense of smaller elevators spread throughout the countryside."

"innovations" were conducted by a producers' group and by private grain companies: not the Pools. As theory predicts, the innovations came from outside the existing power structure.[20]

It is important to recognize that these new facilities are *not* inland terminals as originally conceived. In every case the facilities have been built with *low* storage capacity relative to their throughput. The incentive to do this is provided by the fact that since most of the costs of operating an elevator are fixed, that is, related to the size of the facility, per bushel handling costs could be lowered by reducing the storage capacity. Regrettably, such a facility appears to make the same "mistake" as was made in the 1950s and 1960s. It is designed only for one phase of the world grain "cycle." If and when current demand for grain is exceeded by current supply, the system will once again be required to store large quantities of grain. A network of facilities such as those now being constructed will be ill-designed to handle this task. However, the decision to build such facilities makes sound business sense. Without the extra benefits of rail economies that would have been available with adjustment or removal of the statutory rail rate, inland terminals as originally conceived did not make economic sense. Therefore, economies in construction cost were required to make them financially viable. Further, storage capacity *can* always be added to an existing facility in the event of a demonstrated need. What is more, and perhaps most unfortunate (from the point of view of efficient resource allocation), there is always the possibility that, as with the *Temporary Wheat Reserves Act* in the 1950s, the federal government might "bail out" the system by financing the construction of storage facilities when surpluses abound.

EVENTS SINCE 1975

The success of the new "high throughput" facilities was by no means assured in the two years since 1975. In March of 1976, the Saskatchewan government, in an explicit attempt to *prevent* development of the inland terminals, announced that it intended to *lower* the maximum allowable weight on provincial roads, effectively barring the commercial trucking of grain essential to the success of the inland terminals (Winnipeg Free Press *Report on Farming*, March 27, 1976). Although, in the face of opposition from many quarters, including general for-hire truckers whose activities would also be curtailed, this threat was not acted upon, it served as a reminder that significant opposition to inland terminals still existed and that their successful implementation depended upon still elusive interorganizational cooperation.

The federal government, through the Canadian Wheat Board, con-

---

[20] Of course, Cargill and Bunge were not "outsiders" in the total context of the grain industry, due to their activities in export sales. However, they may be so considered with respect to the primary elevator sector.

tinued to increase its financial contribution to the grain transportation industry. In August of 1976, the Board announced a $2 million plan to encourage expansion of port terminal facilities in Vancouver, whereby the Board would guarantee storage payments on at least 90 percent of new capacity (Canadian Wheat Board Weekly News Review, August 20, 1976). This move was made in response to the fact that capacity limitations in Vancouver had led to costs of $3.1 million in demurrage charges in the 1975-1976 crop year (Canadian Wheat Board Annual Report, 1976). It will be noted, that this action is far from consistent with any long-run plan to promote the development of inland terminals which would themselves alleviate West Coast capacity problems. However, as a medium-term move, the action does make economic sense. The Canadian Wheat Board also continued to purchase grain hopper cars, announcing purchases of an additional 8,000 cars in June of 1977 (Canadian Wheat Board Weekly News Review, June, 1977).

The first of the new facilities, the Weyburn inland terminal, opened in November 1976: its first year of operation was not an overwhelming success, deliveries from producers failing to meet required breakeven volumes (Canadian Wheat Board Weekly News Review). Although little discussion of reasons for this have taken place in the public domain, at least one of the contributory factors was the fact that the 1976 - 1977 crop year did not require a heavy movement of grain. World demand for grain slackened, prices falling from their 1974 peak. In fact, in late 1977 and early 1978 some sales were taking place at prices as low as $2 per bushel, and a final payment of only 22 cents per bushel was paid (above the $3 initial payment) for the 1976 - 1977 crop year. However, world demand cannot be entirely the cause of Weyburn's initial problems. The ability to persuade producers to deliver sufficient quantities over the large distances has yet to be demonstrated. Of course, in the absence of the rail economies possible (unit trains) if the statutory rail rate were to be changed, Weyburn and terminals like it do not constitute a true test of the inland terminal concept.

By far the most significant events in the grain industry in recent years were the *Report of the Commission on the Costs of Transporting Grain by Rail* (Canada, 1976), the "Snavely Commission", and the *Report of the Grain Handling and Transportation Commission* (Canada, 1977), "the Hall Commission." When the federal government's "freeze" on railway abandonments expired in 1975, it set up these two commissions of enquiry. Snavely, a U.S. economist was asked to investigate the costs and revenues of the railways in transporting grain: in effect to determine (once and for all?) whether the statutory rail rates were compensatory. As reported above, he found that they were not: *losses* on grain transport *after* branch line subsidies totalled $90 million in 1974. The revenues of the railways for transporting grain were approximately the same amount (Canada, 1976, Chapter V).

To the Hall Commission was given the task of deciding the future of the 6,300 miles of railway track under consideration for abandonment. (The terms of reference for the Commission are given in Volume 1 of the Commission's Report (Canada, 1977).) The Commission recommended that 2,165 miles be abandoned, 1,813 miles be made part of the "permanent network," and a further 2,344 miles be retained pending further review. It also recommended that an *independent* "Prairie Rail Authority," located in the West, be set up to perform this review. The Hall Commission investigated a wide variety of topics in the course of its deliberations (for example, presenting convincing evidence *against* the hypothesis that rail line abandonment is a prime cause of small community decline), and made the important recommendation that the statutory rail rate be retained, and the railways' losses be fully compensated by the federal government. This conclusion was reached, it would appear, not from economic reasoning, but because "anything else would be a violation of promises made to the producers of Western Canada" (Canada, 1977, I, p. 336).

During the year since the Hall Commission report, the Minister of Transport (who is also currently the Minister responsible for the Canadian Wheat Board) established *not* the independent Prairie Rail Authority (PRA) recommended by Hall, but a "Prairie Rail Action Committee" reporting directly to him (Canadian Wheat Board Weekly News Review, Dec 9, 1977). The Action Committee was supposed to "fill in" until legislation could be drafted to form the PRA, but there exist doubts in the West as to whether the committee is indeed only a temporary creation. This feeling was reinforced by the fact that in September 1977 the Minister signed an agreement to provide a direct grant of $100 million to the railways to rehabilitate rail track, instead of channelling the money through the Prairie Rail Authority who were to set priorities for upgrading (Canadian Wheat Board Weekly News Review, Sept 24, 1977). Although no action has been taken to date, it would appear from the press (Canadian Wheat Board Weekly News Review, Various Issues in 1978) that the federal government is planning to act on Hall's recommendation to compensate the railways for losses due to the Crow rate, leaving the statutory grain rate intact.

The Explanation of Change: Conclusions

There are clearly two sets of conclusions that we may draw from the analysis presented above: conclusions about the theory of change in regulated industries, and conclusions about appropriate policies for the development of the grain transportation system. We begin with the former.

Our analysis has indeed shown that the existence of a superior technology (i.e., an economically more efficient one) was not, in itself, sufficient to result in the adoption of that technology (Hypothesis One). The reason for this was that the "superior technology" was superior in dimensions that did not reflect the dominant goals of the system. Inland terminals offered *movement* cost savings while the dominant goals of the system were maintenance of income for producers and protection of rural communities. Opposition to the new technology was indeed founded upon conflicts of domain, goals and perceptions (Hypothesis Two). The opposition of a potentially powerful participant (the railways) was "bought off" by the channel captain: the granting of branch line subsidies by the federal government (Hypothesis Four).

This equilibrium was disturbed by the gradual emergence of the federal government as the major power holder in the system because of its increasing financial stake in the system (Hypothesis Three and Five). The changing power structure was also explained in terms of the homogeneity of the produce population (Hypothesis Ten),

The reaction of the new channel captain (the federal government) to the shift in goals was to attempt to reduce conflicts of perception about the benefits of the new system (Hypothesis Seven), in the formation of the Grains Group and its subsequent research work. The failure of this action to reduce conflict was primarily due to the lack of credibility in the source (Hypothesis Eight). As predicted, innovation in the system came from outside the established power structure (Hypothesis Six). Finally we have noted that the federal government attempts to introduce change all took place outside of the *directly* political arena. The remaining barrier to inland terminals, the statutory rail rate, was, as predicted, that for which change would require the most overt political action.

It would clearly be with overstatement to suggest that the "model" of change presented here represents a comprehensive and general description of the change process in the context of regulated industries. However, our analysis has served to illustrate the need to draw from a variety of conceptual frameworks to develop a full understanding of the nature of change in regulated industries. In the course of this analysis we have drawn repeatedly on sociological, political and economic principles to explain events in the grain transportation industry.

In this analysis, we have attempted to be reasonably comprehensive in terms of time (explaining all stages of the change process), in terms of the number of participants (the full industry), and in terms of 'relevant factors'. There is much to be said for this approach: only by accumulation and comparison of detailed case studies can the common elements of the change process be identified, and the full development of a conceptual model take place. On the other hand, the specific testing hypotheses related to the conceptual framework is difficult with some case studies, and adequately verified generalizations about the change process will be developed slowly.

CONCLUSIONS: THE FUTURE OF THE GRAIN INDUSTRY

What factors will determine the success and/or speed of the introduction of inland terminals in Canada? We have predicted that the proposed inland terminals are likely to succeed because of the changing goals of the farmer/producer population, that is, a greater concern with income maximization rather than security and traditional social values. It should be noted, however, that a major factor in bringing about this change was the rise in the price of wheat in the period 1972 - 1976, and the consequent relative prosperity of the farm population. It is unlikely that any substantial change in this prosperity could occur without a further readjustment (or return) in producer goals.

More important than this factor, however, in explaining the success of inland terminals, will be the actions of the federal government (and its agencies) in achieving agreement on the future direction of the grain transportation system. In the last few years, as we have seen, the federal government has hesitated to act *directly* to promote inland terminals, while, at the same time, its agencies have taken actions which have promoted the possibility of successful inland terminal operation.

It should be recognized that only by abdicating its 'channel captain' role can the federal government avoid directing the development of the grain transportation system, and if such an abdication takes place, there is no other organization, or group of organizations, large enough to take on the coordinating role necessary for the efficient functioning of the grain transportation system *as a system*. It must also be recognized that the involvement of the federal government in the grain transportation system has grown, since the early 1960s, to a state where it can no longer take a "neutral" action. It therefore has the responsibility to use its decision-making power in a *consistent* manner, and in the best *long-term* interests of the grain transportation industry, the producer community and the general Canadian public. While these various constituencies may (and almost assuredly do) have conflicting interests, no one group's interests will be served by avoiding the task of resolving these interests by policy decision. The action of the Saskatchewan government in taking unilateral action on road weight limits, in an attempt to prevent inland terminals, is evidence that the federal government has failed in its 'channel captain' role of winning the cooperation of all participants in the industry. In large part, this failure is due to the fact that the federal government has attempted to adopt what we interpret as a "neutral" stance on the inland terminal question, a position which we have argued is no longer tenable.

We have referred to the need for *consistent* and *long-run* decision-making. These two considerations have been noticeably lacking in the Canadian grain industry. The evolution of an inland terminal network would involve such large amounts of capital, and such detailed coordination, that it is unlikely to develop successfully in piece-meal fashion. Evidence of this is provided by the fact that virtually all of the inland terminals now under construction have a high throughput capacity to storage capacity ratio. This implies that, if such a trend were to continue, eventually a shortage of storage capacity for weak-market years would exist. Under current tariffs and regulations the incentive exists to build inland terminals, but not sufficient storage capacity to accompany them. That this has resulted is due to the fact that only *some* of the barriers to inland terminals have been removed. Others, like the statutory rail rate, remain. A second example is given by the action of the Canadian Wheat Board in providing incentives for terminal storage capacity in Vancouver (an action reminiscent of the *Temporary*

Wheat Reserves Act program). *If* an inland terminal system with inland cleaning were to develop, such expansion would not be necessary in the long run as important as it is in the short run. The Canadian Wheat Board's action thus appears to be in conflict with the Grain Commission's apparent desire to encourage (or at least, allow) inland cleaning. Taken together, these actions are not consistent. They must stem from different views of the desired direction of the grain transportation system.

A consistent, efficient system can only evolve if the rules and regulations that surround the industry are also consistent. This will involve simultaneous coordination of decision-making by Parliament, the Canadian Grain Commission and the Canadian Wheat Board, among others. The first step in achieving industry agreement and cooperation for the future of the grain transportation system must be agreement, coordination and cooperation among the various federal government decision-making bodies. This agreement and consistency has not always existed.

Of potentially greater concern is the lack of long-run considerations in actions taken by the federal government. The overcapacity of country elevator storage that plagued the industry in the early 1970s is traceable directly to the *Temporary Wheat Reserves Act* program. The branch line subsidy program has also led to various undesirable side effects. These actions failed to recognize the dynamic and cyclical nature of the grain industry. It is obvious, but seldom recognized in policy formation, that the optimal grain transportation system is different for conditions of strong wheat markets and weak wheat markets. In the former, the primary goal must be movement and handling efficiency, while in the latter cheap storage considerations are paramount. The *Temporary Wheat Reserves Act* created a storage-oriented system, which led to crisis when the needs of the market changed. The current activity in inland terminal construction appears to be based on a movement orientation at the expense of future potential storage requirements. It is not difficult to foresee another crisis in the making. The time has come for the conscious design and implementation of a system that recognizes these cyclical and long-run requirements, and decision-making that is based not on short-term measures in response to current pressures, but a reasoned view of what set of rules, regulations and systems will best serve the various interested parties over the long term.

The signs in recent times have not been encouraging. The federal government appears to be adopting a policy of "patching" over the short-term problems by increasingly absorbing the financial burden of the system's built-in inefficiencies. The $100 million grant to the railways is sufficient evidence of this. Even more disillusioning is the possibility that the federal government will absorb the financial losses of the railways due to the low statutory rail rate. As has been argued in this paper, the greatest defect of the statutory rail rate is not that it represents a subsidy to the West, or that it has been an excessive burden on the railways: its greatest defect has been that, by being *fixed*, it has prevented economic forces from providing the incentives to introduce new technology. We can, however, end this analysis on a positive, if spculative, note. If the federal government *does* assume the burden of the unremunerative statutory rate, this burden will be more "exposed" than when it is hidden in the ledgers of the railways. Since the statutory rail rate is fixed in an absolute dollar amount (or, to be ironically precise, an absolute cent amount) the size of the burden can only grow as inflation proceeds. With the burden *directly* on the shoulders of the taxpayer it may soon become politically feasible to achieve an amendment to this unique statutory rate. This factor, together with the trends identified in this paper, suggest that time is on the side of economic rationality.

REFERENCES

Adams, W. and J. B. Dirlam (1968) "Market Structure, Regulation and Dynamic Change" in H.B. Trebing (ed.) *Performance under Regulation,* pp. 131-44 (East Lansing, Mich.: Michigan State University, Graduate School of Business, Division of Research).

Alderson, W. (1957) *Marketing Behavior and Executive Action* (Homewood, Ill.: Irwin).

Alderson, W. (1967) *Dynamic Marketing Behavior* (Homewood, Ill.: Irwin).

Assael, H. (1968) "The Political Role of Trade Associations in Distributive Conflict Resolutions" *Journal of Marketing* 32: April, 21-28.

Averch, H. and L.L. Johnson (1962) "Behavior of the Firm under Regulatory Constraint" *American Economic Review* 52: December, 1052-69.

Baldwin, J.R. (1975) *The Crown Corporation and the Regulatory Agency* (Cambridge, Mass.: Ballinger)

Braybrooke, David and C.E. Lindblom (1963) *Strategy of Decision* (New York: Free Press).

Canada (1959) House of Commons, *Debates,* May 13 (Ottawa: Queen's Printer).

Canada (1961) *Report of the Royal Commission on Transportation,* 2 vols (Ottawa: Queen's Printer).

Canada (1976) *Report of the Commission on the Costs of Transporting Grain by Rail* ("Snavely Commission") Vol. 1 (Ottawa: Information Canada).

Canada (1977) *Report of the Grain Handling and Transportation Commission* ("Hall Commission") vol. 1 (Ottawa: Information Canada).

Canada, *Canadian Wheat Board Act,* R.S.C., c. 44.

Canada Grains Council (1975a) *Statistical Handbook 1974* (Winnipeg: Canada Grains Council).

Canada Grains Council (1975b) *Fact Sheet No. 2* (Winnipeg: Canada Grains Council).

Canada Grains Council (1976) *Statistical Handbook 1975* (Winnipeg: Canada Grains Council).

Canada Year Book (various years) (Ottawa: Supply and Services Canada).

Canadian Grain Commission (1976) *Grain Elevators in Canada: Crop Year 1976/77.*(Ottawa: Information Canada).

Canadian Transport Commission (1972) *Factors Influencing the Choice of a New Delivery Point and Elevator Company by Prairie Farmers Facing Delivery Point Closure,* Report No. 54 (Ottawa: CTC, Economics Branch).

Canadian Wheat Board (various years) *Annual Report* (Winnipeg: Canadian Wheat Board).

Canadian Wheat Board (weekly) *Weekly News Release* (Winnipeg: Canadian Wheat Board).

Candlish, J., A. Mills, R. Martireler, and P. Earl (1973) *Grain Handling and*

Transportation: State of the Industry (Winnipeg: Canada Grains Council).

Capron, W.M. (ed.) (1971) *Technological Change in Regulated Industries* (Washington, D.C.: Brookings).

Fowke, V.C. (1957) *The National Policy and the Wheat Economy* (Toronto: University of Toronto Press).

Goldberg, R.A. (1968) *Agribusiness Coordination* (Boston: Harvard University, Graduate School of Business Administration).

Grain Transportation Committee (1967) *Proceedings of the Grain Transportation Workshop* (Ottawa: Grain Transportation Committee).

Hardin, H. (1975) *A Nation Unaware* (Vancouver: J. J. Douglas)

Heskett, J.L., L.W. Stern and F.J. Beier (1970) "Bases and Uses of Power in Interorganizational Relations" in L.P. Bucklin (ed.) *Vertical Marketing Systems*, pp. 75-93 (Glenville, Ill.: Scott, Foresman).

McCammon, B.C. Jr. (1965) "Alternative Explanations of Institutional Change and Channel Evolution" in S.A. Greyser (ed.) *Toward Scientific Marketing*, pp. 477-90 (Chicago: American Marketing Association).

McCammon, B.C. Jr., and R.W. Little (1965) "Marketing Channels: Analytic Systems and Approaches" in G. Schwartz (ed.) *Science in Marketing*, pp. 321-85 (New York: Wiley).

Maister, D.H. (1976) "Barriers to Change in Distributive Industries: The Canadian Grain Delivery System" D.B.A. dissertation, Harvard University, Graduate School of Business Administration.

Mason, G. (1978) "The Grain Handling and Transportation Commission" *Canadian Public Policy* 4: Spring, 235-45.

Menzies, M.W. (1971) *The Report of the Canadian Grain Marketing Review Committee* (Winnipeg: Canadian Wheat Board).

Mitchell, J.M. and W.C. Mitchell (1969) *Political Analysis and Public Policy* (Chicago: Rand McNally).

Palamountain, J.C. (1955) *The Politics of Distribution* (Cambridge, Mass.: Harvard University Press).

Parsons, G.G. (1975) *Eastern Grain Movement Report* (Winnipeg: Canada Grains Council).

Purdy, H.L. (1972) *Transport in Canada: Competition and Public Policy* (Vancouver: University of British Columbia Press).

Rodgers, E.M. and G.M. Beal (1958) *Reference Group Influence in the Adoption of Agricultural Technology* (Ames, Iowa: Iowa State University).

Ross, P.S. and Partners (1971) *Grain Handling and Transportation Costs in Canada* (Ottawa: Grains Group).

Ruppenthal, K.M. (ed.) (1974) *Transportation Subsidies - Nature and Extent* (Vancouver: University of British Columbia, Centre for Transportation Studies).

Ruppenthal, K.M. and W.T. Stanbury (eds) (1976) *Transportation Policy: Regulation, Competition, and the Public Interest* (Vancouver: University of British Columbia, Centre for Transportation Studies).

Sardy, H. (1974) *The Grain Handling and Transportation System in the Brandon Area* (Winnipeg: Canada Grains Council).

Schultz, R. (1979) *Federalism, and the Regulatory Process* (Montreal: Institute for Research on Public Policy, forthcoming).

Schumpeter, J. (1947) *Capitalism, Socialism and Democracy* (New York: Harper).

Stern, L.W. (ed.) (1969) *Distribution Channels: Behavioral Dimensions* (Boston: Houghton Mifflin).

Stern, L.W. and A.I. El-Ansary (1977) *Marketing Channels* (Englewood Cliffs, N.J.: Prentice-Hall).

Stern, L.W. and R.H. Gorman (1969) "Conflict in Distribution Channels: An Exploration" in L.W. Stern (ed) *Distribution Channels: Behavioral Dimensions* (Boston: Houghton Mifflin).

Stern, L.W. and J.L. Heskett (1969) "Conflict Management in Interorganizational Relationships" in L.W. Stern (ed.) *Distribution Channels: Behavioral Dimensions* (Boston: Houghton Mifflin).

Westfield, F.M. (1971) "Innovation and Monopoly Regulation" in W.M. Capron (ed.) *Technological Change in Regulated Industries,* pp. 13-43 (Washington, D.C.: Brookings).

Winnipeg Free Press (1976) *Report on Farming* March 27.

Yonge, D.L. (1973) "What A Farmer Wants from the System" in G.A. Sparks (ed.) *Proceedings of the Grain Handling and Transportation Seminar,* Two - 1 to Two - 5 (Saskatoon: University of Saskatchewan).

Chapter Six

On the "New" Transportation Policy After Ten Years*

by *John C. McManus*
Department of Economics
Carleton University

INTRODUCTION

In 1967, following the *Report* of the 1961 Royal Commission on Transportation (MacPherson Commission), Parliament passed the *National Transportation Act*, which created the Canadian Transport Commission and much of the dilemma in which the Commission currently finds itself. The Commission's dilemma arises from an internal inconsistency in the 1967 Act. On the one hand, the Act asserts that the objective of regulation is to be an efficient allocation of resources to transportation:

> It is hereby declared that an economic, efficient and adequate transportation system making the best use of all available modes of transportation at the lowest total cost is essential to protect the interests of the users of transportation and to maintain the economic well-being and growth of Canada (1966-67, C. 69, 5.3, Section 3);

but, on the other hand, the Act reverts, in Section 23, to the vague criteria of "the public interest" 23(2), "unfair disadvantage," "undue obstacle," "unreasonable discouragement" 23(3), in evaluating rates set by regulated carriers. The vague wording has predictably invited special interest groups to use the Commission to arbitrate their competing claims with little or no regard for the economic considerations of Section 3. The Section 23 cases that have come before the Commission up to the end of 1976 have forced it into a role of interregional resource allocator without guidelines from Parliament, certainly a thankless if not hopeless task. Ten years after the *National Transportation Act*, it seems we don't know if we have a new transportation policy based on minimizing cost or the old one based on an "equitable" regional distribution of economic activity.

This paper begins with an economic analysis of these two alternative objectives of government regulation. A brief review of the experience up to 1967

---

* This is a substantially revised version of my paper "Federal Regulation of Transport in Canada," (November, 1972) commissioned by the Canadian Consumer Council, Ottawa.

as it may have motivated Parliament to write the 1967 Act follows the economic analysis discussion. Then an attempt is made to offer a critical evaluation of the Act and the record of the Commission to the end of 1976, including brief comments on the Hall Commission *Report* (Canada, 1977) and some recent policy statements by the government.

I will be using the term regulation to mean the presence of a legally constituted, government institution having some discretionary authority to unilaterally impose constraints on private decision-making by individuals and firms in certain activities.

WHY HAVE REGULATION?

From an economic point of view, there are two competing rationale for government regulation of economic activity, which differ mainly in the objectives which the regulatory authority is assumed to pursue. In the traditional, economic case for regulation, it is postulated that the government's objective is to effect a more efficient allocation of resources than would be obtained in the absence of regulation. The MacPherson Commission *Report* (Canada, 1961) lies squarely in this traditional mold. The alternative viewpoint regards regulation as an instrument of public finance. The government, through a regulatory body, manipulates the activities of "private" decision makers in the regulated industry who become, indirectly, tax farmers drawing revenues from one set of consumers and redistributing them, in the form of subsidized goods and services, to other consumers. In this view, regulation is one alternative to the direct taxing and expenditure functions of government. Although a relatively new approach in the United States as shown by Posner (1971, pp. 22-50), the treatment of regulation as an instrument of public finance according to Mackintosh (1964, pp. 24, 170-73) has been the normal approach to transport regulation by Canadian economists with an interest in national policy issues. Regional distribution of resources, encouragement of the export trade, and subsidization of particular East-West commodity movements have historically dominated government policy towards railroads, argues Currie (1954).

In its 1967 *National Transportation Act,* Parliament appeared to have been undecided on which of these two objectives the Canadian Transport Commission should pursue. Section 3 sides with the traditional view in words that could have been taken directly from the MacPherson *Report,* but Section 23 sides with the public finance motive in setting rates. The Act espouses competition among alternative modes, but, contrary to both the spirit and letter of the MacPherson *Report,*[1] contemplates, in Part III, Section 38, "public convenience and necessity" as a licensing requirement, meaning a barrier to entry, for an individual or firm to engage in commercial, interprovincial trucking. And now, to resolve this ambiguity the government is

---

[1] "Regulation in . . . (trucking) . . . should be confined to maintaining standards of safety and performance" (Canada, 1961, Vol. II, p. 10).

asking Parliament to eschew the efficiency objective by passing Bill C-33,[2] which revises Section 3 of the 1967 Act, deleting references to "lowest total cost" and "competition" and adding, as an objective for transport policy, "an effective instrument of support for the achievement of national and regional social and economic objectives." It appears that economic efficiency has had a short-lived acceptance as a goal of transport policy.

To evaluate these two postulated objectives of regulation, let us treat them as competing hypotheses and ask which of the two conforms more closely with regulatory experience.

Regulation and Monopoly

We observe that regulated industries tend to be subject to monopoly control, but at the same time regulatory authorities generally erect barriers to entry, usually licensing, which restrict entry to the regulated activity. One of the traditional arguments for regulation, with the postulated objective of efficient resource allocation, is that the industry is unavoidably susceptible to monopoly control because of scale economies in production, and regulation serves to "do for the industry what universally pervasive competition would do," according to the Royal Commission (Canada, 1961, II, p. 8). However, the regular coincidence of effective, legal barriers to entry with regulation is inconsistent with the hypothesis that efficiency is an objective. If the industry were a natural monopoly, the entry barriers would be redundant. They are not redundant where we find a queue of potential entrants awaiting a licence. Similarly, if regulation served to set a competitive price, there would be no queue of applicants, whether or not the conditions for a "natural monopoly" exist in the industry. Examples of the effectiveness of regulatory entry barriers are cited below.

In the United States where the federal government regulates interstate trucking through the Interstate Commerce Commission, the number of licensed carriers fell from 1945 to 1960 and then remained about the same through 1970 despite a more than *threefold* increase in freight hauled as measured in *ton miles*. Applications for licences run at about 5,000 per year according to Stigler (1971, pp. 5,6). We similarly find effective entry barriers in the regulated airline (Caves, 1962), telecommunications (McManus, 1973), and broadcasting industries (Levin, 1968, pp. 481-501).

These observations of effective entry barriers imply the presence of rents to at least some of the activities conducted within regulated industries. The persistence of rents under regulation is not inconsistent with the postulate that the objective of regulation is to serve as an indirect tax and expenditure mechanism. The rents to certain regulated activities provide the tax base from which "revenues" are implicitly collected and "disbursed" in the form of other services provided at subsidized rates (see Posner, 1971).

---

[2] See the paper by Heaver and Nelson, Chapter Seven of this volume, for an analysis of Bill C-33.

To protect the tax base, the regulator must erect barriers to entry; otherwise, competitive entry would dissipate the rents, even if the regulated rates were maintained.[3] Whether the industry is subject to natural monopoly or not is irrelevant. Once the choice is made to regulate, monopoly will follow. The cross-subsidization among regulated services is not a mistake, as it would be if allocative efficiency were the objective, rather it is the means by which the policy objectives of the government are carried out. Perhaps it was to make transport regulation a more effective instrument of public finance that Parliament, in 1967, chose to attempt to give the Canadian Transport Commission (CTC) powers to license interprovincial trucking. Effective barriers to entry in trucking, a close substitute for rail, would restore the regulator's tax base, and permit it to continue in its traditional role.

The evidence is clearly in favour of the public finance over the efficiency objective. Regulation is not intended to obviate allocative distortions that would be created by an unimpeded monopolist. To the contrary, regulation creates monopoly rents where they would not otherwise exist and directs these rents to serve national policy goals.

Regulation and Market Failure

Even if an industry were not subject to monopoly control, a case for regulating the industry may be constructed if the industry would have effects on others that would not be taken into account in the absence of regulation. We observe that governments regulate many industries which are not, or would not be, subject to monopoly control—commercial trucking, taxicabs, airlines, and broadcasting stations. Such industries may be expected to have "external effects" on others in the society that are great enough to warrant regulation of their activities.

To some extent, this is the basis of railway regulation. Location of lines and the provision of various transportation services affect individuals and regional governments in ways that the railway may not take into account. For example, discontinuance of passenger service can hardly be subject to regulatory control on the grounds that the railway is a "natural monopoly." Regulation may be imposed because it is thought that the railway would not otherwise consider the losses that discontinuance would impose on effected parties or municipalities.

The economic case for regulation of industries generating "external effects" is somewhat similar to the case for regulating a natural monopoly. The reason the industry generates an "external effect" is that some individuals are affected by the actions of the industry but are unable, for some reason or another, to make or receive payments to or from the industry so as to influence its actions. It is important to emphasize that it is the absence of some

---

[3] See Patinkin (1974, pp. 173-205) and Barzel (1947, pp. 73-96) for examples of how free access to a market at a controlled price dissipates the potential rents in that market through cost-increasing, competitive behaviour.

exchange mechanism that is the source of the problem. Because the parties affected by the externality do not engage in exchange with the appropriate industry, the industry's decision makers will not take into account those damages or benefits that they are imposing on others. Therefore, as in the case of the natural monopoly, the industry will produce less "external" benefits and more "external" damages than would be consistent with an efficient allocation of resources. If the establishment of a regulatory agency can bring these external effects to bear on the decisions of the industry, resource allocation will become more efficient. That is, in brief, the standard argument for interfering with the price mechanism when externalities are present.

The Defects In The Argument For Regulation

This argument for regulation suffers from two defects, both arising from common misinterpretations of the concept of externality. The first of these is that not all damages resulting from an action are "external" damages. Any economic action will damage someone simply because resources are scarce. The only damages that count as "external" and attributable to allocative inefficiency are damages to persons or firms who are unable, despite their willingness to pay, to exercise their dollar votes to have the action altered.

As we shall see in our description of some cases before the Canadian Transport Commission, regulatory agencies with control over service offerings commonly regard one of their functions to be the assessment of damages to users and to municipalities that would result from withdrawal of services. For example, the CTC may order (File No. 49467.47, September 30, 1970) the continuance of an uneconomic passenger service if it estimates that the damages to train passengers would be higher than the loss incurred by the railway. But this is an incorrect use of the externality concept. The reason that the service is uneconomic is that consumers are unwilling to pay for the costs of the service, not that they are unable to pay in the sense of having no opportunity to trade with the railroad. The regulatory board is correct in finding that existing users of the service would be damaged if the service were withdrawn; it is incorrect in entertaining the possibility that these damages are higher than the loss. If that were so, a price could be charged that would eliminate the loss.

The damages suffered by the passengers are unavoidable. They would like to have train service but they are not willing to pay for it. If they are provided with a train service at a loss, some other consumers, perhaps users of freight service, are being damaged by having less resources available for their use. These damages arise from scarcity of resources, about which the regulatory agency can do nothing.

The only damages that are relevant to efficiency are those suffered by individuals who have no opportunity to make payments to the railroad and so have an influence on its decisions. For example, a railroad discontinuing passenger service may contribute to increased highway congestion and so impose external damages on highway users who would not find it worthwhile to get together and bribe the railway to continue its service. Of course, these damages are very difficult to estimate.

The second defect in the case for regulating industries which generate externalities is that proponents of regulation often seem to ignore the effects on behaviour of changes in external effects. As I have tried to emphasize, the externality arises because of the absence of a means of making payment between the appropriate individuals or groups. But the absence of a means of payment does not mean that individuals experience external effects without any reaction. Individuals will adjust their behaviour to reduce the external damages caused them by others and to increase external benefits. Residential development will be less intensive downwind of a smoking factory; automobile drivers will demand more comfortable cars as traffic congestion increases; and individuals will alter their locational choices in response to the availability of transport services.

If the regulator acts to reduce external damages or to increase external benefits by altering only the behaviour of the regulated industry, the externality remains and there may be no gains from the change in behaviour due to regulatory intervention. Individuals will adjust their actions in response to the effects of regulation in a way that will reduce the gains that would otherwise result from regulation, says Coase (1960, pp. 30-34).

To illustrate the problem, suppose that a subsidized commuter service is instituted to relieve traffic congestion on a public highway.[4] As a first approximation, the gains from the passenger service may be estimated to be equal to the value of reduced travel time to automobile commuters following from the reduction in the number of vehicles using the public highway; but that would ignore predictable changes in behaviour due to the new service. For example, suppose that travelling on the toll-free highway between Burlington and Toronto, a trip of about 40 miles, took 80 minutes in rush hour in 1966 before a commuter train service was instituted. The travel time was in equilibrium given the relative real estate prices and other attributes of the two locations. Their relative populations will have adjusted so that for at least some individuals, living in Burlington and driving for 160 minutes to and from Toronto each day was equivalent to living in Toronto and paying higher real estate prices.

Suppose the government in 1967 institutes a subsidized commuter train service between the two points. For a period of time congestion will be relieved and travel time reduced, say to 40 minutes. But at 40 minutes some Torontonians will choose to move to Burlington and drive or commute to Toronto. How many will move? If we assume no change in the relative price of real estate in the two places, and assume a sufficiently large number of people who had viewed the two locations as equivalent when it took 80 minutes to make the trip, then a number of Torontonians will move to Burl-

---

[4] Although not directly germane to the question of federal regulation, the GO commuter trains operating along the lakeshore both east and west of Toronto may be an appropriate example.

ington until congestion on the new highway increases the travel time to 80 minutes.

Similarly, the rail commuter service will be used by a proportion of the Burlington commuters such that, in equilibrium, given the fare, the inconvenience, crowding, and other attributes of the rail service as seen by commuters, at least some of them will regard driving as equivalent to taking the train. The subsidized passenger service would have no effect on highway congestion and the losses incurred in its operation would produce no offsetting gains at all. The congestion problem on the highway is due to the absence of tolls, not to the lack of alternative transportation facilities (see Knight, 1924).

In the illustration, the potential benefits from the policy were completely dissipated because we assumed an indefinitely large elasticity of demand for the Burlington location at the equilibrium travel time holding everything else constant. Normally the response will be less elastic and the potential benefit of such a policy will not vanish, but the realized benefit will always be less than the potential, and will be necessarily less than the cost of the policy if no one can be excluded from the beneficial effects of the policy. Excepting pure public goods, all government policies that provide a "free good" to the public will have a benefit to cost ratio less than one (Baumol, 1972, pp. 307-22).

We have two conditions, rarely met in observed practice, for a regulatory authority to improve economic efficiency when externalities are present. First, evidence of individuals' willingness to pay at least the costs of the change; and second, some constraint on the beneficiaries to prevent dissipation of the gains.

In the above illustration, we have confined ourselves to partial equilibrium analysis, assuming that the regulatory policy in question had measurable effects only on the limited targets to which the policy was directed. We have assumed away problems of second best, and the general equilibrium effects that a regulatory intervention might have.

To take into account a more complex, general equilibrium framework could substantially change one's evaluation of a regulatory intervention. But it would require a case-by-case examination of specific policies, and would be limited by the practical impossibility of taking everything into account, both for an outside observer and for a regulatory authority, according to the Royal Commission on Transportation (Canada, 1961, II, pp. 81-82). There is, however, one effect of regulation that we can predict in a general equilibrium framework. An increased incidence of regulation as a constraint on individual decision-making will reduce the effectiveness of market prices to allocate resources, and tend to create perceived external effects. As regulatory constraints on decision-making are increased, the substitution possibilities available to individuals are reduced, which lowers the responsiveness of behaviour to changes in prices according to Samuelson (1965, pp. 36-39). Individuals will find the market a less effective means of coordinating their actions with others, as compared with non-market methods of coordination, which include making more use of the regulatory authority.[5]

For example, I would conjecture that the statutory rate on grain shipments from the West has had something to do with the secular increase in the incidence of regulation over the grain trade, to include box car allocation, shipping quotas, maintenance of branch lines, and to crops such as rapeseed and flax not covered in the original Crow's Nest Pass Agreement. It also has something to do with the diminution of market forces upon the economy of the West.

In an area as intensively subject to regulation as is transportation, it is more likely that regulation has created "external effects" rather than ameliorating the waste due to unavoidable market failure. Barely, if ever, does the regulator test intervenors for their willingness to pay, even in cases in which it would seem to be simple to do so. In the issue of line abandonment, for example, it would seem to be possible to offer the parties affected by a particular line the subsidy currently paid to the railways and let them choose to use the monies to maintain the line or use it in other ways and let the line go. Rarely, if ever, does the regulator attempt to avoid competitive dissipation of the potential benefits from its decisions. The Feed Freight Assistance Program, for example, bears a close resemblance to our hypothetical Burlington-Toronto example. The major impact of the policy as reported by the Grain Handling and Transportation Commission (Canada, 1977, I, pp. 301-05) is to shift the location of livestock feed lots, increasing rents in some regions and reducing them in others with no apparent net gain.

It again appears that the objective of regulation is to serve as an instrument of public finance rather than to serve the objective of economic efficiency. Many of our transportation policies are clearly directed towards maintaining the level of economic activity in different regions at the expense of economic efficiency, and regulation of transport is one of the means to accomplish regional policy objectives, as is explicit in Bill C-33.

Summary

Economists have a history of beating upon dead horses. We have since 1776 condemned tariffs, monopolies, regulatory practices, price controls, and other barriers to free exchange, all of which remain with us. In our microeconomics textbooks, government fares so badly that students must wonder why we have it at all. Only recently have we begun to treat government policies as scientific observations, instead of irrational aberrations, which refute the empirical implications of neo-classical economic theory, and principally the neo-classical assumption that markets are costless.

The hypothesis that regulation's objective is efficient resource allocation in the neo-classical sense is clearly refuted by the evidence at hand. The alternative hypothesis, that regulation is an instrument of public finance, seems

---

[5] This is essentially the argument of Hayek (1944, especially Chapter VII) and McManus (1975, pp. 334-50).

to have received some support from the evidence but lacks clearly refutable empirical implications in the absence of a specification of policy objectives, which we don't have. Accepting the latter hypothesis does not vitiate an economic analysis of regulation. Government presumably seeks out the most efficient means of serving its policy goals; but it does mean that the effects of regulation cannot be usefully evaluated by comparison with a perfectly functioning price mechanism.

Transaction costs make for a more profane world than the one envisaged by neo-classical economics, and one in which it is much more difficult, and perhaps impossible, to make a clear evaluation of regulatory practices with which all reasonable men must agree. Instead of attempting that, I shall confine myself to a few observations on regulation as a tax-expenditure mechanism and forewarn the reader that any evaluations of Canadian transport policy below are personal and conjectural.

THE PROBLEMS FACING THE REGULATION OF RAILWAYS IN THE EARLY SIXTIES

In the postwar period, technical changes in transportation frustrated the traditional exercise of railway regulation. The most important disturbance was that the cost of trucking fell sufficiently to make road transport a substitute for rail for an increasing number of shippers. For example, in 1959 a refrigerator truck service carrying dressed meat began to operate between Alberta and Eastern Canada and the rail rate on dressed meat fell from $2.39 to $2.00 a hundredweight from Winnipeg to Toronto, as reported in the Royal Commission on Transportation (Canada, 1961,II, pp. 117 and 123). This is only one of many examples of reduced costs of non-rail modes of transport reducing demand for rail services or increasing its elasticity.

The MacPherson Commission's *Report* of 1961 (Canada, 1961, I, pp. 3-9) called for changes in the regulation of railways to permit railway management to adjust more rapidly to the rise of intermodal competition in the transportation industry. In the view of the Commission, the cost of trucking had fallen by enough over the 1950s that trucking had become an effective substitute for much of the railways' business. The combination of increased competition and inflexible, regulatory constraints on railway management was hampering the ability of the railways to maintain positive net revenues. The principal source of the difficulty was that the railways were being used to provide unremunerative services to some consumers out of revenues earned in selling services for which the railway had some monopoly power. "Value of service" pricing was being used to cross-subsidize some users of rail services. Both government legislation and the practice of regulation used the railways as an instrument of public finance.

Through the 1950s, increased competition from other modes of transport reduced the ability of the government to impose taxes via railway freight rates, but the railways continued to bear obligations to subsidize some shippers and passengers by providing service at a loss. The result was that regulation, which had been based on constraining the total earnings of the railway companies to a maximum permissible rate of return, was forced to turn towards maintaining a reasonable minimum level of earnings.

Inflation through the 1950s worsened the railways' earnings and led to their application to the Board of Transport Commissioners in 1958 for a general increase in rates on non-competitive traffic. The Board in its *Rulings* awarded a 17 percent increase in rates to the CPR (Canada, 1958) following which the federal government passed the *Freight Rates Reduction Act* which reduced the increase awarded by the Board's Judgement of August 1, 1959 to 10 percent and granted the railways a general subsidy, for 1959, of $20 million. This subsidy, asserted at the time to be temporary, had risen to $100 million per year in 1966 in order to keep the overall level of freight rates at its 1959 level. According to Purdy (1972, p. 160), from 1959 to 1966, about $500 million was provided by the federal government to keep freight rates lower than they would otherwise have been.

At the time of the passage of the *National Transportation Act* of 1967, there was a considerable subsidy to resources in rail transportation, which must have led to many locational decisions being made that would have been different if the real economic costs of railway services had been reflected in rates. This situation resulted from an attempt to use transportation, by both government and its regulatory agency, to serve as a policy tool in attaining certain political goals. However, the *Freight Rates Reduction Act* may not have been simply an attempt to avoid a general increase in rates; such an interpretation does not make much sense, either economic or political. It is more likely that the government expected that a general increase in rates, given the rate structure, would not produce an increase in earnings that would maintain investment in the CPR.

Certainly the U.S. experience in the 1950s would have suggested that general rate increases would not resolve the railway's problem. Despite successive rate increases awarded by the Interstate Commerce Commission in the early 1950s, by 1957 the Eastern railroads in the United States were in worse financial condition than in 1932 and 1933 and their losses had led to physical deterioration (Hilton, 1969, p. 13). The general subsidy may have been the only way to avoid the same thing in Canada, short of a radical change in regulatory practices. The cause of the problem was the same in both countries—growing competition from trucking had reduced the potential rents that could be squeezed out of railways to serve political objectives and had practically forced a change in the national policy towards transportation.

Direct and Indirect Government Subsidies

In addition to the *Freight Rates Reduction Act,* there were in 1967 the following government subsidies, direct and indirect, to specific freight movements:

1. The *Maritime Freight Rates Act,* first passed in 1927, provides to

shippers a 30 percent reduction of freight rates on "preferred movements in the select territory." The "select territory" includes all the Maritime provinces, Newfoundland and that part of Quebec east of Levis and Diamond Junction to the Quebec boundary and south of the St. Lawrence River. "Preferred movements" do not include traffic to or from the United States, eastbound traffic into the "select territory," imports from abroad or passenger traffic. In 1970 the subsidy was applied to truck movements from and within the select territory. For both rail and truck movements, subsidies to intra-select territory shipments are less than for shipments outside the territory. This policy is one of many intended to stimulate economic activity in the Maritime provinces. The subsidy totalled about $40.5 million in 1976 (CTC, Annual Report, 1976), and about $17 million in 1967.

2. The movement of feed grains from the Prairies east and west had been subsidized since 1941 when a "temporary" Order-in-Council granted shippers of feed grain by rail and/or water routes a subsidy of from $5 to $11 per ton. In 1960, the cost of the subsidy to the federal government was about $20 million. The allocative effect of the subsidy is to lead to more livestock raising in the East and in British Columbia and more feed grain production in the Prairie provinces. The subsidy is not generally available for truck movements of grains (Canada, 1961, I,pp. 119-29).

3. Statutory rates apply to the movement of grain and flour from the Prairies for export and from the Prairies to eastern markets. Rates are set at their level of 1899. These rates have been maintained at a level set as a result of the Crow's Nest Pass Agreement of 1896. The Royal Commission on Transportation found that the statutory rates are lower than the cost of shipping grain and recommended that a subsidy totalling about $16 million be paid to the CN and CPR to cover the cost of moving grain and flour under the statutory rates (Canada, 1961, I, p. 30).

4. The "bridge subsidy" was a payment of not more than $7 million, shared about equally between the CN and the CPR for maintaining their trackage across Northern Ontario. The Board of Transport Commissioners ordered reductions in rates on both east and west-bound traffic so that the subsidy would be reflected in lower rates between the East and the Western provinces (Canada, 1961, II, pp. 113-18).

5. The At-and-East subsidy freezes rates on grain and flour moving in bulk for export to any eastern port at their levels of 1960 and 1966 respectively. In 1966, the subsidy payment totalled about $2 million. The principal effect of the subsidy is to reduce the export of Canadian grain through American ports. The subsidy is based on the difference between the frozen rates and the variable costs of haul as determined by the Canadian Transport Commission (Purdy, 1972, pp. 155-57).

These government policies and subsidies illustrate how important a role the industry has played as an instrument of public finance. Transportation policy has been used to equalize regional differences, to stimulate exports, and to increase domestic trade between the provinces. The real cost of these policies is the resource misallocation that results from them, and one's impression is that the cost may have been high in the early 1960s because of the slow reaction of policy to the railways' declining role as a mode of transport and the erosion of its tax base.

A NEW TRANSPORT POLICY?

The general nature of the changes in policy towards regulating transportation found in the *National Transportation Act* can be classed into two categories. First, as at least a partial substitute for cross-subsidization based on "value-of-service" pricing, direct subsidies are paid for certain services, and some matching subsidies are paid to truckers where they compete against rail at a subsidized rate. Second, there is a reduction in regulatory control over the railway companies and an increase in potential regulatory control over other modes, particularly trucking. Rail rates are no longer subject to maximum rate-of-return regulation and the Canadian Transport Commission will accept rates as filed unless the rate is contested under the appropriate sections of either the *National Transportation Act* or the *Railway Act*.

Subsidies

Railway Subsidies

The *National Transportation Act*, following the recommendations of the MacPherson Commission, phased out the general subsidy over the period from 1967 to 1974. Railways were free to adjust the general level of rates which had been frozen since 1959. In addition, specific subsidies are to be paid on services which are unremunerative but which must be maintained, either by statute or by the decision of the Canadian Transport Commission. With the exception of the bridge subsidy, the statutory subsidies described above, as they appear in the *Report* of the Grain Handling and Transportation Commission (Canada, 1977, I, pp. 301-5), have been retained, although the feed grain subsidy has been reduced. A government subsidy is paid for grain and flour shipments under statutory rates which is administered by the CTC. Except for shipments subject to statutory rates, the primary sources of operating losses are maintenance of branch lines and the operation of passenger services. Railway companies receive subsidies equal to 100 percent of their loss on branch lines and 80 percent of their loss on passenger train service. The companies apply to the CTC to have the services declared uneconomic; if the CTC agrees that a service or a line is uneconomic but does not permit discontinuance or abandonment, the Treasury compensates the companies for the losses incurred. These losses in turn are certified by the CTC. By the end of 1971, the CNR and CP Rail had filed applications for the discontinuance of all of their passenger train services (CTC, *Annual Report*, 1971, p. 14). The total subsidies paid to the two major railways in 1976 was about $260 million. There is no maximum on such payments provided for by the *National Transportation Act*.

The CTC's role in administering these subsidies is to certify the railway companies' estimates of cost on which the subsidies are based and to rule on the continuance of an uneconomic service. With respect to costing procedures, I have little to say. Allocation of costs to various railway services is necessarily arbitrary to a certain extent and is not worth discussing here. More important is the indirect effect that the subsidy may have upon cost. Compensating railways for losses on an annual basis, even 80 percent of losses where costs include items of joint cost such as track maintenance and general administration, reduce the pecuniary incentive for railway management to minimize their losses. The effect of these subsidies will depend on the potential discretion management has with respect to cost. Such discretion may be very low in the maintenance of a branch line, higher in the transport of grain and flour at statutory rates, and even higher in the operation of passenger services.

The administration of subsidies to railways under the *National Transportation Act* removes from the railways the burden of maintaining losing services and reduces their role as an instrument of public finance which, as we have seen, they have become increasingly unable to fill through the postwar period. The current policy also has the advantage of making the subsidy explicitly related to the relevant service rather than hidden in the structure of rates.

Trucking Subsidies

The major subsidy to truckers is administered by the CTC under the *Atlantic Region Freight Rate Assistance Act* (ARFRAA), which came into effect in 1970, when payments of $1.4 million were made (CTC, *Annual Report*, 1970, p. 13). By 1976, these payments totalled $23.4 million of which amount about three-quarters was paid for trucking within the Atlantic provinces and the remainder for truck shipments to other areas of Canada (CTC, *Annual Report*, 1976, p. 35). The only other direct federal payment to truckers was not a subsidy, but a transfer of payment of $10 million made in March 1976 as a result of a voluntary rail freight rate freeze requested by government and in force from January 30, 1972 to December 31, 1974. The railway companies received $117.9 million for their compliance with the freeze.

Advantages And Disadvantages Of Subsidizing
Trucking And Rail

Subsidizing trucking and rail, to the extent the former is a fairly close substitute for rail, has the allocative advantage of maintaining a closer correspondence between the relative costs of the two modes and their relative value to shippers. A subsidy paid only to rail for the purpose of moving goods would partially have the effect of displacing trucking, and for a given payment, would result in a lower response by shippers than if the same payment were divided between the two competing modes, provided that the joint supply curve is more elastic with respect to price than the supply of transport services provided only by rail. For example, there seems to be more long-haul grain trucking in Minnesota and the Dakotas than in the Canadian Prairies, partially due to the application of the statutory rates to rail shipments only. We would expect to move the same amount of grain for a lower total payment if a subsidy to trucks were instituted. Such a subsidy might also ease the problems of line abandonment and box car allocations.

The only clear allocative disadvantage of subsidizing trucking is that a subsidy to commercial hauling will induce some shippers to shift from private to commercial trucking, with the associated loss of the advantages of coordination within a single firm or a single proprietorship. Although statistics on private trucking in the Maritimes are not available, undoubtedly some of the increase in ARFRAA payments from 1970 to 1976 has been due to an increase in the proportion of trucking done commercially. In addition, the ARFRAA subsidy applies to some goods for which rail and truck are not close substitutes and is a more extensive subsidy to transportation than the *Maritime Freight Rate Assistance Act.*

Maintenance Of Lines And Continuance Of Service

The two major Treasury expenditures under the 1967 Act are for maintaining branch lines, about $82.5 million in 1975, and continuing passenger services, about $162.5 million in 1975 (CTC, *Annual Report, 1975*). Both of these subsidies seem to have acquired sacred cow status. The abandonment of branch lines is a thorny political issue, particularly in the West, because of the reliance of many small communities on the local grain elevator and the rail line. Since 1962, the Board has deferred consideration of Western abandonment cases at the request of the federal government. In 1967, an Order-in-Council listed about 6,274 miles of branch lines in the three Prairie provinces which were to be maintained through the end of 1974. In 1973, 1,839 miles of Prairie branch lines were added to the guaranteed list by Order-in-Council. In December 1974, 12,413 miles of rail line were protected by Order-in-Council to the year 2000, and 6,283 miles to the end of 1975 (CTC, *Annual Report, 1974*, p. 2). According to the CTC's *Annual Report,* the government's policy left only 525 miles of track, "none of it currently in use, open to abandonment procedures set out in the Railway Act" (1974, p. 2).

Much of this political difficulty is indirectly due to the Crow rate. As the Hall Commission (1977, I, Chapter 3) noted in its chapter, "Social and Community Implications of Railway Abandonment," "There may be a tendency by people making representations to the Commission to equate the significance of the railway of 30 to 50 years ago with its significance today." The Commission wrongly took the people's view to be exaggerated. On the contrary, the railway is likely much more important today at the subsidized price, than in the pre-war period.

Similar considerations of social and economic side effects enter into decisions by the CTC regarding the continuance of uneconomic passenger services. All of the passenger services in Canada, excepting commuter trains, are the subject of applications for discontinuance and will eventually appear before the Commission. From 1967 to the end of 1976, there were seventy-two applications for discontinuance before the Commission of which eleven passenger services were discontinued.

In these cases, the Commission takes into account the expected subsidy if the service is continued as against a host of other considerations. They include the availability of substitute services and "the inconvenience to the public caused by the discontinuance of the operation" (CTC, *Rulings*, 1967, 57, p. 95). The inconvenience factor consists of such things as increased traffic congestion[6] and the "quality of life" in a community;[7] the effect that discontinuance is expected to have upon the development of a community or region;[8] and the number of individuals that would be affected by discontinuance.

There can be little doubt that the Commissioin is making decisions regarding passenger services on a political rather than an economic basis. For all Canadian passenger services, costs are greater than revenues.[9] There is no explicit trade-off between the amount of the subsidy and the social effects of discontinuance, and a fairly clear unwillingness on the part of the Commission to permit discontinuance which would have measurable locational effects. The eleven decisions for discontinuance, with the possible exception of the Newfoundland service, all involve either a small number of riders[10] or availability of a very close substitute service. No very difficult decisions to discontinue have yet been made.

In these cases, the Commission defines to be "uneconomic" a service "which is incapable of being rendered profitable to the railway under any feasible alterations in railway operating practises (CTC, *Rulings*, 1969, 59, p. 403). Although it is unlikely that the Commission would be able to find potential profit where the companies could not, attempts are being made by the Commission to effect cost savings on some services by "rationalizing" the operations of CN and CP Rail.

These plans have not yet been completed; but, although some cost savings may be made, it seems likely that most of the existing passenger services

---

[6] See the Decision of September 30, 1970, File No. 49467.47, p. 52.

[7] See the Decision of May 31, 1971, File No. 49466.24, p. 29 which states "We accept the statement of one witness that the quality of transportation available to some important degree determines the quality of development in an area, and hence the amenities or quality of life. In this regard, it seems to us that there is truth in the statement that the North-East quadrant of the Toronto region is not now as well served for transportation both by railways and commuter services, as it could be."

[8] For example, the Decision of May 31, 1971, File No. 49467.99, p. 7 says "Because this area (Camrose, Drumheller) is growing, albeit slowly, it is essential that no impediment be placed in the way of future growth."

[9] Railway companies are free to set passenger fares without regulatory approval.

[10] The extreme case is a daily average of two passengers leaving Windsor towards London on CP Rail's train.

will be retained by the Commission at an annual pecuniary loss of about to-day's level plus inflation.

The payment of direct subsidies has changed the way in which transport regulation is used to fulfill policy objectives. Transport no longer has a tax base which can be tapped via railway rates, unless trucking can be brought under CTC jurisdiction, which appears unlikely at present. The role of the industry has been confined to an expenditure function, explicitly subsidizing commodity movements in the Maritimes and for export, and inter-city passenger traffic. There appears to have been no change in policy objectives. The only other change of substance is that the payment of open-ended subsidies from the Treasury appears to have virtually eliminated a budget constraint upon the regulatory authority, which perhaps explains why difficult decisions regarding passenger train discontinuance are not being made.

Rates

The various nature of the considerations which influence decisions regarding uneconomic branch lines and passenger services are most pronounced in rate cases that have arisen under Section 23 of the *National Transportation Act*. Under Section 23, a person may appeal to the Commission to have a rate changed, and the Commission is instructed to conduct an investigation of the rate if it finds that a *prima facie* case has been made to establish that the rate (or any act or omission) of a carrier "may prejudicially affect the public interest." The considerations which the Commission is instructed to take into account in its investigation are at least vague as the concept of "the public interest." They include for example, "unfair disadvantage," "undue obstacle," and "unreasonable discouragement" to "the interchange of commodities between points in Canada" or "to the development of primary or secondary industries or to export trade in or from any region of Canada or to the movement of commodities through Canadian ports," according to the *National Transportation Act* (Canada, 1967, S. 23 (3)). The Commission may order a change in any rate found to be preudicial.

There have been eight cases under Section 23 before the Commission; only one has been finally decided. All of the cases involve the transport of a commodity by rail which is produced in different regions of the country. The applications for an investigation under Section 23 of the Act have been made by a group of producers in one region and have met opposition from competing producers in other regions. For example, the Province of Ontario has opposed applications for leave to appeal rates on pulp by Prince Albert Pulp Company Limited (which competes in the Minnesota market with mills in Thunder Bay and Dryden) and on newsprint by seven Quebec mills, supported by the Province of Quebec, which compete with Ontario mills in New England (see CTC, *Cases, 1972*, S. 23.13). The CTC has interpreted Section 23 so liberally that it has put itself in the position of an interregional distributor of economic rents, a position from which it will be hard to escape unscathed.

The length of these cases attests to their tendentiousness. The only case decided, *Saskatchewan Wheat Pool et al. v. Canadian National et al.*, (see CTC, *Cases,* 1970-71, 316; 1973, 250) was before the Commission for about two years, involved thirty-seven days of public hearings, leading to an interim decision in 1973 which included a continuing investigation of rates and which was finally revised, in 1976, by a Cabinet decision. Perhaps the best feature of Section 23 of the Act is that cases are so expensive that few applicants could expect to gain by appealing a rate.

The first application to the Commission for an investigation of a rate under Section 23 was made October 1970 by the Saskatchewan Wheat Pool and three processors of rapeseed with plants located in each of the Prairie provinces. The applicants, supported by their respective provincial governments, argued that the rates on rapeseed oil and other products of rapeseed (which are agreed charges) are so high relative to the rate on rapeseed itself (which is a statutory rate) as to hinder the development of processing facilities on the Prairies which they assert to be prejudicial to the public interest. Opposition to this application was raised by four eastern oil seed processors and the provincial government of Ontario who argued that the applicant had not established a *prima facie* case that the rates in question were prejudicial to the public interest. Following a long interpretation of the meaning of a *prima facie* case, the Commission accepted as a definition: "at first sight." The remaining definitional problem involves the term "public interest." It is not clear from this Decision of October 29, 1971 (File No. 30637.2, 1970-71, 316) what meaning is attached to that term. The following excerpt from the Decision will illustrate the Commission's state of confusion regarding the nature of the "public interest." "The Commission is concerned with public as distinct from private interest except to the extent that private interest can be shown to be part of the interest of the public" (CTC, *Cases,* 1970-71, 317). At any rate, the application was granted and the Railway Transport Committee undertook to investigate the rates on rapeseed products.

In its 1973 decision (CTC, *Cases,* 1973, 250), some of the rates in question were found prejudicial to the public interest. An interim order of the Commission directed lower rates on oil and meal for export and lowered rates on domestic meal moving East to the rate on seed (CTC, *Cases,* 1973, 263, 316), and directed a continuing investigation of these rates following which a final decision was to be made. No change was made on the rate on oil.

In 1976, a Cabinet decision on an appeal by the western processors directed the CTC as recorded in its *Annual Report* (1976, p. 11) to establish minimum compensatory rates on oil and meal from Western Canada. In this case, as in the others, the Commission put itself in the role of arbitrator between eastern and western processors, a policy-making function for which the Commission is not equipped. It is also interesting to note how the side effects of the Crow rates keep reappearing in many issues of contention between the CTC and various Prairie interests.

All of these three general issues before the Commission—abandonment, discontinuance and rates prejudicial to the public interest—involve decisions that are essentially political rather than economic because they involve a redistribution of income at the expense of a less efficient allocation of resources. The costs of decision-making by Parliament and by the Governor-in-Council may warrant delegation of specific political decisions regarding branch lines and passenger trains to the CTC, but it is hard to believe that the general considerations that will arise under Section 23 of the *National Transportation Act* are appropriately decided upon by the Commission. In the decisions that have been made, one cannot tell what criteria is used by the Commission to define the "public interest," particularly in settling inter-regional differences of opinion, but it is difficult to understand how a *prima facie* case of "public interest" exists in the *Saskatchewan Wheat Board et al. v. CNR et al.* case unless the Commission intends to introduce regional con-siderations. Section 23 is sufficiently vague that it confers on the Commission much more potential power to make political decisions than existed before 1967 under the *Railway Act*. Similarly, the open-ended subsidy to uneconomic services amounts to an increase in the powers of the Board to in-fluence the allocation of resources.

Trucking

Part III, Sections 36 to 42 of the *National Transportation Act* estab-lished, for the first time, federal regulatory control over interprovincial trucking. The Motor Vehicle Transport Committee of the Canadian Transport Commission has broad potential powers under the Act to regulate trucking. The Commission may require that interprovincial common and contract carriers be licensed and may stipulate schedules, routes, places of call, commodities carried, and insurance provisions. Section 38, subsection 2 of the Act requires that such licences be issued only if "required by the pres-ent and future public convenience and necessity." The Commission as described in Section 39, subsection 3 also has regulatory control over tariffs and may order changes in tariffs that it considers to be either non-compensatory, exploiting a monopoly situation or "not justified by the public interest." Private trucking, that is, the carriage of one's own property, is ex-cluded from the provisions of the Act and is not subject to federal regulatory authority. Private trucking is exempted from regulatory control in both Canada and the United States because of the practical impossibility of en-forcing rate regulation upon firms to whom the rate is an internal price. The potential entry controls on trucking have not been established because they have evoked strong opposition from the provinces. Entry controls are sup-ported by licensed carriers (Purdy, 1972,p. 312). The Motor Vehicle Transport Committee has not actively exercised its powers which are, in ef-fect, limited to approving acquisitions.

In the absence of a Canadian record, a brief comment on federal regulation of trucking in the United States may be instructive. The Interstate Commerce Commission (ICC) appears to have erected relatively high barriers to the entry of new firms. The effect of rate regulation has been to cause rates to be about 20 percent above competitive levels (Hilton, 1969, p. 205). These conditions create incentives for shippers to avoid the effects of regulation by substituting private for commercial carriage, according to Harbeson (1969, p. 335), which has created all kinds of enforcement problems for the ICC. Unlicensed truckers try to avoid regulation by engaging in "buy-sell" operations, taking title to goods in transit. Some operators lease trucks with drivers to shippers. Hilton (1969, pp. 172-85) also says that shippers who own trucks form into cooperatives which lease trucks from the members, provide transportation services to them, and prorate the profits among the members. Similar problems arise because of regulatory restrictions to prevent carriers from offering cheap backhauls which result in increases in the number of empty backhauls. It is not surprising that a powerful incentive to cheat exists.

Among the provinces in Canada, a study by Sloss (1970, p. 346) similarly showed that "rates per ton-mile received by Canadian motor carriers were materially increased when and where there was regulation by provincial transport commissions." Although there is no published evidence to confirm it, one would presume that, as in the United States, the provinces regulating trucking have relatively less commercial to private hauling, except in the Maritimes where the ARFRAA subsidy would work in the opposite direction. If private is a close substitute for commercial haul for a sufficiently large number of shippers, the CTC would do little to enhance its tax base by extending its control to trucking, and would encounter the same kind of enforcement problems found in the United States.

Summary

There has been no apparent change in the objectives of transport policy except for a most cursory flirtation with efficiency, and the changes in method have been predictable for a long time. A quote from Mackintosh's 1939 study for the *Rowell-Sirois Report* continues to pretty well describe the present objectives:

> the direction of (transportation) policy has been unmistakable. It has been toward low rates on basic commodities—rates lower than comparable rates in the United States—and toward the reduction of regional differentials or in the case of the Maritimes the restoration of favourable differentials. (1964, p. 172)

Although there has been a change in the ability of transport policy and regulation to serve these objectives, and a consequent change in the choice among the options, the current status of transport policy was perceived at least as early as 1939.

> It is necessary to note that such a policy (removing regional differentials) would in-

volve the following accompaniments:

(1) complete jurisdiction by a single authority over all alternative modes of transportation, water, rail, road, and air; and

(2) the raising of rates on basic commodities and of rates generally in the regions most subject to highway and water competition; or

(3) the meeting of a part of railway costs out of taxation through payment of railway deficits by government.

The second is not possible without the first and if the first two are rejected, the third is very difficult to avoid (Mackintosh, 1964, p. 173).

CONCLUSION

Although we seem to have the same old transport policy in new clothing, the first fitting in 1967 has been found wanting and some modifications will be made.

As we have seen, the statutory rates on grain exports create policy problems elsewhere, from line abandonment to processing rapeseed. Many of the concerns of the Hall Commission (Canada, 1977) are attributable to the presence of these subsidized rates, which the Commission wants retained. These "problems" are unavoidable—a subsidy to one activity or region is equivalent to a tax on others, and it would be unfortunate and futile for the government to try to subsidize all of us.

If that is accepted, the unavoidable trade-offs would more clearly impinge on the decisions of the regulator, the Canadian Transport Commission, if it were subject to clearer constraints than provided by the 1967 *National Transportation Act,* which proffered the CTC open access to the Treasury and no direction other than to pursue that will-o'-the-wisp, the public interest.

REFERENCES

Baumol, W.J. (1972) "On Taxation and the Control of Externalities" *American Economic Review* 62: 307-22.

Barzel, Y. (1974) "A Theory of Rationing by Waiting" *Journal of Law and Economics* 17: 73-96.

Canada (1958) Board of Transport Commissioners, *Judgements, Orders, Regulations and Rulings (Rulings)* (Ottawa: November).

Canada (1961) *Report of the Royal Commission on Transportation Vol. I and II* (Ottawa: Queen's Printer).

Canada (1967) *National Transportation Act* (Ottawa: Queen's Printer).

Canada (1977) Report of the Grain Handling and Transportation Commission, *Grain and Rail in Western Canada* I (Ottawa: Supply and Services Canada).

Canadian Transport Commission (1967) *Judgements, Orders, Regulations and Rulings (Rulings)* 57.

Canadian Transport Commission (1969) *Judgements, Orders, Regulations and Rulings (Rulings)* 59.

Canadian Transport Commission (1970) *Decision and Order* September, File No. 49467.47.

Canadian Transport Commission (1970) *Annual Report.*

Canadian Transport Commission (1970-71) *Canadian Transport Cases.*

Canadian Transport Commission (1971) *Annual Report.*

Canadian Transport Commission (1971) *Decision and Order* May, File No. 49466.24 and No. 49467.99.

Canadian Transport Commission (1971) *Decision and Order* October, File No. 30637.2.

Canadian Transport Commission (1972) *Canadian Transport Cases.*

Canadian Transport Commission (1973) *Canadian Transport Cases.*

Canadian Transport Commission (1974) *Annual Report.*

Canadian Transport Commission (1975) *Annual Report.*

Canadian Transport Commission (1976) *Annual Report.*

Caves, R.E. (1962) *Air Transport and Its Regulators: An Industry Study* (Cambridge, Mass.: Harvard University Press).

Coase, R.H. (1960) "The Problem of Social Cost" *Journal of Law and Economics* 3: 30-34.

Currie, A.W. (1954) *Economics of Canadian Transportation* (Toronto: University of Toronto Press).

Harbeson, Robert W. (1969) "Toward Better Resource Allocation in Transport" *Journal of Law and Economics* 12: 321-38.

Hayek, F.A. (1944) *The Road to Serfdom* (Chicago: University of Chicago Press).

Hilton, George W. (1969) *The National Transportation Act of 1958* (Bloomington, Ind.: University of Indiana Press).

Knight, F.H. (1924) "Some Fallacies in the Interpretation of Social Cost" *Quarterly Journal of Economics* 38: 582-606, reprinted in G. Stigler and K. Boulding (1951) *Readings in Price Theory* (Chicago: Irwin).

Levin, H.J. (1968) "The Radio Spectrum Resource" *Journal of Law and Economics* 11: 481-501.

Mackintosh, W.A. (1964) Study for the Rowell-Sirois Report (1939) as it appears in *The Economic Background of Dominion-Provincial Relations*, Carleton Library Edition (Toronto: McClelland and Stewart).

McManus, J.C. (1973) "Federal Regulation of Telecommunications in Canada" in H.E. English (ed) *Telecommunications for Canada* (Toronto: Methuen).

McManus, J.C. (1975) "The Cost of Alternative Methods of Organization" *Canadian Journal of Economics* 8: 334-50.

Patinkin, Don (1947) "Multiple-Plant Firms, Cartels and Imperfect Competition" *Quarterly Journal of Economics* 51: 173-205.

Posner, R.A. (1971) "Taxation by Regulation" *The Bell Journal of Economics and Management Science* 2: Spring, 22-50.

Purdy, H.L. (1972) *Transport, Competition and Public Policy in Canada* (Vancouver: University of British Columbia Press).

Samuelson, P.A. (1965) *Foundations of Economic Analysis* (New York: Atheneum).

Sloss, J. (1970) "Regulation of Motor Freight Transportation: A Quantitative Evaluation of Policy" *The Bell Journal of Economics and Management Science* 1: Autumn, 327-66.

Stigler, George J. (1971) "The Theory of Economic Regulation" *The Bell Journal of Economics and Management Science* 2: Spring, 5-6.

Chapter Seven

The Roles of Competition And Regulation In Transport Markets: An Examination of Bill C-33*

by *Trevor D. Heaver*
Faculty of Commerce and Business Administration
University of British Columbia
and
James C. Nelson
Professor Emeritus
Washington State University

INTRODUCTION

The extent of constraints on the freedom given to individuals and corporations in a country is a matter of public choice. The extent and form of constraints are varied because of the range of ends which a society may strive to achieve through regulation. In view of the diversity of public objectives in any nation, it is not surprising that the regulation of corporations may be looked on to achieve several objectives.

There is nothing inherently wrong in a nation deciding to regulate the economic activities of an industry to achieve non-economic goals, even if it is at the cost of efficiency in the industry. The criterion by which such intervention with an industry may be judged is the cost-effectiveness of achieving the national objectives in that way rather than in some other way.

Since 1973, the national transportation policy passed in the *National Transportation Act* (NTA) of 1967 (Canada, 1967) has been the subject of much study. In 1975 the Department of Transport issued a report in which new statements of policy and of policy principles were set down (Canada, 1975). It is not the purpose of this paper to comment on the merits and shortcomings of that report. In 1977, Bill C-33, an act to amend the NTA and other legislation, was introduced into Parliament (Canada, 1977a). The Bill, which was not enacted into legislation, included the objectives of transport

---

* The authors acknowledge, with thanks, the comments on a draft of this paper by W.G. Waters II.

policy and the principles applicable to its application similar to those of the 1975 report. In the absence of evidence to the contrary, it appears that the Government of Canada still has intentions of bringing forward new statements of transportation policy objectives and principles similar to those in Bill C-33.

The thesis of this paper is that it is misguided for the Canadian government to make those changes in the objectives of the national transport policy *and* to require the regulation of freight transport by the Canadian Transport Commission (CTC) consistent with the revised transport policy. The changes run the risk of leading to decisions contrary to the efficient provision of transport services while exacerbating regional dissatisfactions as a result of the failure of reality to match the expectations which the revised statement of policy may engender. (A cynical critic might suggest that the experience of many decades should prevent the development of much optimism in Canada for any policy oriented to the resolution of regional problems!)

In presenting an argument that the existing national transport policy sets the appropriate objectives for the regulation of freight transport, this paper argues in favour of regulation to facilitate the efficient working of competition in transport markets and against the regulation of commercial rates and services by the CTC to achieve non-economic objectives. However, this argument does not deny that it may be appropriate for the government to give the CTC the task of judging whether it is in the public interest to retain unprofitable branch lines and passenger services. In these instances, the CTC is not required to trade off the revenue needs of the railways with national social objectives as the retention of the services is accompanied by the payment of compensation to the railways. Nor does the argument deny the need for the government to achieve non-economic ends through its investment and subsidization policies in transport. The argument of this paper is directed to the regulation of freight rates and service conditions set commercially.

The paper is in five parts. First, it examines the existing national transportation policy and the policy set down in Bill C-33. The implications of the policies for the criteria by which transport would be regulated are described. The second part of the paper reviews the working of transport markets and of regulation since the NTA of 1967. The views of this part of the paper are drawn from the research reported by T.D. Heaver and J.C. Nelson (1977, p. 344). Thirdly, the paper examines the decisions of the CTC which would be affected significantly by the change in the criteria for regulation. The results likely from the application of the new criteria are considered in the fourth section. Conclusions are reached in the final part of the paper by comparing the experience with the present policy and the probable results of the policy proposed in Bill C-33.

REGULATION AND NATIONAL TRANSPORTATION POLICY

The statement of transportation policy sets down the objectives and main principles which guide government actions in respect of its promotional, operational and regulatory roles. The significance of the statement for transport regulation lies, in part, in the influence which the policy has during the formulation of statutes and, in part, in the influence which the statement has on the criteria for the regulatory decisions of the CTC. Examination of the effects of the policy statement on regulatory decisions requires a careful examination of both the policy statement and its applicability to the regulatory responsibilities of the CTC.

The Transport Policy of the 1967 Act

The NTA of 1967 includes the statement of transportation policy which is given in Appendix 1. The statement sets out the objective of the policy to achieve " . . . an economic, efficient and adequate system making the best use of all available modes of transportation at the lowest cost is essential to protect the interests of users of transportation and to maintain the economic growth and well-being of Canada, . . ."[1] This statement is consistent with the view that transportation can serve the various needs of the country best if the carriage of passengers and freight is achieved in the most efficient way. Efficiency in transportation is vital to the wealth of the country and, therefore, to the nation's ability to achieve its quantitative and qualitative goals.

The policy statement goes on to set down the conditions necessary for the objectives " . . . most likely to be achieved . . ." Regulations should not restrict the ability of modes to compete freely. Carriers should not be burdened with imposed public duties without compensating subsidies, nor be subsidized by the provision of facilities without compensating user charges. Rates charged by carriers should not constitute an "unfair disadvantage" or "undue obstacle" to the carriage of traffic. Each of these conditions should be pursued "having due regard to national policy and to legal and constitutional requirements."

In the NTA and other Acts, relevant to the CTC, the statement of transportation policy is referred to only in Section 23 of the NTA. Only in that Section is it prescribed that the public interest includes the objective and conditions of the policy statement. However, it is reasonable to expect that the national transportation policy guides the CTC whenever the public interest is a relevant criterion. The emphasis in the existing policy is, clearly, on achieving efficiency in the transportation industry.

The Transportation Policy of Bill C-33

The revision to Section 3 of the NTA set down in Bill C-33 is in Appendix 2. The changes in wording carry major implications for the regulatory criteria to be used by the CTC. In this section the major changes in wording of potential significance to regulatory decisions are pointed out.

---

[1] Canada (1967) *National Transportation Act* (hereafter cited as NTA) (R.S.C. N-17, s.3).

The statement of the transportation policy is significantly different from that of 1967. While transport is to be "efficient," it is also to be an "instrument of support for the achievement of national and regional social and economic objectives" and provide "accessibility and equity of treatment for users."[2] The Bill sets out a more detailed set of principles necessary to achieve the objectives than is set out in the NTA. Some of the eleven principles impact on regulating criteria more than others.

The encouragement of intramodal as well as intermodal competition is acknowledged,[3] as is the desirability of commercial viability.[4] Competition is relied on to regulate the provision of services in some markets but "where no effective competition exists, transportation rates and services should be so regulated as to give transportation users the same protection as they would have if effective competition existed."[5]

The existence of conflicts between public and private interest is recognized. Such conflicts are to "be resolved in favour of the public interest,"[6] but "where implementation of a *particular* policy of the Government of Canada requires departure from the objective of commercial viability . . ., the benefits and costs involved should be identified and the relevant additional costs assumed by that government."[7] (Emphasis added.)

The Bill provides that the Governor-in-Council (i.e., the Cabinet) may issue directions to the CTC to achieve the objective of the transportation policy.[8] The CTC is explicitly charged with the responsibility of carrying out its responsibilities "having due regard to the objective described in subsection 3(1) and the principles described in subsection 3(2)" and complying "with all directions issued by the Governor-in-Council pursuant to Section 3.2."[9] However, apart from directing the CTC to give attention to the statement of policy, Bill C-33 proposes no changes in the relevance of the public interest to regulatory matters.

In summary, the current objective of transportation policy is focussed clearly on achieving an efficient transportation system. The relevance of national policy and the broad public interest to government and CTC decisions is acknowledged. However, the guidelines to the CTC in interpreting the public interest are limited because of the emphasis on efficiency.

Bill C-33 proposes that transport (including transport regulation), be an instrument to achieve non-transport efficiency objectives in the nation and it prescribes a number of conditions for transport to meet the public interest.

---

[2] Canada (1977a) *An Act to Amend the National Transportation Act* [*and other legislation*] (hereafter cited as Bill C-33) s. 1.

[3] Bill C-33, s. 1 (revised NTA, s. 3 (2) (d)).

[4] *Ibid.*, (revised NTA, s. 3(2)(g)).

[5] *Ibid.*, (revised NTA, s. 3(2)(i)).

[6] *Ibid.*, (revised NTA, s. 3(2)(f)).

[7] *Ibid.*, (revised NTA, s. 3(2)(h)).

[8] *Ibid.*, (revised NTA, s. 3(2)(a)).

[9] Bill C-33, s. 2 (revised NTA, s. 21(1)).

These conditions include the objective of accessibility and equity of treatment for users and the principle of regulation to achieve the results of effective competition, even where effective competition is absent. These concepts are discussed later.

The changes proposed in Bill C-33 change the meaning of the public interest for the CTC. For example, it is believed, generally, that the policy objectives in Bill C-33 are substantively different from those in the NTA. However, prior to assessing the effects of these changes it is desirable to examine the working of railway markets and the regulatory process today.

THE WORKING OF RAILWAY MARKETS

Railway rates in Canada are made in the context of the complex working of dynamic competitive forces. Competitive pressures take many forms and elicit responses from the railways in terms of rate and service actions and marketing and technological innovations.[10] When the response of the railways is insufficient shippers may resort to the use of other carriers, to the use of other production and distribution systems, or to the regulatory process.

It is common knowledge that, overall, the railways do not enjoy a monopoly power today that enables them to earn monopoly profits. Indeed, the earnings of CP Rail are well below its cost of capital and below the rate of return allowed for public utilities.[11] In their multitude of markets the railways are faced with heterogeneous competitive conditions and they attempt to price in those markets in a manner to maximize their profitability. They price their services according to the competitive pressures which can affect their volume of traffic and their revenues.

The incidence and intensity of competitive pressure are multifarious.[12] Competition is most often evident when two or more modes of transport serve a market and vie to serve more of the market. However, competition may be just as effective when it takes the form of the *potential* presence of a competitor. For example, opposition to the restriction of coastal shipping to Canadian flag ships has come from shippers who have obtained lower railway rates than would otherwise be possible on the basis of the argument that shipping *could be used* to meet their logistical requirements.

Important competition exists between carriers within a mode of transport. Although intramodal rate competition is exceptional in Canadian railway markets, intramodal service competition is very important. The com-

---

[10] The working of dynamic competition, as developed by John M. Clark in *Competition as a Dynamic Process* (Washington, D.C.: Brookings, 1961) is explained in relation to Canadian railway markets in Heaver and Nelson (1977, pp. 134-37).

[11] CP Rail reported a 6.7 percent return on net rail investment in 1977 compared with a return of 6.3 percent in 1976.

[12] For a more detailed description of the working of intermodal, intramodal and market competition see Heaver and Nelson (1977, pp. 157-231).

plaints voiced by shippers dependent on only one railway are evidence, in a reciprocal sense, of the merits of two or more railways.

Even in the absence of potential or actual carrier competition for a movement, shippers may use many arguments about the logistics of their business to demonstrate to the railways the constraints which apply to the level of freight rates. The use of alternate sources of supply or sale to alternate markets may constrain freight rates, or a ceiling may be placed on freight rates by the competitiveness of a market. "The evidence is clear that market competition in its various forms is a significant controlling factor on the level of railway rates throughout the country and on a wide range of commodities." (Heaver and Nelson, 1977, p. 181).

The result of the working of these competitive forces is a complex discriminating rate structure in which the profitability of individual traffic movements to the railway varies greatly with the rate and cost of the traffic. The presence of discriminating pricing, although not consistent with the theoretical ideal world of economists' perfectly competitive market model, is essential for the commercial viability of the railways and the most efficient pricing structure possible in view of the nature of railway costs. The need for discriminatory pricing today is heightened by the financial burden placed on the railways by the unprofitable Crow's Nest Pass rated traffic.

In spite of less than adequate returns in recent years, the railways are confident that reliance of this market system, with the burden of unremunerative public services removed from them, can produce financial results consistent with the support of the capital investments necessary to meet the needs of the Canadian economy. However, arranging rate and service conditions on the basis of negotiation between shippers and carriers have not worked smoothly at all times. In some instances, shippers have resorted to the CTC before they have experienced a satisfactory level of negotiation with the railways. In some instances, shippers have proceeded through with an application to the CTC under Section 23 of the NTA. However, in spite of these few failures of complete reliance on the free commercial process to produce results acceptable to the parties, and in spite of some dissatisfaction with the slow processing of Section 23 cases, most shippers are strongly in favour of reliance on the existing transportation policy. (Heaver and Nelson, 1977, pp. 240-45 and 331-35). They are opposed to the use of transport as an instrument of national policies and are concerned about the regulation of transport subject to possible "directions" from the Governor-in-Council.

The major complaints about the transportation policy have come from the premiers of the western provinces.[13] Subsequent analyses of the complaints and proposals of the western premiers have shown that, with the exception of the impact of statutory Crow's Nest Pass rates on grain processing industries, there is no general feature of rates and services resulting from the existing transportation policy, which works to the detriment of the develop-

---

[13] See, for example, *Transportation Paper* (1973).

ment of industry in western Canada.[14] However, in western Canada, as in any part of the country, the impact of particular rates on particular industries may be matters of concern at particular times.

THE REGULATION OF RATES AND SERVICES AND THE PUBLIC INTEREST

Bill C-33 not only changes the concept of the public interest but it ensures its application to all responsibilities of the CTC. This paper does not deal with the possible impact of the proposed policy on the assessment of retaining unprofitable branch lines or passenger services in the public interest (Canada, 1976; 1977b). The paper deals only with the regulation of commercially determined levels of freight rates and services. However, within this limited context, it is appropriate to clarify the relevance of the policy statement.

The Regulation Under the Public Interest Section of the NTA

In the regulation of the railways, the existing statutes only require the CTC to take into account the statement of national transportation policy under Section 23 of the NTA. This section allows for the regulation of any acts or omissions of carriers under the jurisdiction of Parliament and of any rate established pursuant to the NTA or the *Railway Act* (Canada, 1970a), when the acts, rates or omissions are prejudicial to the public interest. The public interest is defined as including "without limiting the generality thereof, the public interest as described in section 3,"[15] that is, the policy statement (Appendix 1).

The Regulation of Minimum and Maximum Rates

The regulation of minimum and maximum rates is carried out under sections 276 to 278 of the *Railway Act* on the basis of the technical criterion of the relationship of rates to costs. Minimum rates should not be below variable costs and maximum rates are determined by a formula in relatin to variable costs. The revisions proposed in Bill C-33 to these sections of the *Railway Act* may have been prompted by some of the concepts in the policy statement of the Bill. However, the working of maximum and minimum rate regulation under the present statutes or as proposed in Bill C-33 are not affected by the policy statement.

The relationship between maximum rate regulation and the policy statement is not clear. Policy principle (i) states that "transportation rates and services should be so regulated as to give transportation users the same protection as they would have if effective competition existed."[16] When

---

[14] For a summary analysis see Heaver and Nelson (1977, pp. 45-52 and 245-49).

[15] NTA, s. 23 (1).

[16] Bill C-33, s. 1 (revised NTA, s. 3(2)(i)).

evaluating the merits of Bill C-33, is it to be assumed that Section 178 provides the protection intended for shippers by policy principle is inconsequential to the regulation of the railways at this time. The crucial matter in that
case is Section 278. However, Section 278 deals only with rate and not service
levels. In the absence of ministerial clarification neither shippers, carriers or
the CTC can know whether section (i) has meaning beyond justification for
maximum rate regulation. It is argued later that it is impractical to give section (i) wider application.

The Regulation of Agreed Charges

Agreed charges, which are authorized by Part IV of the *Transport Act*
(Canada, 1970b), are not regulated like other railway rates. They are not
subject to Section 23 of the NTA, but they are subject to change or cancella-
tion if found to be contrary to the public interest under Section 33 Of the
Transport Act. Therefore, it appears that the possible effects fo the policy
statement are the same for the regulation of agreed charges, under Section 33
of the *Transport Act*, and for regulation of other rates, under Section 23 of
the NTA.

Control of Proposed Consolidations of Carriers

The CTC is responsible for making decisions "in the public interest"
concerning the consolidation by various means of transportation enterprises
under the federal jurisdiction when an objection is made to the CTC concerning the consolidation. The legislation allows objections to be made to the
CTC against an acquisition "on the grounds that it will unduly restrict competition or otherwise be prejudicial to the public interest."[17] It seems unlikley
that the policy statement in Bill C-33 would affect the criteria by which the
consolidations are judged. This aspect of the control of commercial services
is not considered further.

IMPLICATIONS OF BILL C-33 FOR RATE REGULATION IN THE PUBLIC INTEREST

The policy statement of Bill C-33 raises insurmountable problems for
application to the regulation of rates in the public interest. The problems
come from three major sources. First, the statements of objectives and principles involve conflicts and, therefore, ambiguities which it is impractical to
expect the CTC to resolve. Second, individual objectives or principles require
political policy judgments which the CTC is not qualified or justified in making. Third, application of the objectives and principles are contrary to the interests of the railways, competing carriers, shippers overall and the general
public interest in the availabilty of goods and services at low cost.

---

[17] NTA, s. 27 (3).

Conflicts in the Bill C-33 Policy Statement

Regulation in the public interest is always difficult because the public interest is multi-faceted. Inherently, the public interest involves conflicts of interests between objectives and between interest groups. Therefore, it is impossible to come up with constant criteria. Decisions must be made on the merit of arguments in individual cases conducted in a quasi-judicial hearing which can run on for years. This is one of the factors underlying the widespread criticism of the working of many independent regulatory commissions.[18]

The regulation of railway rates in the public interest since 1967 has revolved around the correctness of the response of the railways to competitive and cost factors affecting shippers. In particular, Section 23 cases have involved difficult instances of the effects of freight rates on the competitive position of shippers in a common market.[19] The length of time for the CTC to reach a decision in these cases may have been unduly long. Nevertheless, there is not general criticism of the way in which the CTC has carried out its responsibilities.[20]

Bill C-33 encompasses the types of objectives and principles for the regulation of railway rates in the public interest which require the gathering of evidence and making of trade-offs between many diverse effects. The CTC is not likely to make choices between efficiency, various national policies, accessiblity and equity, consistent with provincial and federal government views in judging the reasonableness of a particular rate. The CTC is not likely to know when the principle of commercial viability is paramount over public interests as defined in the many different ways in which Bill C-33 requires them to be defined. In short, the CTC would face the impossible task of using the objectives and principles set down in Bill C-33 in a way to match the intentions of the legislators (if the legislators had considered the specific problems associated with the application of the concepts). In the face of this task, it seems likely that the CTC would render discussions which might be seen as inconsistent, contrary to the public interest, and too protective of carrier interests.[21]

Ambiguity of Concepts in Bill C-33

Many of the individual concepts in the policy statement of Bill C-33 are ambiguous. It is not peculiar to this Bill, that concepts which sound laudable are being proposed for a statute with the pious hope that over time they can be given an operational meaning, and that the meaning will be consistent

---

[18] See, for example, Ruppenthal and Stanbury (1976, p. 232).

[19] For a review of the decisions to 1977, see Heaver and Nelson (1977, pp. 249-72).

[20] For support of the existing legislation and the CTC, see Edgar (1977). See also Heaver and Nelson (1977, pp. 240-45).

[21] For a general discussion of the problem of commission regulation "in the public interest", see Waters (1976, pp. 9-33).

with the ill-defined notion of the original legislators. It is not an acceptable position for government to suggest that the meaning of words and expressions in Bill C-33 will be defined over time as the CTC renders its decisions. With this response, it is impossible to judge the merits of the legislation until it is enacted and used. Two examples of ambiguous terms in Bill C-33 are selected for discussion. They are concepts of "equity" and "effective competition."

The notion of equity is laudable. Presumably, we all believe in fair play! However, what does equity in prices mean? If the railways are efficient and are not earning a rate of return equal to the cost of capital, is any holddown of railway rates equitable when it shifts profits from the railways to shippers? Is it equitable when the profitability of some traffic to the railways is greater than the profitability of other traffic? Is it ever equitable for some traffic to be carried at a loss? Does the term "equity," as used in Bill C-33, refer to the establishment of rates and services consistent with the avoidance of "unfair advantage" and "undue obstacle" to the carriage of traffic and development of industry as already laid down in Section 23 of the NTA? Or is equity in the public interest more than this? If equity is limited to those concepts already spelled out in Section 23, the addition of the term "equity" to the statement of national transportation policy does not represent any change in regulatory policy. That would be consistent with the continued regulation of the railways to produce efficient transportation. Only the government can answer these questions because equity is a concept to be defined by the political process and not one to be defined by an independent regulatory commission such as the CTC. Attempts by the CTC to regulate rates under an ill-defined concept of equity would surely prove British economist W. Arthur Lewis to exclaim that, in rate determination, "equity is the mother of confusion."[22]

Providing protection for all shippers equivalent to that provided by "effective competition" sounds idyllic. However, what is effective competition as intended in Bill C-33? An economist might view effective competition as that level of competition causing rates to equal marginal costs. But this is impractical for the railways with their need to practise price discrimination. Does effective competition include the influence of market, intramodal and intermodal competition? Since these types of competition working singly and collectively produce a wide range of responses from carriers, including a wide range of railway cost/rate relationships, at what point is competition to be judged effective by the CTC? How are the results of effective competition for rates and services to be provided to all shippers when it is the railways which are responsible for the provision of a particular service level at a particular rate? While the meaning of effective competition is not known, it is reasonable to conclude that regulatory attempts to hold down rates, without compensating service reductions, will be to the detriment of the commercial viability of the railways by shifting revenue from the railways to shippers.

---

[22] Lewis (1951, p. 23) quoted in Bonbright (1961, p. 126).

Such an income transfer would not further efficiency in the economy and might result in income transfers from a Canadian Crown corporation to a foreign-owned subsidiary company.

The Interests of Carriers and Shippers in the Regulatory Process

Carriers and shippers expect to be responsible for the commercial viability of their enterprises. They do not expect to be burdened with special public service obligations without compensation. They expect the regulatory process to work to encourage efficient competitive practices, to place a limit on rates in true monopoly conditions and to provide remedies against errors of judgment in the supply of regulated services. For example, the environment in which the railways judge the appropriate rate to charge in the face of competitive conditions is imperfect and errors, particularly with respect to the influence of market competition, are likely to occur. A regulatory process to correct such errors is accepted.

The experience since 1967 has shown that the reliance on commercial market forces has been conducive to the development of efficiency in the Canadian transportation and distribution systems. Competitive responses by carriers have been facilitated, with beneficial results for innovation in technology, organization and procedures, especially pricing. The responsiveness of carriers has facilitated and encouraged the development of shipper expertise in the organization and management of sophisticated logistical systems, carefully matched to market requirements and transportation opportunities (Heaver and Nelson, 1977, pp. 295-344).

This is not to deny that commercial and regulatory problems have been present since 1967. The railways have at times attempted to introduce rate and service charges without due consultation with shippers. In the case of the rates on rapeseed and rapeseed products, the rate differential was found to be contrary to the public interest. However, instances of these problems are few. The solutions to these problems do not seem to lie in the revised policy statements of Bill C-33.

The Bill threatens to give rise to decisions which, while supposedly in the "public interest," are based on the views of a few "prudent men" in the CTC. Personal judgments will need to be made on the definition and weightings of conflicting objectives and principles. Some examples of this have been given already. However, one further example is given here to demonstrate the problems raised by the use of transport to achieve national policies other than the promotion of efficient transport and the placing of certain public interests over private interests. A hypothetical Section 23 case can be used to make the point.

A forest products establishment in a remote location protests rail rates under Section 23 of the NTA. A case is made conclusively that lower rail rates will enable the firm to increase sales in the U.S.A., but not sufficiently to maintain the same profitability of the traffic in total to the railway. However, the traffic would still be profitable to the railway (although less so after a rate reduction) and the total increase in wages paid in the remote community, which exceed the loss in profits to the railway. Under the proposed policy statement, a strong case could be made for reducing the freight rate, thereby foregoing railway revenue for the sake of job creation. This would be equivalent to using the assets and earning power of the railways as a source of funds to deal with unemployment.Unless the government compensates the railways financially for the holddown in railway revenues caused by the CTC for reasons of national social objectives, the efficiency of the railways would be impaired and a financial burden thrown on other shippers.[23] Calculation of the amount of such a compensatory payment would not only involve the usual difficult problems of ascertaining railways costs, but would often require judgment about the amount of the rate holddown justified by social considerations and the amount justified by the CTC's assessment of the appropriate impact of competitive conditions on the railway rates.

If it is argued that such a rate reduction would not be required because the railways are not so profitable overall as to be able to afford to forego profits, then it is being argued that commercial interests would only be subservient to public interests when railway earnings are at least equal the cost of capital. Since this prospect is not immediately eminent, this interpretation would not see regulatory decisions being made in favour of broad social objectives for many years.

The conclusion to be reached is that the legislation does not make clear the conditions under which the public interest should take precedence over the private interest and the profitability of traffic to the railways. It is not clear how, if at all, the railways would be compensated for losses of revenue caused by such CTC decisions as the principle of compensation (principle (h) in Bill C-33) relates to "a particular policy of the Government." Nor is it clear who would bear the responsibility for the financial well-being of the railways.

The application of decisions by the CTC giving preference to national policies over the commercial interests of the railways would impact on competing carriers, some of whom may not be under federal jurisdiction. The result would be impacts through the transport system equivalent to that of previous unimodal interventions of government policy. Under the legislation proposed in Bill C-33, the interpretation of all these matters for regulatory decisions would be the responsibility of the CTC.

In summary, the effects of the proposed policy statement on the regulation of railway rates and services are uncertain. Conflicts between and ambiguities in policy objectives and principles are left to the CTC to resolve. The concepts of "equity" and "effective competition" are not concepts that can be defined and used by the CTC in the absence of specific parameters for these concepts set down by Parliament. Decisions by the CTC, where the

---

[23] A current analogy is the government policy of allowing the railways to shoulder the burden of Crow's Nest Pass grain rates.

public interest in national policies exceeds the private interest in commercial profit, would raise issues of intermodal competition and the overall commercial viability of the railways. The uncertainty and delays in administration of regulations under such a wide-ranging policy statement would make the difficulties of reaching decisions on the public interest on branch lines and passenger services, appear minor!

CONCLUSIONS

The brief review of the existing and proposed legislation, and of the market experience since 1967 compared with the uncertain implications of the proposed legislation, provides scant grounds for firm conclusions. The paper does not attempt a substantial analysis but contrasts the positive results of the existing regulatory policy for efficiency in transport with the uncertainties, conflicts and problems predictable with attempts to implement Bill C-33. The evidence seems so overwhelming that this paper lends its full support to the opposition registered by carriers and shippers against the application of the proposed policy principles to the regulation of transport. Indeed, in face of the opposition to the policy since 1975, at least, it is surprising that it is still necessary to argue against the radically new approach to regulation encompassed in Bill C-33.

The regulation of railway rates and services by the CTC to achieve social and political ends would not be conducive to efficiency in the transportation industry, and therefore, in Canadian production and distribution systems. Nor would it witness consistent and effective progress towards the achievement of social and political ends.

The conclusion is clear that in today's market conditions regulation should be relied on only to facilitate the working of competitive forces and that the broader social and political objectives of the nation that go beyond the provision of efficient transport, should be achieved through direct government operational and subsidization programs.

The apparent intransigence of the government to give up the application of a new transportation policy to the regulation of transport can come from several sources. One may be lack of appreciation of the complex and interrelated factors which work together and constitute the transportation system. Another may be the failure of the government to differentiate between the objectives and principles which it can follow in its operational and promotional roles as compared with the objectives and principles to be applied by a regulatory commission. Third, but by no means least, may be the belief in a political imperative to accede to regional demands for federal concessions in respect of transport policy, even if the medicine to be administered is untested and unlikely to produce the results hoped for.

Passage of legislation comparable to Bill C-33 would leave a legacy on which lawyers would grow rich but shippers, carriers and even provincial politicians would grow frustrated. Attempts to reach decisions consistent with objectives and policy principles as vague as those in Bill C-33 would surely produce cases which would require a longer time to adjudicate than the rapeseed case. Dissatisfaction would likely result in scorn being showered on the CTC for failure to carry out a task, whereas the failure would lie with the legislators who had assigned an impossible task.

The year 1978 is an appropriate one to set aside an approach to the solution of western economic development which is at least 100 years old. In 1878, the Conservative Party, under John A. Macdonald, was swept to power on a platform based on the expansion of Canada through the construction of the CPR in the West and the provision of tariffs to protect Canadian manufacturers. The apparent dichotomy of interests in Canada in transport concessions for the West as a trade-off against tariff protection for eastern manufacturers persists to this day. In the carousel of Canadian politics, when the wheel spins so that the federal ear is attuned to the West, concessions to transport policy are called for. In 1973, it was predictable that changes in transport policy would be called for even if they were not appropriate to the issues at hand (Heaver, 1973, pp. 13-15).

In 1978, like 1878, Canada is concerned with transport policy and with an overall economic development policy. The solution to the regional concerns, attributed to transport regulation, does not lie in the application of the transport policy in Bill C-33 to transport regulation. Perhaps, yet, there will be an election in 1978 and a party will come forward with a general strategy that will let Canada get off a century-old carousel without falling on her face.

REFERENCES

Canada (1967) *National Transportation Act* (R.S.C. 1970, c. N-17).

Canada (1970a) *Railway Act* (R.S.C. 1970, c. R-2).

Canada (1970b& *Transport Act* (R.S.C. 1970, c. T-14).

Canada (1975) Transport Canada, *Transportation Policy, a Framework for Transport in Canada: Summary Report* (Ottawa: Information Canada).

Canada (1976) *Report of the Commission on the Costs of Transporting Grain by Rail* ("Snavely Report") (Ottawa: Information Canada).

Canada (1977a) *An Act to Amend the National Transportation Act* [and other legislation] (Bill C-33), first reading 27 January.

Canada (1977b) *Report of the Grain Handling and Transportation Commission* ("Hall Commission") (Ottawa: Information Canada).

Edgar, J.R. (1977) "To Regulate or Not to Regulate" an address to the Third Annual Meeting of the Western Transportation Advisory Council, Regina, 17-18 March.

Heaver, Trevor D. (1973) "Wrong Way to Solve Ill-defined Problems" *Executive,* June-July, 13-15.

Heaver, Trevor D. and James C. Nelson (1977) *Railway Pricing under Commercial Freedom: The Canadian Experience* (Vancouver: University of British Columbia, Centre for Transportation Studies).

Lewis, W. Arthur (1951) *Overhead Costs,* quoted in James C. Bonbright (1961) *Principles of Public Utility Rates* (New York: Columbia University Press).

Ruppenthal, Karl M. and W.T. Stanbury (eds.) (1976) *Transportation Policy: Regulation, Competition and the Public Interest* (Vancouver: University of British Columbia, Centre for Transportation Studies).

Transportation Paper (1973) paper submitted jointly by the Premiers of Saskatchewan, British Columbia, Manitoba and Alberta at the Western Economic Opportunities Conference, Calgary.

Waters, W.G. II (1976). "Public Policy and Transport Regulation: An Economic Perspective" in Karl M. Ruppenthal and W.T. Stanbury (eds.) (1976) *Transportation Policy: Regulation, Competition and the Public Interest* (Vancouver: University of British Columbia, Centre for Transportation Studies).

Appendix 1

Excerpt from the *National Transportation Act* of 1967

NATIONAL TRANSPORTATION POLICY

National transportation policy

3. It is hereby declared that an economic, efficient and adequate transportation system making the best use of all available modes of transportation at the lowest total cost is essential to protect the interests of the users of transportation and to maintain the economic well-being and growth of Canada, and that these objectives are most likely to be achieved when all modes of transport are able to compete under conditions ensuring that having due regard to national policy and to legal and constitutional requirements

(a) regulation of all modes of transport will not be of such a nature as to restrict the ability of any mode of transport to compete freely with any other modes of transport;

(b) each mode of transport, so far as practicable, bears a fair proportion of the real costs of the resources, facilities and services provided that mode of transport at public expense;

(c) each mode of transport, so far as practicable, receives compensation for the resources, facilities and services that it is required to provide as an imposed public duty; and

(d) each mode of transport, so far as practicable, carries traffic to or from any point in Canada under tolls and conditions that do not constitute

(i) an unfair disadvantage in respect of any such traffic beyond that disadvantage inherent in the location or volume of the traffic, the scale of operation connected therewith or the type of traffic or service involved, or

(ii) an undue obstacle to the interchange of commodities between points in Canada or unreasonable discouragement to the development of primary or secondary industries or to export trade in or from any region of Canada or to the movement of commodities through Canadian ports;

and this Act is enacted in accordance with and for the attainment of so much of these objectives as fall within the purview of subject-matters under the jurisdiction of Parliament relating to transportation. 1966-67, c. 69, s. 1.

POLITIQUE NATIONALE DES TRANSPORTS

Politique nationale des transports

3. Il est par les présentes déclaré qu'un système économique, efficace et adéquat de transport utilisant au mieux tous les moyens de transport disponibles au prix de revient global le plus bas est essentiel à la protection des intérêts des usagers des moyens de transport et au maintien de la prospérité et du développement économique du Canada, et que la façon la plus sûre de parvenir à ces objectifs est vraisemblablement de rendre tous les moyens de transport capables de soutenir la concurrence dans des conditions qui assureront, compte tenu de la politique nationale et des exigences juridiques et constitutionnelles,

a) que la réglementation de tous les moyens de transport ne sera pas de nature à restreindre la capacité de l'un d'eux de faire librement concurrence à tous les autres moyens de transport;

b) que chaque moyen de transport supporte, autant que possible, une juste part du prix de revient réel des ressources, des facilités et des services fournis à ce moyen de transport grâce aux deniers publics;

c) que chaque moyen de transport soit, autant que possible, indemnisé pour les ressources, les facilités et les services qu'il est tenu de fournir à titre de service public commandé; et

d) que chaque moyen de transport achemine, autant que possible, le trafic à destination ou en provenance de tout point au Canada à des prix et à des conditions qui ne constituent pas

(i) un désavantage déloyal à l'égard de ce trafic plus marqué que celui qui est inhérent à l'endroit desservi ou au volume de ce trafic, à l'ampleur de l'opération qui y est reliée ou au type du trafic ou du service en cause, ou

(ii) un obstacle excessif à l'échange des denrées entre des points au Canada ou un découragement déraisonnable du développement des industries primaires ou secondaires ou du commerce d'exportation dans toute région du Canada ou en provenant, ou du mouvement de denrées passant par des ports canadiens;

et la présente loi est édictée en conformité et pour la réalisation de ces objectifs dans toute la mesure où ils sont du domaine des questions relevant de la compétence du Parlement en matière de transport. 1966-67, c. 69, art. 1.

Appendix 2

2nd Session, 30th Parliament, 25 Elizabeth II,
1976-77

2ᵉ Session, 30ᵉ Législature, 25 Elizabeth II,
1976-77

THE HOUSE OF COMMONS OF CANADA

CHAMBRE DES COMMUNES DU CANADA

BILL C-33

BILL C-33

An Act to amend the National Transportation Act and the Department of Transport Act for the purpose of defining the objective of the transportation policy for Canada and authorizing the consequential rearrangement of powers and duties relating to transport and to amend the Transport Act and the Railway Act in respect of freight rates and other matters

Loi ayant pour objet de définir l'orientation de la politique canadienne des transports et autorisant en conséquence la redistribution des pouvoirs et fonctions relatifs aux transports et modifiant à ces fins la Loi nationale sur les transports, la Loi sur le ministère des Transports ainsi que les taux de transport de marchandises et autres dispositions prévus par la Loi sur les chemins de fer et la Loi sur les transports

Her Majesty, by and with the advice and consent of the Senate and House of Commons of Canada, enacts as follows:

Sa Majesté, sur l'avis et du consentement du Sénat et de la Chambre des communes du Canada, décrète:

R.S., c. N-17

NATIONAL TRANSPORTATION ACT

LOI NATIONALE SUR LES TRANSPORTS

S.R., c. N-17

1. Section 3 of the *National Transportation Act* is repealed and the following substituted therefor:

1. L'article 3 de la *Loi nationale sur les transports* est abrogé et remplacé par ce qui suit:

5

Objective of the transportation policy for Canada

"**3.** (1) It is hereby declared that the objective of the transportation policy for Canada is to achieve a transportation system that

«**3.** (1) Il est par les présentes déclaré que la politique canadienne des transports a pour objet la mise en place d'un système de transport qui

Orientation de la politique canadienne des transports

10

(*a*) is efficient,

a) soit efficace,

(*b*) is an effective instrument of support for the achievement of national and regional social and economic objectives, and

b) contribue efficacement à la réalisation des objectifs sociaux et économiques tant au niveau national que régional, et

15

(*c*) provides accessibility and equity of treatment for users,

and it is further declared that achievement of the objective of the transportation policy for Canada requires the integration of services employing the most appropriate modes for each service and that it is the responsibility of governments to attend to the provision of the transportation system.

c) offre à des conditions uniformes, des services facilement accessibles aux usagers,

et il est en outre déclaré que la réalisation de cet objet suppose l'intégration des moyens les plus appropriés de chaque service et que c'est aux gouvernements qu'il incombe de veiller au maintien d'un bon système de transport.

20

Principles applicable to implementation of transportation policy

(2) For the purpose of achieving the objective of the transportation policy referred to in subsection (1) and having due regard to the requirements and objectives of the public and private sectors and to legal and constitutional requirements, the following principles apply:

(2) L'objet énoncé au paragraphe (1) devra, compte tenu des exigences et objectifs des secteurs public et privé ainsi que des contraintes d'ordre juridique et constitutionnel, être réalisé conformément aux principes suivants:

Principes régissant la mise en œuvre de la politique des transports

5

(*a*) the Government of Canada should establish national policies respecting the various constituent parts of the transportation system and it is the responsibility of the Commission, within its statutory jurisdiction, to ensure adherence to such policies;

a) le gouvernement du Canada définit la politique nationale relative aux divers éléments constitutifs du système de transport et la Commission, dans les limites de sa compétence, veille à sa mise en œuvre;

10

(*b*) in major aspects of the process relating to the development and economic regulation of the transportation

b) les divers niveaux de gouvernement du pays concourent, aux étapes importantes, à l'élaboration des principes régissant le développement et la réglementation économique du système de

15

system, there should be cooperation be- 20
tween the different levels of government
as well as consultation with the public;

(*c*) in the planning and development of
transportation services designed to
achieve a particular purpose, consider- 25
ation should be given to all means of
achieving that purpose including means
that do not involve a mode of transport;

(*d*) competition within and between
modes of transport should be 30
encouraged where economic and technical factors permit;

(*e*) in the provision of transportation
services there should be opportunity for
both public ownership and private own- 35
ership of carriers and also for national,
regional and local carriers with Canadian control of privately owned carriers
being an objective;

(*f*) any conflict between public and pri- 40
vate objectives should be resolved in
favour of the public interest;

(*g*) commercial viability should be an
objective both in the operation of transportation services and in the provision of 45
facilities and services in direct support
thereof;

(*h*) where implementation of a particular policy of the Government of Canada
requires departure from the objective of
commercial viability referred to in paragraph (*g*), the benefits and costs
involved should be identified and the
relevant additional costs assumed by 5
that government;

(*i*) where effective competition exists,
transportation rates and services should
be established through the working of
the market mechanism, but where no 10
effective competition exists, transportation rates and services should be so
regulated as to give transportation users
the same protection as they would have
if effective competition existed; 15

(*j*) where competitive services are available, but public assistance is considered
necessary to support a policy of the Government of Canada, such assistance
should be made available in such a way 20
as not to distort the selection by the user
of the most appropriate mode of transport; and

(*k*) special measures, in so far as they
are necessary, should be adopted to 25
avoid undue disruption of transportation
services essential to the national
interest.

Minister's
responsibilities

(3) It is the responsibility of the Minister to undertake the necessary measures to 30
achieve the objective of the transportation
policy referred to in subsection (1) having
due regard to the principles described in
subsection (2) and, without restricting the
generality of the foregoing, it is the re- 35
sponsibility of the Minister to

(*a*) inquire into and undertake measures to ensure the effective and efficient
development of the various modes of
transport over which Parliament has 40
jurisdiction;

(*b*) inquire into the relationship between the various modes of transport
within, to and from Canada and undertake measures to achieve coordination in 45

transport et le public est consulté sur 20
ceux-ci;

c) lors du développement de services de
transport visant à accomplir un objet
déterminé, toutes les possibilités sont
étudiées, notamment celle de ne recourir 25
à aucun moyen de transport;

d) la concurrence au niveau d'un moyen
de transport et entre les divers moyens
de transport est favorisée dans la mesure
compatible avec les conditions économi- 30
ques et les facteurs techniques;

e) l'organisation du service de transport
fait appel à la participation d'entreprises
de transport nationales, régionales et
locales tant du secteur public que du 35
secteur privé, le contrôle des entreprises
privées par des Canadiens étant un
objectif;

f) toute incompatibilité entre les objectifs du secteur privé et ceux du secteur 40
public est tranchée en regard de l'intérêt
public;

g) les services de transport et les installations et services complémentaires
visent à la rentabilité commerciale; 45

h) lorsque le gouvernement du Canada
prend une décision dont la mise en
œuvre est incompatible avec l'objectif de
rentabilité énoncée à l'alinéa *g*), les profits et pertes doivent être identifiés et il
doit absorber les pertes impliquées;

i) dans les situations de concurrence
efficace, les taux et les services de transport sont laissés aux règles du marché; 5
dans le cas contraire, ils doivent être
réglementés de façon à donner aux usagers la protection dont ils seraient
privés;

j) lorsqu'il y a libre concurrence, une 10
aide jugée nécessaire à l'application
d'une politique du gouvernement du
Canada peut être fournie à un service,
pourvu qu'elle ne fausse pas le choix de
l'usager quant au moyen de transport le 15
plus approprié; et

k) des mesures extraordinaires doivent
être prises, en cas de nécessité, pour
empêcher une perturbation excessive des
services de transport essentiels à l'intérêt 20
national.

(3) Il incombe au Ministre de prendre
les dispositions nécessaires à la réalisation
des objets exprimés au paragraphe (1) en
conformité avec les principes énoncés au 25
paragraphe (2) et, notamment,

a) de prendre, après enquête, les mesures susceptibles d'assurer un développement efficace des divers moyens de
transport qui ressortissent à la compé- 30
tence du Parlement;

b) d'étudier l'interaction des divers
moyens de transport régionaux, nationaux et internationaux qui desservent le
Canada et de prendre les mesures néces- 35
saires pour coordonner l'exploitation, le
développement, la réglementation et le
contrôle de ceux-ci;

Responsabilités
incombant au
Ministre

the operation, development, regulation and control of those various modes of transport;

(*c*) undertake studies and research into and, where appropriate, undertake 50 measures respecting any aspect of all modes of transport within, to or from Canada, including

(i) standards and criteria to be used in the determination of investment by 5 the Government of Canada in equipment and facilities in or in support of the various modes of transport and the determination of desirable financial returns therefrom, 10

(ii) the development of revenue from the use of transport equipment, facilities and services provided or operated by any department, branch or agency of the Government of Canada, 15

(iii) financial assistance required in support of any mode of transport and the method of administration of such assistance, and

(iv) the effects and requirements 20 resulting from participation in or ratification of international agreements;

(*d*) administer subsidies voted by Parliament for any mode of transport in 25 Canada the administration of which has not been assigned by law to any other department, branch or agency of the Government of Canada; and

(*e*) participate in the work of intergov- 30 ernmental, national or international organizations dealing with any mode of transport over which Parliament has jurisdiction.

Delegation of responsibilities to Commission

(4) The Minister may cause any of the 35 powers, duties and functions conferred or imposed on him by law, including those described in paragraphs (3)(*a*) to (*e*), to be exercised or performed by the Commission on his behalf. 40

Transfer of powers, etc.

3.1 (1) For the purpose of achieving the objective of the transportation policy referred to in subsection 3(1), the Governor in Council may, by order, transfer to the Minister any powers, duties or func- 45 tions conferred or imposed on the Commission by this Act or any other Act, but this section does not authorize the transfer of any power, duty or function mentioned in subsection 22(1).

c) de prendre les mesures jugées nécessaires à la suite d'études et de recher- 40 ches sur toute question relative aux moyens de transport régionaux, nationaux ou internationaux qui desservent le Canada, notamment sur

(i) les normes et critères qui doivent servir à la détermination des investissements du gouvernement du Canada 5 en matériel et installations rattachés, directement ou indirectement, à la prestation de services de transport ainsi qu'à la détermination des rendements financiers qu'il serait souhaita- 10 ble d'en obtenir,

(ii) les possibilités d'augmenter les revenus tirés du matériel, des installations ou des services de transport fournis ou exploités par tout minis- 15 tère, département, direction ou organisme du gouvernement du Canada,

(iii) l'aide financière nécessaire à un moyen de transport et l'administration de celle-ci, et 20

(iv) les conséquences qui résultent de l'adhésion aux conventions internationales ou leur ratification;

d) d'administrer les crédits votés par le Parlement pour un moyen de transport 25 au Canada lorsque la loi n'en a pas confié l'administration à un autre ministère, département, direction ou organisme du gouvernement du Canada; et

e) de participer aux travaux des orga- 30 nismes intergouvernementaux, nationaux ou internationaux qui portent sur un moyen de transport ressortissant à la compétence du Parlement.

Délégation de responsabilités à la Commission

(4) Le Ministre peut déléguer à la Com- 35 mission les pouvoirs et fonctions que toute loi lui confère, notamment, ceux qui sont prévus aux alinéas (3)*a*) à *e*).

Transfert de pouvoirs

3.1 (1) Afin d'atteindre l'objectif de la politique des transports énoncée au para- 40 graphe 3(1), le gouverneur en conseil peut, par décret, transférer au Ministre, les pouvoirs et fonctions que la présente loi ou une autre loi confère à la Commission, à l'exclusion de ceux qui sont prévus au para- 45 graphe 22(1).

EXPLANATORY NOTES

Clause 1: This amendment would redefine the objective of the transportation policy for Canada and set forth principles applicable to the implementation of that policy. It would also set forth the responsibilities of the Minister of Transport in relation to the transportation policy for Canada, provide for delegation of powers, duties and functions of the Minister to the Canadian Transport Commission and for the transfer of certain powers, duties and functions of that Commission to the Minister. The proposed section 3.2 would authorize the Governor in Council to issue directions to the Commission in relation to the transportation policy for Canada. The proposed section 3.3 would provide for the exemption of certain conduct from the application of section 32 of the *Combines Investigation Act.*

NOTES EXPLICATIVES

Article 1 du bill: Cette modification définit la nouvelle politique canadienne en matière de transport ainsi que les principes applicables à sa mise en œuvre, précise les responsabilités du ministre des Transports en ce domaine, prévoit la délégation, à la Commission canadienne des Transports, des attributions du Ministre et le transfert, au Ministre, des certaines attributions de la Commission. Le nouvel article 3.2 autorise le gouverneur en conseil à donner à la Commission des directives concernant cette politique et le nouvel article 3.3 dispense certains actes de l'application de l'article 32 de la *Loi relative aux enquêtes sur les coalitions.*